# THE ALL-NEW BLUE RIBBON COOKBOOK

# THE ALL-NEW BLUE RIBBON COOKBOOK

Prize-Winning Recipes from America's State Fairs

Catherine Hanley

HPBooks

HPBooks
Published by The Berkley Publishing Group
200 Madison Avenue
New York, NY 10016

Copyright © 1997 by Catherine Hanley
Book design by Rhea Braunstein
Cover design by Joe Lanni
Cover photograph by Envision

First edition: August 1997

Published simultaneously in Canada.

The Putnam Berkley World Wide Web site address is http://www.berkley.com

Library of Congress Cataloging-in-Publication Data
Hanley, Catherine.
    The all-new blue ribbon cookbook  :  prize-winning recipes from
America's state fairs / Catherine Hanley. — 1st ed.
        p.   cm.
    Includes index.
    ISBN 1-55788-270-3
    1. Cookery.   2. Cookery, American.    I. Title.
TX714.H362   1997
641.5973—dc21                                                    96-52653
                                                                      CIP

Printed in the United States of America

10   9   8   7   6   5   4   3   2   1

*This book is for Jim,*
*who made it possible,*
*and in memory of Phyllis McFarland,*
*for all her support*

# Acknowledgments

The valuable assistance of the following fair administrators made this book possible:

**California:** Barbara Farnsworth, Entry Supervisor, Kern County Fair; Silvia Bishop, Home Arts Coordinator, Los Angeles County Fair
**Indiana:** *Virginia Gale, Culinary Arts Department Coordinator, Indiana State Fair
**Iowa:** *Arlette Hollister, Food Superintendent, and *Jacquie Holm, Publicity Coordinator, Iowa State Fair
**Kansas:** Cleta Dewey, Competitive Exhibits Supervisor, Kansas State Fair
**Minnesota:** *Evelyn Hagen, Superintendent, Creative Activities, and Valori Trantanella, Competition Assistant, Minnesota State Fair
**Missouri:** Mary E. Quinn, Exhibits Director, Ozark Empire Fair
**New York:** Mary Catherine Somerset, Director, Art and Home Center, New York State Fair
**Ohio:** Kathryn Bennett, Director, Canfield Fair, and Sande Haldiman, Director, Special Events, Ohio State Fair
**Oregon:** Coralee Cox, Demonstrations Coordinator, Oregon State Fair
**Texas:** Glenna Myatt, Superintendent of Culinary Department, South Plains Fair
**Vermont:** Linda Sanderson, Superintendent, Culinary Department, Champlain Valley Fair
**Washington:** Stephanie Hagarty, Open Class Superintendent, Evergreen State Fair

My special gratitude to others who supplied information or helped in a variety of ways, sometimes without knowing it—Marlene Johnson, Ann Kapaun and Lynda Kamps, The Pillsbury Company, Minneapolis, Minnesota; Lydia Botham, Land O'Lakes, Inc., Arden Hills, Minnesota; Cecelia Deck, Hershey Kitchens, Hershey, Pennsylvania; Donald Keaton, Archway Cookies, Inc., Battle Creek, Michigan; Marvin Sparks, Archway Ellison Bakery, Inc., Ft. Wayne, Indiana; Joyce Agnew, Agnew Communications, Inc., Minneapolis, Minnesota; The American Egg Board, Chicago, Illinois; Jan Roberts-Dominquez and Barbara Durbin, *Portland Oregonian*; Al Sicherman, *Minneapolis Star-Tribune*; Karal Ann Marling, Anne Hanley, Stuart Hanley, Gladys Mikkola and Joanne Murphy, all of Minneapolis, and the exemplary Hennepin County (Minnesota) Library System.

* Special thanks to these people for supplying valuable historical material.

# Contents

# Introduction

## How It All Began

A strong desire to educate farmers was the driving force behind what is believed to be the first fair in America. In the early nineteenth century, a wealthy farmer and businessman, Elkanah Watson, exhibited fine Merino sheep in Pittsfield, Massachusetts. He wanted farmers to be able to come together to learn to improve their livestock and their farming methods.

Watson even encouraged women to attend and to be involved. He wanted to improve their lives as well as the lives of their husbands. This was a revolutionary idea that didn't catch on in some parts of the country for nearly two centuries.

Although today there are not many big state fairs in the East, agricultural expositions first flourished there. By the middle of the nineteenth century, the newly formed states in the Midwest were following their lead and organizing their own agricultural fairs.

Apparently women's activities continued to be recognized at eastern expositions. In 1854, while Minnesota was still a territory, an official with that first agricultural fair wrote, "There will be no women's building, since only fifty ladies reside in the district, few of whom had time to do the fancy work traditionally displayed at agricultural shows back east."

## Indiana Is Enlightened

In what has been described as the "golden age of the fair in America" from 1850 to 1870, Indiana must have been one of the most enlightened states to recognize the contributions women were making to farm and small-town life. Even their first fair in 1853 recognized "what women's industrious hands can produce: the churn, the homespun, table delights and the arts earned diplomas and cash premiums, alongside the toils of the field."

Early Indiana exhibits centered around the most practical aspects of home life. Food exhibits emphasized preserving food—both canning and drying—and making butter and cheese at home. A Mrs. Powell Howland was awarded a prize of ivory-handled knives and forks for the best 10 pounds of butter and her second-best 25-pound block of cheese.

By 1900 a category called "table luxuries" had been added to the premium list, an indication that life in rural Indiana was becoming easier. This group also included everything from maple syrup, wheat bread, rusk, fruit cake, cheese straws, Saratoga chips, spiced pears and peaches, catsup, and "gelatine dessert." Cheese also was included in the table luxury class, but presumably the homemaker no longer had to tote a 25-pound block to the fair.

After World War I, a Women's Advisory Committee representing women active in organizations ranging from the Indiana Farmers' Federation to the Indiana Federation of Women's Clubs was set up. This organization gave the signal that the agricultural fair was enlarging to include urban women as well as those from farms and small towns.

By that time the Indiana women had their own building. The ancient frame Art Hall had been replaced by an imposing concrete and brick Women's Building. Ironically, though, it took more than two decades before a woman was put in charge of that department.

Indiana has done a far better job than most states in documenting the history of food exhibits at the fairs. In researching culinary history at the big state and regional fairs, it has been disturbing to see how most published histories of the big state and regional fairs treat what is perceived as "women's work" as inconsequential by ignoring it.

## Culinary Arts Are Thriving

But as the status of agriculture fades at fairs across the country, the culinary arts are thriving. They have reflected the times, from showing the best of the practical, life-sustaining home activities of preserving food and churning butter to emphasizing creativity and cooking for fun. Unless fairs do a better job of documenting this aspect of their history, it will soon be lost.

The only reason we know as much of the Minnesota history as we do is thanks to Karal Ann Marling, professor of art history and American studies at the University of Minnesota. In 1990 the University of Minnesota Press published her *Blue Ribbon: A Social and Pictorial History of the Minnesota State Fair*. Dr. Marling is an unabashed fan of state fairs. She is not only a scholar, but she is a droll chronicler of popular culture. It becomes clear in her book that the men running the Minnesota fair wanted to keep women in their place, which was at home, while the feisty "new women" of Minnesota were determined that their place was participating in fair activities.

By 1908, 20 percent of the total entries from the entire fair were the quilts, needlework and food exhibited in what made up the Women's Department. Finally the department had to get its own building. The exhibits had become too numerous to remain where they had been, in a spare corner surrounded by vendors of vegetable cutters and sewing machine needles.

## Homemaking Is a Science

In Minnesota as in Indiana, the Federation of Women's Clubs became involved. They insisted that homemaking was a rational science. They pushed for demonstrations and lectures to help women learn domestic science in the same way that farmers at the fair learned about breeding cattle and selecting feed. The Agricultural Society, which ran the fair, finally had to acknowledge reality and invite practicing home economists to give public lectures.

The club women wanted to make household tasks easier, to free women and give them time to pursue an independent life of learning and service, including the opportunity to become active in the suffragette movement. This idea did not make a big hit with the men.

A member of the Agricultural Society remarked on the changes: he noted that the time had passed when "the fairer sex" were expected only to bring "their prize sponge cakes and fussy little tidies" to exhibit.

Gradually, under the leadership of the first female superintendent of the Women's Department, the premium list was expanded to include prizes for more entries that were creative as well as purely practical. People who decorated cakes or put up jam for the fun of it now had a venue, along with the down-to-earth home arts the men had encouraged.

The Depression brought a return to more mundane concerns, but by the 1940s and 1950s, blue ribbon royalty reigned. Each year brought a new Queen of Angel Food, Bread, Pie Crust or Preserves.

Cooking had become more of a hobby. As a social historian, Karal Ann Marling credits external forces like magazine ads for new kitchen appliances and articles describing new cooking methods for these changes.

The premium list from the 1960s and 1970s reflects these new ideas. Canning and bread baking lost ground to the preparation of special-occasion foods like sweet rolls and coffee cakes for the neighborhood coffee klatch.

Interestingly, today the pendulum is swinging back. Bread baking definitely has returned, but as a hobby rather than a necessity. Preserving food is more popular than ever. Men and women are making salsa, chutney and the kinds of relishes and sweet preserves found in specialty food shops. And while blue ribbon winners may watch fat and cholesterol in their everyday diets, they bake elaborate cookies, cakes and pies with love, butter and lots of nuts! Furthermore, the food is as beautiful as it is delicious.

## What's New

The Gedney Company, a Minnesota-based food processor of high-quality pickles, brought out a premium line of home-style pickles which they labeled "State Fair." Each variety of pickles had won a blue ribbon at the Minnesota State Fair. The winner is identified on the label by her photograph and a few lines of copy about her pickles.

From a marketing standpoint, it is significant that customers immediately recognized "State Fair" on the label as an indication that this was a premium product, even without emphasis on the blue ribbon. It also is of special interest to state fair culinary mavens, because it points up a change in state and regional contests, big-stakes competitions sponsored by food companies.

When I first realized how many of these contests had started up in the decade between the publication of *Blue Ribbon Winners* and *The All-New Blue Ribbon Cookbook,* I was concerned. My original premise in writing *Blue Ribbon Winners* was that fairs offered the only noncommercial cooking contests left. Despite modest cash prizes that often didn't even cover the cost of ingredients, tens of thousands of men and women were willing to compete for the ribbons and the thrill of the competition.

Would prizes of $100, $50 and $25 turn the fair competitions into just another contest that would reflect the biases of the company sponsors? What I have learned is gratifying, and the answer is a decided "No." The contests actually are adding vitality to culinary arts competitions.

The fairs, which have a number of food company–sponsored prizes, have found that they are getting more entries in their regular fair-sponsored open competitions. In states with few or no company-sponsored categories, entries are down.

Arlette Hollister, food superintendent at the big Iowa State Fair, says they had seven thousand entries in 1996, one thousand more than in 1995. She attributes this to the increased interest because of sponsored events. The main reason these commercial contests have worked out so well is the way the judging is done. The food professionals who judge the open competitions also judge these special contests. They use the same tough "by the book" scoring that they use for all the regular categories.

At the 1996 Minnesota State Fair, the Gedney Company, which also is bringing out a new line of premium State Fair preserves, offered a $100 prize for the best strawberry spread and the best raspberry spread. They hoped to work with the winners, as they had done previously with the pickle winners, to develop commercial recipes as close as possible to the winners' homemade versions. These lower-sugar spreads then would join their new line of preserves.

According to Evelyn Hagen, superintendent of creative activities, the tough judges got out their score cards, went through the standard judging procedure and said they didn't consider any of the entries worthy of a blue ribbon. So Gedney's $100 prizes were not awarded that year.

At the Iowa State Fair, they occasionally use a celebrity judge for publicity. A star of the road show of *State Fair,* which is based on the Iowa fair, was a judge for one category when the musical played in Des Moines. But Arlette Hollister said in these cases she pairs the celebrity with one of her expert judges, like a *Better Homes & Gardens* test kitchen home economist or an extension home economist.

Joyce Agnew, whose Minneapolis company, Agnew Communications, Inc., each year manages more than 250 of these sponsored events at more than 90 fairs throughout the country, says her clients find that this is a great way to stay in touch with grass-roots cooking and baking trends throughout the country.

Marlene Johnson, director of product communications at Pillsbury, agrees. The company sponsors a pie-baking competition where fair contestants must use the food company's refrigerated pie crusts. These commercial crusts would never be allowed in the open pie competition, where everything must be made from scratch. But here the judges concentrate on judging the fruit fillings, and the company comes away with a better idea of the kinds of fruit fillings that are popular throughout the country.

Pillsbury Bake-Off Contest recipes in which these crusts are used are more unusual, since those recipes must be original, according to Lynda Kamps, publicity coordinator. But she adds, "Those women and men who enter at the fairs are the *real* bakers. In terms of techniques and quality of the finished product, their products can't be beat."

## Sponsored Contests Are Increasing

The number of sponsored contests has increased. Iowa State, whose 100 plus sponsors range from Fortune 500 food companies to the Inn of the Six-Toed Cat and Cy, the Iowa State University mascot, tops the list by far. However, many of these prizes are from small companies, and these prizes are modest. But they still offer an extra incentive to the competitors.

Giving commercially sponsored prizes actually is not a new phenomenon. Evelyn Hagen has a 1948 Minnesota premium book that shows that King Midas Flour gave what was then an impressive $25 prize for the best loaf of white bread. As a newly hired superintendent, she approached Kerr in the early 1950s when she discovered that the company was offering canning jars to ribbon winners in some other states, and persuaded them to add Minnesota to their list. From 1950 to 1960 General Mills promoted its new recipe for chiffon cake by offering a silver tray to that blue ribbon winner.

Indeed, while the original purpose of the nineteenth-century expositions was education, a look at their history shows that they always have been a place where new agricultural products and technologies were introduced. Now it seems that food companies have begun to recognize the talent and expertise that have always been exhibited in culinary arts and are taking advantage of it.

## Where These Recipes Came From

This book could not exist were it not for the generosity of the men and women who were willing to share their recipes. As I did for *Blue Ribbon Winners*, I wrote some of the major fairs asking for their premium books. After identifying categories I was especially interested in, I wrote to the fair for the names and addresses of those blue ribbon or sweepstakes winners.

This time I also had the advantage of being able to go back to some of the outstanding winners from the first book. A few of them are no longer competing, but most of them still are winning ribbons and a number of them are back in this book with new recipes. I also asked these previous winners for their recommendations for some of the best winners from their fair.

Since all the recipes in this book had to be different from *Blue Ribbon Winners*, unfortunately, I had to turn down a number of recipes that were too similar. *Blue Ribbon Winners* concentrated on the best of the basics and regional specialties. The *All-New Blue Ribbon Cookbook* supplements these with more special-occasion and ethnic recipes. I believe this selection is in line with the way many of us are cooking today: quick and simple meals during the week, while we concentrate our time and effort on special dishes for family and friends. Many people also are baking bread and making preserves as a hobby, and they are interested in more out-of-the-ordinary recipes. The result is that some of these recipes are somewhat involved. But that is noted, so you won't start making one of them when you are feeling rushed or under pressure.

The recipes are written so you can do one step at a time, in the most efficient way. In some, you can (or must) even divide the work over two days, which fits many busy schedules.

Obviously the recipes as received had to be rewritten—and often reorganized—into a more-or-less standard form. In some cases, the winners' directions were so helpful—or so engaging—that they are written into the recipe, even though this deviates from the established recipe style.

In a few cases, their methods are unusual. This is noted, and their method used, on the theory that it worked when I tested it, and that's the way they won their blue ribbons.

I think you will agree that this is a truly outstanding collection of recipes, with many you will want to make again and again. As you do, please join me in thanking these generous-spirited women and men who were willing to share their winning secrets.

# Sweet Yeast Breads, Rolls & Coffee Cakes

Baking sweet rolls and coffee cakes at home appears to be coming back into fashion. Well into the 1970s, the weekly routine of making a panful of caramel pecan rolls for Sunday breakfast or a streusel coffee cake for the neighborhood coffee klatch was traditional in many homes.

But as more women entered the work force, there was less time for home baking of any kind. Busy families turned to the bakeries. In-store bakeries started up and flourished, competing with the neighborhood shops. In this competitive climate, the quality of the products was satisfactory, if not quite up to homemade.

But then something happened: with rapidly rising wages and ingredient costs in the 1980s, bakeries turned to frozen doughs to save labor costs and time, instead of mixing their own doughs. Gradually heavy-textured rolls and coffee cakes that were sweet, but with little flavor, became the norm. Customers switched to muffins and bagels, but that alluring smell and taste of cinnamon rolls fresh from the oven or light, flaky Danish pastry were impossible to forget. We learned that the only way to get the quality we wanted was to do it ourselves.

Since state fair entries tend to reflect baking trends in their area, it's not surprising that the categories where sweet breads compete are growing. In addition to the usual sweet roll and coffee cake entries, there is a growing interest in ethnic yeast baking, which brings in many festive breads and rolls. Baking with honey is another category that attracts sweet yeast entries.

Although the blue ribbon winners represented here may favor nutritious, whole-grain loaves for their daily bread, when they bake sweet rolls and breads, the emphasis is on indulgent treats.

Roll recipes range from a heritage recipe for orange-glazed cinnamon rolls to real Danish pastry. Some of the festive loaves and coffee cakes, like Maple Yeast Coffee Cake, feature show-stopping shaping, with directions that make it easy to duplicate.

For those with not quite so sweet a tooth, European-style breads like Czechoslovakian Egg Braid or Mile-High Poppy Seed Bread emphasize the flavor of the luxurious egg-rich doughs.

Be forewarned: recipes as good as these demand your time and attention. Most of them are treats to make when you want to serve something special and are willing to take the time to do it well.

For those occasions when you want to serve something delicious, but want it to be out of the oven in less than an hour, we have included four prize-winning quick-bread coffee cakes.

## LOAF PAN SIZES

Blue ribbon bakers know that it is important to use the correct sized pan to get the well-shaped product that state fair judges look for. Unfortunately, the capacity of baking pans isn't standardized, even when they are marked the same. Loaf pans are among the most inconsistently sized.

We tested a medium-weight aluminum, a glass and a heavier no-stick aluminum loaf pan. Each was from a well-known manufacturer. Each was marked 8½ × 4½-inches or the metric equivalent and measured that size across the top. Yet the capacities varied from 5 to 7 cups.

If you are a less experienced baker or have bought new pans, it's a good idea to measure the liquid capacity of a pan and mark it on the bottom with nail polish.

Here are some guidelines. If a recipe specifies:

| | |
|---|---|
| 9 × 5-inch loaf pan | Best for 2-pound loaves. An 8½-inch pan that holds 7 cups can be substituted, but one that holds 5 cups is too small. This pan makes a flatter-topped country loaf. Fair bakers usually prefer a high-crowned loaf. |
| 8½ × 4½-inch loaf pan | Best for 1½- or 1-pound loaves. |
| 7½ × 3½-inch loaf pan or 6½ × 4½-inch loaf pan | These recipes do not call for these sizes, which hold about 3 cups of liquid, but some fair bakers use them for quick breads. You can make two loaves from any recipe that can be baked in a 9 × 5-inch pan. |

# Czechoslovakian Egg Braid

For nearly two decades Cheryl Christiansen has been honing her baking skills by competing with some of the best cooks in Kansas at the state fair. In a state famous for wheat, it's not surprising that the yeast baking categories are some of the most competitive.

A winner in the international breads category, her braided loaves typify the tender, egg-rich dough made from precious white flour that took the place of cake for festive occasions in many European homes. Her braids also received special prizes from the Kansas Wheat Commission and a regional flour company.

*1½ cups milk*
*½ cup water*
*¼ cup margarine*
*¼ cup sugar*
*1 tablespoon salt*
*7 to 7 ½ cups all-purpose flour*

*2 (¼-oz.) packages active dry yeast*
  *(5 teaspoons)*
*3 eggs*
*1 egg yolk*
*2 tablespoons water*

In a medium saucepan, heat milk, ½ cup water, margarine, sugar and salt to 120F (50C), or very warm, stirring frequently. In a large mixer bowl, combine 3 cups flour and yeast. Add milk mixture to flour mixture. Beat for several minutes, then beat in the whole eggs. Add enough flour to make a dough that cleans the sides of the bowl. Turn out on a lightly floured surface. Knead until smooth, 5 to 10 minutes.

Wash and grease a large bowl. Place dough in greased bowl and turn dough to grease top. Cover with plastic wrap and let rise in a warm place until double, about 45 minutes. Punch dough down.

Turn out on a lightly floured surface. Divide dough in half. Grease a 15 × 10-inch baking sheet or two smaller baking sheets. Divide 1 piece of dough into 3 equal parts. Roll each into a rope about 12 inches long. On the baking sheet, braid the three parts, loosely fastening ends. Repeat with remaining dough. Cover and let rise until light (braids will not be doubled).

Preheat oven to 400F (205C). Make egg wash by mixing egg yolk and 2 tablespoons water just enough to combine. Brush braids with egg wash. Bake until bread is a deep golden brown and loaves sound hollow when tapped on the bottom, 30 to 40 minutes.

Makes 2 braids.

### Temperature Is Important
Using liquid at the correct temperature to activate yeast is one of the most important steps in bread baking. When yeast is combined with some of the dry ingredients before adding the liquid, rather than softened in water, the liquid must be hotter—120 to 130F (50 to 55C). Most blue ribbon yeast bakers say a good thermometer is one of their most useful pieces of equipment.

CHERYL CHRISTIANSEN    MCPHERSON, KANSAS    KANSAS STATE FAIR

# Cinnamon Raisin Bread

Between 4-H and adult competition Ruth Bristol can count fifty years of entering the Champlain Valley Fair. She says it's still the highlight of her summer. She always brings home blue ribbons, one of which was for her Cinnamon Raisin Bread, which also was awarded the sweepstakes in yeast baking.

The bread, from her grandmother's recipe, is made by the old-time sponge method. Many bread bakers believe this preliminary fermentation improves the flavor of the bread. This sweet, raisin-filled bread certainly is exceptionally good tasting. An interesting difference in this recipe is the brown sugar–spice filling.

| | |
|---|---|
| ¾ cup milk | 1 egg, slightly beaten |
| ⅓ cup solid vegetable shortening | 3½ cups bread flour |
| ½ cup granulated sugar | 1½ cups raisins, rinsed and drained |
| 1 teaspoon salt | 6 tablespoons light brown sugar |
| 1 (¼-oz.) package active dry yeast | 2 teaspoons ground cinnamon |
| (scant 1 tablespoon) | ¼ teaspoon grated nutmeg |
| ¼ cup warm (105 to 115F; 40 to 45C) | 2 tablespoons butter, melted |
| water | |

In a medium saucepan, heat milk to 120F (50C), or very warm. Add shortening, granulated sugar and salt; stir until dissolved. Pour into a large bowl and cool to lukewarm. In a small bowl, sprinkle yeast on the warm water, stir to dissolve and let stand until bubbly. Stir yeast and egg into lukewarm milk mixture. Beat in about half the flour. Cover and let rise in a warm place about 1 hour or until double in size.

Gradually beat in the remaining flour to make a stiff dough, adding raisins with final addition. Turn dough out onto a lightly floured surface and knead about 10 minutes, until dough is smooth and elastic. Wash and grease large bowl. Place dough in greased bowl. Cover with plastic wrap and let rise about 1 hour or until double in size.

In a small bowl combine brown sugar, cinnamon and nutmeg. Grease 2 (8½ × 4½-inch or 9 × 5-inch) loaf pans.

Divide dough in half. On a floured surface, roll into a 14 × 9-inch rectangle. Spread with 1 tablespoon melted butter and half the sugar mixture. Starting with the short end, roll tightly and place in greased pan. Repeat for remaining dough. Cover and let rise until just doubled, about 50 minutes.

Preheat oven to 350F (175C). Bake 45 to 50 minutes or until golden brown and until loaves sound hollow when tapped. Remove from pans and cool on a wire rack.

**Makes 2 (1½-lb.) loaves.**

### 🏵 *Setting a Sponge*
The sponge method is one in which only part of the flour is mixed with the yeast and liquid. This is allowed to rise (ferment) until it is bubbly, about an hour at warm room temperature. "Setting a sponge" was a common practice when yeast was less reliable, because the bubbly dough enhanced the proofing action. Now the method is used to develop flavor. Slower fermentation gives bread more of the wheaty flavor of the flour and less yeast flavor.

RUTH BRISTOL     ESSEX JUNCTION, VERMONT     CHAMPLAIN VALLEY FAIR

# Mile-High Poppy Seed Bread

"Mile high" is a slight exaggeration, but Lynda Mackey's delicious cakelike bread rises so high in the oven, you may want to bake it on the lower rack.

In her professional life, Lynda is a writer and editor. Her creativity flows over into her cooking. She especially enjoys making up original recipes for the special food company–sponsored contests at the Ohio State Fair, where she regularly carries off top prizes.

| | |
|---|---|
| 1 (¼-oz.) package active dry yeast (scant 1 tablespoon) | ¼ cup butter, cut into chunks |
| ¼ cup warm (105 to 115F; 40 to 45C) water | 1 teaspoon salt |
| ½ cup water | 1 tablespoon poppy seeds |
| 2 tablespoons sugar | 3 to 3½ cups bread flour |
| | 2 eggs |
| | 2 egg yolks |

In a small bowl, sprinkle yeast on the warm water, stir to dissolve and let stand until bubbly. In a medium saucepan, heat the ½ cup water, sugar, butter, salt and poppy seeds to 115F (45C), stirring to mix ingredients. Pour into a large mixer bowl. Add 1½ cups flour and the yeast mixture. Beat until well mixed. Beat in eggs and egg yolks. Mix in enough additional flour to make a soft dough that pulls away from the sides of the bowl.

Turn out onto a lightly floured surface and knead 8 to 10 minutes, until smooth and satiny. Wash and grease a large bowl. Place dough in greased bowl and turn to grease top. Cover with plastic wrap and let rise in a warm place until double, 45 to 60 minutes.

Punch down dough. Grease a 1½-quart casserole dish or an 8½ × 4½-inch loaf pan.

Turn dough out onto a lightly floured surface, form into a ball and place in greased casserole dish or form into a loaf and place in greased pan. Cover with plastic wrap and let rise until just double, about 45 minutes.

Remove top oven rack. Preheat oven to 375F (190C). Bake on lower rack 35 to 40 minutes or until crust is deep golden brown. Let bread cool in pan 1 to 2 minutes for easier removal.

Makes 1 (1½-lb.) loaf.

### 🎗 *Storing Poppy Seeds*

Tiny poppy seeds are high in oil and can develop a rancid, almost bitter flavor, which is evident in baked products. Begin by buying fresh seeds. If you buy in bulk, taste them. Then store the poppy seeds in a tightly closed container in the refrigerator or freezer. Mark the purchase date on the container and taste any seeds that are more than 6 months old before using.

LYNDA MACKEY     COLUMBUS, OHIO     OHIO STATE FAIR

# Apricot-Filled Envelopes

Linda Pauls used to cook for her husband's custom combining crew, traveling from Texas to Montana. In the process she acquired an interesting collection of regional and ethnic recipes. This sweet roll is from a German community where it was called a *kuchen*. These envelope-shaped rolls may remind others of Czechoslovakian *kolaches*. But whatever the name, this is an outstandingly good sweet roll, which brought raves from everyone who tasted it.

Be sure to include the small amount of apricot gelatin. It definitely enhances the flavor of the filling as well as provides a little thickening.

1 (¼-oz.) package active dry yeast
   (scant 1 tablespoon)
¼ cup warm (105 to 115F; 40 to 45C)
   water
1¼ cups undiluted evaporated milk or
   light cream
¼ cup sugar
1 teaspoon salt
1 egg
¼ cup butter or margarine, softened
3½ to 3¾ cups all-purpose flour

APRICOT FILLING
1 cup (⅓ lb.) dried apricots, quartered
1 cup water
¼ cup sugar
1½ teaspoons cornstarch
2 tablespoons apricot gelatin
   (from 3-oz. package)

TOPPING
½ cup sugar
½ cup all-purpose flour
½ cup butter, melted

In a small bowl, sprinkle yeast on the warm water, stir to dissolve and let stand until bubbly. In a small saucepan, heat evaporated milk, sugar and salt to warm 105 to 115F (40 to 45C), stirring constantly. Pour warm milk mixture into a large mixer bowl; beat in dissolved yeast, egg, butter and 2 cups flour to make a soft sponge. Cover with plastic wrap and let rise about 1 hour, until dough is bubbly.

Stir in the rest of the flour to make a soft dough, mixing until dough begins to leave the sides of the bowl. Cover with plastic wrap and let rise again until doubled, 45 minutes to 1 hour.

Prepare filling and topping. Lightly grease large baking sheets. Punch dough down. Turn dough out on lightly floured surface; knead a few minutes and form dough into a smooth ball. Cut the dough into 3 equal parts.

Working with 1 piece of dough at a time, roll the dough into a 12-inch square. Cut the dough into 12 (3-inch) squares. Place 1 teaspoon of filling in the center of each square. Bring the corners to the center to enclose the filling, gently pinching to seal. Dip the top of the roll in melted butter, then in sugar and flour mixture. Place on baking sheet, reshaping roll if needed, and sprinkle with a little more topping (or place roll on baking sheet and brush with melted butter and sprinkle generously with topping). Cover rolls with plastic wrap and let rise for about 45 minutes, until your fingerprint remains when you touch the dough.

Preheat oven to 400F (205C). Bake for 10 to 12 minutes, until rolls are golden brown. Cool on wire rack. Serve warm or at room temperature. Rolls freeze well.

Makes 3 dozen rolls.

### FILLING

In a small saucepan over low heat, combine apricots and water. Simmer, covered, about 10 minutes, until apricots have softened, stirring occasionally. In a small bowl, mix sugar and cornstarch. Stir into apricot mixture, and simmer, stirring constantly, a few minutes more, until the mixture thickens. Stir in gelatin until thoroughly blended. Remove from heat, puree in the blender and set aside to cool.

### TOPPING

In a pie pan or other shallow container mix sugar and flour. Pour melted butter into another shallow container.

### Big-Batch Baking

When you are making a large number of shaped and filled rolls, it's a good idea to divide the dough into portions to make no more than a dozen rolls at a time. Use a separate baking sheet for each group of rolls, so they will all rise at the same time.

If you are baking in a single oven, divide it into thirds with the two racks. Then switch racks when you put in the second pan. By the time the third pan of rolls is ready for the oven, the first one should be baked. If your kitchen is very warm, you may want to refrigerate the last portion of dough until you are ready to use it.

LINDA PAULS     BUHLER, KANSAS     KANSAS STATE FAIR

# Old-Fashioned Cinnamon Rolls

Sue Smart has been making her mother's recipe for cinnamon rolls since she was a teenager. They won a blue ribbon the first time she entered the New Mexico State Fair, and she has triumphed with them over some of the best yeast bakers in the country at the Minnesota State Fair.

The rich, no-knead dough is soft, but reasonably easy to work with. Drizzling the glaze over the hot rolls allows the sweet orange flavor to run down into the cinnamon-sugar filling, creating an irresistible flavor combination.

*2 (¼-oz.) packages active dry yeast*
  *(5 teaspoons)*
*2 cups warm (105 to 115F; 40 to 45C)*
  *water*
*2 cups sugar*
*1½ teaspoons salt*
*6 to 7 cups all-purpose flour*
*2 eggs*

*½ cup vegetable oil*
*1 teaspoon ground cinnamon*
*½ cup margarine, softened*

*GLAZE*
*1½ cups powdered sugar, sifted*
*½ teaspoon grated orange peel*
*3 to 4 tablespoons milk*

In a large bowl, sprinkle yeast on the warm water, stir to dissolve and let stand until bubbly. Stir in ½ cup of the sugar, salt and 2 cups of flour; beat until smooth. Beat in eggs and vegetable oil. Slowly add remaining flour, mixing well after each addition. Dough will pull away from the bowl but remain soft.

Grease a large bowl. Turn dough into greased bowl, cover with plastic wrap and let rise in a warm spot 20 minutes.

Combine remaining 1½ cups sugar and cinnamon. Grease 2 (13 × 9-inch) baking pans.

Punch down dough. Turn out on a floured surface. Divide dough and shape into 2 balls. Put one in the greased bowl while rolling out the other. Roll into an 18 × 12-inch rectangle. Spread half the soft margarine on the dough and sprinkle with half the sugar-cinnamon mixture. Starting from the long side, carefully roll the rectangle jelly-roll fashion. Pinch edges to seal. Cut roll crosswise into 12 slices. Arrange in prepared pan. Repeat with remaining dough and filling ingredients. Cover pans with plastic wrap and let rise in a warm place 45 minutes to 1 hour, until doubled in size.

Preheat oven to 350F (175C). Bake rolls about 25 minutes or until golden brown.

Prepare glaze while rolls are baking. Turn baked rolls out on serving plates or trays, top side up. Drizzle glaze over hot rolls.

**Makes 24 rolls.**

**GLAZE**

In a small bowl beat together powdered sugar, grated orange peel and enough milk to make a thin glaze.

**VARIATION**

If you don't have 2 (13 × 9-inch) pans, bake half the rolls in greased muffin cups.

### Sue's Smart Tips for Blue Ribbon Results

At most fairs, contestants just receive the judges' scorecard, which rates the product for a number of qualities and may have a comment or two. A smaller number, like the New Mexico State Fair, have open judging, with the public invited to observe the proceedings.

Sue Smart took advantage of this learning experience and discovered you should never underestimate the taste buds of expert judges. Flavor counts for the greatest number of points in most categories, and a single point can mean the difference between a first- or second-place ribbon or no ribbon. Here are some suggestions:

- Don't clean your oven just before you do your fair baking. Judges have been known to taste the flavor of the oven cleaner and lower the rating because of it.
- Use your trusty old baking pans, not shiny new ones. Sensitive taste buds can pick up the slight flavor some new pans can give.
- Always use the real thing. Judges will identify flavors like artificial vanilla and butter-flavored products.
- Taste nuts, seeds and dried fruit before you use them to make sure they are fresh. Be sure whole-grain flours and spices are fresh-tasting and full-flavored.

SUE SMART     APPLE VALLEY, MINNESOTA     MINNESOTA STATE FAIR

# Apricot Danish Pastries

Making Danish pastry can be considered a challenge, and John Chovan admits he is obsessed with bread baking. But if you understand the principles of making the flaky pastries and follow the recipe exactly, you will have a big batch of delicacies that will make great eating.

Don't worry if they aren't all perfectly shaped the first time. The flavor and texture still will be memorable. Note that it takes two days—or longer, if you prefer—to duplicate his recipe, because the dough goes through several essential chilling processes.

*2 (¼-oz.) packages active dry yeast*
   *(5 teaspoons)*
*3¼ to 3¾ cups all-purpose flour*
*½ cup sugar*
*¼ cup warm (105 to 115F; 40 to 45C)*
   *milk*
*¼ cup warm (105 to 115F; 40 to 45C)*
   *water*
*1 teaspoon salt*
*1 teaspoon vanilla extract*
*½ teaspoon ground cinnamon*
*2 tablespoons butter, melted*
*1 pound butter, chilled*
*¼ cup all-purpose flour*

*Apricot Filling (see below)*
*1 egg*
*1 tablespoon water*
*Pearl sugar (optional)*

*APRICOT FILLING*
*1½ cups (8 oz.) dried apricots, cut*
   *into quarters*
*2 cups orange juice*
*6 tablespoons sugar*
*1 teaspoon vanilla extract*
*Dash salt*
*¼ cup butter*

In a large bowl, combine yeast and 3 cups flour. Stir in sugar, milk, water, salt, vanilla extract, cinnamon and melted butter. Turn dough out on a floured surface and add remaining flour, kneading until dough is smooth. Return dough to a bowl, cover with plastic wrap and refrigerate overnight.

The next day, knead or cream the 1 pound butter with the ¼ cup flour until well blended. (John Chovan suggests "giving the butter a few good whacks with the rolling pin to loosen it up.") If the kitchen is warm, cover and refrigerate the butter while rolling out the dough.

Turn chilled dough out on a lightly floured surface. Dust with flour and roll or lightly pound out to a rectangle about ½ inch thick. Brush away any excess flour and spread the butter mixture over ⅔ of the surface. Fold ⅓ of the dough to the center and fold the other ⅓ over the top, making 3 layers. Press edges to seal. Turn the folded dough toward you so one of the narrow ends faces front (this is one turn). Repeat the process four more times. If the dough gets soft, refrigerate it 30 minutes or put it in the freezer 10 to 15 minutes or until it is firm enough to roll. Wrap the dough tightly and refrigerate for several hours or up to several days.

Prepare filling. About 15 minutes before baking, preheat oven to 400F (205C). Make egg wash by mixing egg and water in a small bowl. Line large ungreased baking sheets with kitchen parchment paper.

Divide the dough into 6 equal pieces. Work with 1 piece at a time and refrigerate the rest. On a floured surface, roll each piece into a 12 × 8-inch rectangle. Cut each rectangle into 6 (4-inch) squares. Arrange on a baking sheet. Place 1 tablespoon of filling in the center of each square. Bring 1 corner of the dough over filling; bring the opposite corner to the center of the fold. Secure with a dab of water and press gently to seal. Brush each pastry with egg wash and sprinkle lightly with pearl sugar, if using.

Bake about 15 minutes or until golden brown. Remove to a wire rack. Best served fresh or warm briefly before serving. Pastries also freeze well.

**Makes 3 dozen pastries.**

### APRICOT FILLING

In a medium saucepan over low heat, combine apricots and orange juice. Simmer, covered, about 30 minutes, stirring occasionally. When apricots are soft, add sugar, vanilla, salt and butter, and cook, stirring, until sugar dissolves. Remove from heat. Puree in blender. Cool.

## Secrets for Making Danish Pastry

- Make Danish pastry when your kitchen is cool and you don't feel rushed. If you are making it for the first time, read the recipe carefully before you even think about starting it. Both the method and the timing are different from those of other yeast baking.
- The basic idea in Danish pastry is to incorporate a lot of butter (no substitutes) into the dough by a method that involves rolling and folding the dough in a specific way described in the recipe. This makes the characteristic rich, flaky, layered dough.
- The dough and butter need to be cool. If they start to warm up, you must stop and chill the dough until it is firm enough to handle.
- At some stages the dough and butter may be so firm that you need to pound the dough with the rolling pin to soften it. This is a good way to release tensions and doesn't hurt the dough.
- Usually the shaped pastries are baked without proofing, or they may be refrigerated for an hour or two before baking. [Both Danish Walnut Loaf (page 12) and Bear Claws (page 13) are exceptions to this rule. They also have a somewhat different texture.]

JOHN CHOVAN    COLUMBUS, OHIO    OHIO STATE FAIR

# Danish Walnut Loaf

Fran Hurayt has taken Danish pastry dough and turned it into raised loaves of nut-filled sweet bread that make for superb eating. The bread has a wonderfully rich, buttery flavor and a texture that is flakier than ordinary sweet yeast dough but not layered like Danish pastries. Her method is a little different from John Chovan's Apricot Danish Pastries (page 10), but you still need to refrigerate the dough overnight before shaping. The big recipe makes four loaves, which freeze beautifully, or you can use part of the dough for Bear Claw Rolls (page 13). See Secrets for Making Danish Pastry (page 11) for more information about making Danish pastry.

*1 pound butter*
*½ cup all-purpose flour*
*2 (¼-oz.) packages active dry yeast*
   *(5 teaspoons)*
*½ cup plus 1 teaspoon sugar*
*½ cup warm (105 to 115F; 40 to 45C)*
   *water*
*4¼ cups all-purpose flour*
*1 teaspoon salt*
*¾ cup cold milk*
*2 eggs, slightly beaten*

*WALNUT FILLING*
*¼ cup honey*
*2 tablespoons margarine*
*¼ cup milk*
*½ teaspoon vanilla extract*
*½ cup packed light brown sugar*
*4 cups ground walnuts*
   *(1 pound shelled walnuts)*

*TOPPING*
*¼ cup sugar*
*¼ cup ground walnuts*
*1 egg white*

In a large mixer bowl, beat butter until softened. Add flour and mix well. Place mixture between two sheets of waxed paper. Roll out into a 12 × 10-inch rectangle. Place on a baking sheet and refrigerate. Wash and dry bowl.

In a small bowl, sprinkle yeast and 1 teaspoon sugar on the warm water, stir to dissolve and let stand until bubbly.

In a large mixer bowl, combine 3 cups of flour, salt, ½ cup sugar, milk, eggs and the yeast mixture. Beat at medium speed 3 minutes. With a wooden spoon, beat in remaining flour until dough is shiny and elastic. Scrape down sides of bowl. Cover with plastic wrap and refrigerate 30 minutes.

Turn dough out on a floured surface. Sprinkle a little flour on top of dough and roll out into a 22 × 14-inch rectangle. Remove butter mixture from the refrigerator. Peel off top sheet of waxed paper. Place butter on the center of the dough. Peel off remaining waxed paper. Fold unbuttered dough over to completely enclose butter. Fold dough in half to make a 22 × 7-inch rectangle. Fold crosswise in half. Sprinkle flour over any butter that oozes out.

Roll out into a 22 × 14-inch rectangle. Repeat folding and rolling two more times (if the dough becomes soft, wrap and chill between rollings). Wrap dough tightly with plastic wrap and refrigerate overnight.

Prepare filling. Generously grease 4 (8½ × 4½-inch) loaf pans. Cut the chilled dough into quarters. Work with 1 piece at a time and refrigerate the rest until ready to use.

On a lightly floured surface, roll the dough into a 12 × 10-inch rectangle. Cut it into 3 (10 × 4-inch) strips. Spread a scant ⅓ cup of the filling down the center of each strip. Starting at a long side, roll up jelly-roll style, pinching seams to seal. Braid strips together. Pinch ends and fold under to seal. Gently place braid in prepared pan. Repeat with remaining portions of dough and filling.

Let the loaves rise until light, about 1½ to 2 hours (loaves are light when an impression of your finger remains when you touch them). Preheat oven to 375F (190C) at least 10 minutes before first loaf is ready to bake.

Prepare topping. Brush each loaf with egg white and sprinkle with ¼ of the sugar and nut mixture.

Bake 35 to 45 minutes or until the braid is deep golden brown and dough between braids looks baked. Cool the loaves in the pan on a wire rack. When cool, gently turn out onto the rack.

**Makes 4 loaves.**

### WALNUT FILLING

In a medium saucepan, heat honey, margarine and milk just to warm; add vanilla and sugar. Cook, stirring, until sugar is dissolved. Add walnuts; mix well. Cool before using.

### TOPPING

In a small bowl, lightly beat egg white enough to blend. In another small bowl, combine sugar and walnuts.

### *Making the Filling*

While it's tempting to save time by making the filling ahead, a mixture that contains egg and brown sugar quickly begins to thin out and is difficult to spread. Chop the nuts ahead of time (easiest in a food processor or blender), but mix in the other ingredients just before rolling the dough.

### VARIATION

#### BEAR CLAWS

Using a nut filling is traditional in Danish pastry with this shaping. They also are called Coxcombs.

Fran Hurayt gives her rolls a final proofing before baking, which gives them a puffier, less layered texture. Rather than letting the Bear Claws rise, they also can be refrigerated for an hour, then baked, for a flakier texture.

Prepare all the Danish Walnut Loaf dough, filling and topping (page 12) to make 24 Bear Claw rolls, or make 2 loaves from half the dough and 12 Bear Claws from the other half.

To form 12 bear claws using half the dough, line a large baking sheet with kitchen parchment paper. On a floured surface, roll out the prepared dough, which has been chilled overnight, into a 16 × 12-inch rectangle. With a sharp knife or pizza cutter, cut the rectangle into 12 (4-inch) squares.

Spread a generous tablespoonful of filling on half the square to within ½ inch of the edges. Fold the square in half, pressing the edges lightly to seal. Make 4 slits across the folded edge, cutting ¾ of the way through.

Place on the baking sheet, curving the roll slightly to form a crescent shape (this opens the slashes). Cover with plastic wrap and let rise 45 minutes.

Preheat oven to 400F (205C). Brush rolls with egg white and sprinkle lightly with the sugar and walnut mixture. Bake at 400F (205C) 3 minutes, then reduce the temperature to 350F (175C) and bake 15 to 20 minutes, until the rolls are golden and puffy. Remove to a wire rack to cool.

**Makes 12 pastries.**

FRAN HURAYT     AUSTINTOWN, OHIO     CANFIELD FAIR

# Maple Pecan Twist

Special food-company contests have become an important factor at major fairs. Their significant money prizes attract many contestants like Alan Reid, who also is a frequent blue ribbon winner in the regular culinary arts competitions at the Michigan State Fair.

The Land O'Lakes quick bread contest is a favorite with many blue ribbon bakers. After all their state prizes are awarded, their home economists test all the first-place winners and select a national grand prize winner. Alan Reid's interestingly shaped Maple Pecan Twist was awarded that honor and they have shared his recipe.

This is a large coffee cake, made with a rich, soft biscuit dough. For easier handling, shape it on a big baking sheet. Be sure to use pure maple syrup, not pancake syrup, for the delicious, rich flavor it gives.

*Filling (see opposite)*
*2¾ cups all-purpose flour*
*2 tablespoons sugar*
*1 teaspoon baking soda*
*½ teaspoon salt*
*½ cup butter*
*1 cup sour cream*
*¼ cup milk*
*1 egg, slightly beaten*
*1 tablespoon butter, melted*

*FILLING*
*1⅓ cups finely chopped pecans*
*¼ cup pure maple syrup*
*3 tablespoons packed light brown sugar*

*GLAZE*
*1 cup powdered sugar, sifted*
*1 tablespoon pure maple syrup*
*3 to 4 teaspoons milk*

Heat oven to 450F (230C). Line a 16 × 14-inch baking sheet with kitchen parchment paper. Prepare filling.

In a large bowl, combine flour, sugar, soda and salt. With a pastry blender, cut in butter until crumbly. In a medium bowl, combine sour cream, milk and egg; beat with a wire whisk until smooth. Stir sour cream mixture into flour mixture just until dough forms.

Turn dough out onto a lightly floured surface; knead 12 to 15 times. On parchment-lined baking sheet, roll or pat dough into a 15 × 12-inch rectangle; brush with melted butter. Sprinkle filling over half the length of the dough to within 1 inch of the edges. Fold other half of dough over filling. Trim edges evenly.

Cut dough into 15 (1-inch) strips, cutting to within 1 inch of the folded edge. Twist each strip 3 times, pressing ends to seal. Bake 12 to 15 minutes or until golden brown. Prepare glaze while coffee cake is baking.

Cool coffee cake on baking sheet on wire rack until just warm. Remove to wire rack. Drizzle glaze over the twists.

Makes 1 large coffee cake.

## FILLING

In a small bowl, stir together all ingredients.

## GLAZE

In a small bowl, combine all ingredients.

### Thinking Recipes Through

When you are an experienced cook, there's a great temptation to start making a recipe before you have read it all the way through. For Maple Pecan Twist, for example, a 16 × 14-inch baking sheet is necessary to hold the 15-inch-long coffee cake. A jelly roll pan is too small. This can be a distressing discovery if you find it out after you've formed the coffee cake.

An experienced baker will know from the recipe that this is a soft, rich dough. Thinking it through, you realize it will be much easier to shape it right on the baking sheet, rather than trying to transfer it. And if you roll the dough, rather than pat it out, you must use a baking sheet without sides.

ALAN REID    DETROIT, MICHIGAN    MICHIGAN STATE FAIR

# Orange Coconut Coffee Ring

After David George celebrated his eightieth birthday, he decided it was time to give up state fair baking competition. Then, shortly before fair time, a friend sent him this coffee cake recipe. Just reading the ingredients, he knew it could be a winner and entered it. Judges agreed.

The filled and glazed ring not only is delicious, but is an exceptionally attractive pastry. The dough is soft but easy to roll out. The baked rolls are rich and tender.

David George spent twenty-six years as a national flour salesman, but he didn't start baking competitively until he retired. After helping introduce bread flour to the consumer market, it's the only kind he uses now for yeast baking.

1 (¼-oz.) package active dry yeast
   (scant 1 tablespoon)
¼ cup warm (105 to 115F; 40 to 45C)
   water
2 eggs, beaten
¼ cup sugar
1 cup regular or light sour cream
6 tablespoons butter, melted
1 teaspoon salt
2¾ to 3¼ cups bread flour
Coconut Filling (see opposite)
Orange Glaze (see opposite)
¼ cup flaked coconut

COCONUT FILLING
2 tablespoons butter
¾ cup sugar
¾ cup flaked coconut
2 teaspoons grated orange peel

ORANGE GLAZE
¼ cup sugar
¼ cup regular or light sour cream
2 tablespoons orange juice
2 tablespoons butter

In a large bowl, dissolve yeast in warm water. Stir in eggs, sugar, sour cream, melted butter, salt and 2 cups flour. Beat until smooth. Gradually mix in remaining flour until dough pulls away from the sides of the bowl.

Turn dough out on a lightly floured surface. Wash and grease large bowl. Knead dough until smooth and elastic, 5 to 8 minutes, adding additional flour if necessary to make a moderately soft dough. Place dough in the large bowl, and turn to grease top. Cover with plastic wrap. Let rise in a warm place, 45 minutes to 1 hour, until doubled.

Meanwhile, prepare filling and glaze. Coat 2 (9-inch-round) cake pans with nonstick cooking spray.

Punch down dough and turn out on a lightly floured surface. Divide dough in half; shape each piece into a ball. Cover and let rest 10 minutes.

Roll 1 ball into a 12-inch circle. Brush with 1 tablespoon of melted butter and sprinkle half the filling evenly over the circle. Cut the circle into 12 wedges. Roll up each wedge starting at the wide end. Arrange in the pan, large end out and point side down. Repeat with remaining dough and filling. Cover, let rise in a warm place until light, about 30 to 40 minutes.

Preheat oven to 350F (175C). Bake 25 to 30 minutes or until a deep golden brown. Let rest in the pans on a cooling rack 5 minutes. Then carefully turn out on cooling racks. Set racks on waxed paper to catch glaze drips. Spoon cooled glaze over warm coffee cake and sprinkle with coconut. Serve warm or at room temperature.

Makes 2 coffee cakes, 12 servings each.

### COCONUT FILLING

Melt butter; set aside. In a small bowl, combine sugar, coconut and orange peel.

### ORANGE GLAZE

In a small saucepan, combine sugar, sour cream, orange juice and butter. Bring to a boil over medium heat, stirring constantly. Reduce heat and cook 3 minutes, stirring constantly. Let cool before spooning on warm coffee cake.

### *Learning from the Judges' Comments*

Only a few major fairs hold open judging in the food categories. There, contestants can come to the judging and listen to the judges' comments, in addition to seeing their scorecard. In many more cases, the scorecard attached to the food must serve as a silent instructor.

Many blue ribbon winners say that they started entering with no hope of winning a ribbon but simply to learn from experts how to improve their baking techniques.

David George was pleased to get a fifth place gold ribbon on the orange rolls that were his first entry. But he wasn't going to be satisfied until he could bring home a coveted blue ribbon.

From that first scorecard he realized, among other things, the judges thought the rolls should be baked longer. That was easily remedied. So the next year, at seventy-two, he received his first blue ribbon, winning with the same orange roll recipe.

Judging criteria for all categories are included in the fair premium book. They are similar, if not identical, for all fairs. It's easy to tell from the points allotted what things are most important.

Fair judges are chosen because they are experts in their field. While personal opinion inevitably will enter in, these specialists tend to judge "by the book." When dozens of the same product may be entered in a category, a single point often makes the blue ribbon difference. If you want to be a winner, study the judging criteria, learn from the judges' comments—and keep trying.

DAVID GEORGE    RICHFIELD, MINNESOTA    MINNESOTA STATE FAIR

# Maple Yeast Coffee Cake

Barbara Polk's attractive big round coffee cake looks like it came from an upscale bakery, but the taste is deliciously homemade. She uses a pizza pan to bake a three-layer filled coffee cake that is cut into wedges which are twisted before baking. It's not difficult to do, and the dough is easy to handle.

Barbara says she had to practice a few times to get picture-perfect shaping for her blue ribbon winner. Even if you have to practice, like her family, you'll love eating the test results.

1 (¼-oz.) package active dry yeast
   (scant 1 tablespoon)
¼ cup warm (105 to 115F; 40 to 45C)
   water
1 cup milk, scalded
¼ cup sugar
¼ cup vegetable oil
1 teaspoon salt
3¼ to 3¾ cups bread flour
1 egg

*FILLING*
½ cup sugar
1 teaspoon ground cinnamon
1 teaspoon maple flavoring
½ cup chopped pecans
6 tablespoons butter, melted

*DRIZZLE ICING*
1 cup powdered sugar, sifted
½ teaspoon maple flavoring
1 tablespoon milk

In a small bowl, sprinkle yeast on the warm water, stir to dissolve and let stand until bubbly. In a large bowl, combine milk, sugar, oil and salt, mixing until sugar is dissolved. Beat in 1½ cups of flour. Add egg and yeast mixture; beat until blended. Gradually mix in remaining flour until dough pulls away from the sides of the bowl.

Turn dough out on a lightly floured surface. Wash and grease a large bowl. Knead dough until smooth and elastic, about 8 minutes. Place dough in bowl and turn dough to grease top. Cover with plastic wrap. Let rise in a warm place, about 45 minutes, until doubled. Meanwhile, make filling.

Punch dough down and turn out on a lightly floured surface. Grease bottom and sides of a 12-inch pizza pan. Divide dough into 3 equal parts. Roll or pat one part into a 10-inch circle. Fit it into the bottom of the pizza pan. Brush dough with 2 tablespoons melted butter and sprinkle with ⅓ cup of filling. Repeat with two more layers.

Use a juice glass to mark the center of the coffee cake. With a scissors or sharp knife cut in wedges from the outside edge of the coffee cake just to the glass, making 2-inch-wide slices. Twist each of the 3-layer wedges once, so the bottom is now the top. Cover, let rise in a warm place until light, about 40 minutes.

Preheat oven to 350F (175C). Bake about 35 minutes or until top is a deep golden brown.

While the coffee cake is baking, make icing. Let coffee cake rest in the pan on a wire rack

10 minutes, then very carefully transfer to the wire rack. With the tip of a spoon, drizzle icing over the slightly cooled coffee cake.

**Makes 1 (10-inch-round) coffee cake.**

### FILLING

In a small bowl, combine sugar, cinnamon, maple flavoring and pecans. Melt butter.

### DRIZZLE ICING

In a small bowl, mix together the powdered sugar, maple flavoring and milk.

BARBARA POLK       ALBUQUERQUE, NEW MEXICO       NEW MEXICO STATE FAIR

# German Nut Roll

Nuts play an important part in German holiday baking, but this special pastry is such a favorite in Valalee Weber's extended family, she makes it all year long. The dough is soft, yet easy to roll out until very thin. There is a generous amount of filling. Don't be concerned if a little leaks out while the pastry bakes. Valalee says this still occasionally happens to her. She just trims it off and has won a blue ribbon with the result.

*1 (¼-oz.) package active dry yeast*
  *(scant 1 tablespoon)*
*⅓ cup plus 1 tablespoon sugar*
*1 cup warm (105 to 115F; 40 to 45C) milk*
*3 to 3½ cups all-purpose flour*
*1 egg*
*3 tablespoons butter, melted*
*½ teaspoon salt*

*WALNUT FILLING*
*3 eggs*
*1 cup sugar*
*½ teaspoon ground cinnamon*
*½ teaspoon vanilla extract*
*4 cups walnuts, finely chopped*

In a large mixer bowl, sprinkle yeast and the 1 tablespoon sugar on the warm milk, stir to dissolve and let stand until bubbly. Beat in 1½ cups flour until mixture is smooth. Let rest 30 minutes or until light and bubbly. Beat in egg, melted butter, ⅓ cup sugar and salt. Gradually add flour until dough pulls away from sides of bowl.

Turn out on lightly floured surface and knead about 5 minutes, until dough is smooth and elastic, adding more flour if needed. Wash and grease bowl. Place dough in greased bowl; cover with plastic wrap. Let rise in a warm place until doubled in size, about 45 minutes.

Grease a 15 × 13-inch baking sheet. Punch down dough. On a lightly floured surface, divide dough into 3 equal parts. Cover with plastic and let rest while mixing filling.

Roll 1 piece of the dough into a rectangle about 10 × 8 inches. Spread ⅓ of filling within 1 inch of the edges. Starting at a long side, roll, jelly-roll style, as tightly as possible, tightly sealing seam and edges. Carefully transfer roll, seam side down, to baking sheet. Repeat with remaining dough and filling, leaving 2 inches between loaves on baking sheet. Cover and let rise until light (will not be double in size), about 30 minutes.

Preheat oven to 350F (175C). Bake about 30 minutes or until loaves are golden brown. Carefully remove loaves to wire rack.

Makes 3 loaves.

**FILLING**

In a medium bowl, beat eggs, sugar, cinnamon and vanilla until well blended. Fold in the nuts.

### Chopping Nuts

The easiest way to finely chop nuts for a filling is in a food processor using a steel blade. Be sure the bowl is completely dry. Chop no more than 2 cups at a time. Place the nuts in the processor bowl, rather than feeding them through the tube, for the most uniform results. Process by quickly starting and stopping the machine. It takes only seconds to chop the nuts fine—and only seconds more to turn them into an unusable paste.

To chop in a blender, process only 1 cup at a time. You may have to chop some pieces a second time. Be careful not to overprocess; the nuts in the bottom of the blender container will be chopped finer than the rest.

VALALEE WEBER        ST. PAUL, MINNESOTA        MINNESOTA STATE FAIR

# Raisin Potato Bread

Potato bread might sound like ordinary country fare, but Linda Shaw's sophisticated brandied raisin version could star at a special tea or breakfast. You need to plan ahead to do it her way, however, because she soaks the raisins overnight in brandy until they become plump and flavorful. With both buttermilk and mashed potatoes in the dough, the bread is especially moist and tender and keeps well.

| | |
|---|---|
| *1 cup raisins* | *3 tablespoons sugar* |
| *¼ cup brandy or orange juice* | *2 tablespoons margarine* |
| *1½ cups water* | *2 teaspoons salt* |
| *1 medium potato, peeled and cut into* | *6 to 6½ cups all-purpose flour* |
| *small cubes (about ¾ cup)* | *2 (¼-oz.) packages active dry yeast* |
| *1 cup buttermilk* | *(5 teaspoons)* |

In a small bowl, toss raisins with brandy. Cover and let stand overnight before making the bread.

In a medium saucepan, combine water and potato. Bring to a boil and cook, covered, 12 to 15 minutes or until potatoes are very tender. Mash potatoes in the water. Pour into a pint measuring cup and add enough water to make 1¾ cups liquid.

Return mixture to saucepan; stir in buttermilk, sugar, margarine and salt. Heat mixture to 120 to 130F (50 to 55C), or very warm.

In a large mixer bowl, combine 2 cups flour and yeast. Blend in warm liquid at low speed until flour is moistened. Beat 3 minutes at medium speed, scraping down bowl. By hand, stir in raisins and any liquid and enough flour to form a stiff dough.

Turn out onto a lightly floured surface and knead in enough flour to make a smooth, elastic dough, about 5 minutes. Wash and grease a large bowl. Place dough in greased bowl and turn to grease top. Cover with plastic wrap and let rise in a warm place until doubled, about 40 to 45 minutes. Grease 2 (8½ × 4½-inch) or 2 (9 × 5-inch) loaf pans.

Punch down dough. Turn out onto a floured surface; divide in half. Shape into loaves by rolling each dough half into a 14 × 8-inch rectangle. Roll up starting with the shorter side. Dip the top of the loaf lightly in flour. Place in pan flour side up. Smooth top carefully to finish shaping. Cover and let rise in a warm place until nearly doubled in size, 30 to 40 minutes.

Preheat oven to 375F (190C). Bake in preheated oven about 40 minutes, until loaves sound hollow when tapped and are lightly browned.

Makes 2 (2-lb.) loaves.

### Bread Pan Sizes

Raisin Potato Bread makes big 2-pound loaves. Either a 9 × 5-inch pan or an 8½ × 4½-inch pan can be used. The larger pan size makes a wider loaf that is not as high as one baked in the 8½-inch pan. For fair competition, many blue ribbon winners prefer the appearance of the bread baked in the smaller pan, but they like the larger pan for country-style breads they bake for their families.

LINDA SHAW     UPLAND, CALIFORNIA     LOS ANGELES COUNTY FAIR

# Pineapple-Apricot Coffee Cake

Growing up on a Texas ranch where her family grew, canned or baked almost everything they ate, Charlene Reardon declared that she would never have a garden and would always have store-bought bread. Fortunately, she soon discovered the joys of baking and followed her parents' advice to "do it often, do it well and you will make something good."

Her fruit-swirled cakelike coffee cake certainly qualifies as something good. Since it uses ingredients that are easy to keep on hand, it's a good recipe when you need something special to serve in a short time.

*Streusel Topping (see opposite)*
*1 (8-oz.) can crushed pineapple,*
  *well drained (⅔ cup)*
*¼ cup apricot jam*
*1¼ cups all-purpose flour*
*2 teaspoons baking powder*
*¼ teaspoon salt*
*½ cup margarine or butter, softened*
*½ cup sugar*

*1 egg*
*1 teaspoon vanilla extract*
*½ cup milk*

*STREUSEL TOPPING*
*⅓ cup chopped nuts*
*¼ cup packed light brown sugar*
*2 tablespoons margarine or butter, softened*
*⅛ teaspoon ground cinnamon*

Preheat oven to 350F (175C). Grease and lightly flour an 8-inch-square baking pan. Prepare topping and set aside. In a small bowl, combine crushed pineapple and apricot jam and set aside.

In a small bowl, stir together flour, baking powder and salt. In a medium bowl, beat margarine or butter until creamy. Beat in sugar, egg and vanilla until well combined (batter may appear curdled). Stir in flour mixture and milk, alternately, mixing only until combined.

Spread batter in prepared pan. Dollop the pineapple mixture by teaspoonfuls on top of the batter. With a narrow-bladed knife, swirl the pineapple mixture into the batter. Sprinkle with the topping. Bake 30 to 35 minutes or until a wooden pick inserted near the center of the coffee cake (not the pineapple mixture) comes out clean and the coffee cake begins to pull away from the sides of the pan. Serve warm.

Makes 1 (8-inch-square) coffee cake.

### STREUSEL TOPPING

In a small bowl, combine all ingredients and set aside.

### Soft or Softened Margarine?

If you bake with butter, you know that "softened butter" means to use it at room temperature or beat it until it is soft. But when you use margarine, can you save time by substituting the kind that comes in tubs or one of the softer low-fat spreads?

Baked goods made with these lower-fat products tend to dry out quicker and become stale faster. So for blue ribbon results, especially if you don't plan to serve all of the baked product immediately, stick with an "80-percent fat product," which means regular margarine or butter (also an "80-percent fat product"). Read the package label to see what you are buying.

CHARLENE REARDON     SHAFTER, CALIFORNIA     KERN COUNTY FAIR

# Banana Streusel Coffee Cake

Joyce Dubois made an old favorite streusel sour cream coffee cake even better by adding mashed banana. Instead of baking it the traditional way in a tube pan, she uses two round cake pans. You can have one coffee cake to eat warm from the oven and another for the freezer. The banana flavor is particularly good combined with a generous amount of nut streusel.

*Streusel Mixture (see opposite)*
¼ *½ cup solid vegetable shortening*
½ *1 cup sugar*
1 *2 eggs*
½ *1 cup mashed ripe bananas*
¼ *½ teaspoon vanilla extract*
¼ *½ cup sour cream*
1 *2 cups all-purpose flour*

½ *1 teaspoon baking soda*
½ *1 teaspoon baking powder*
⅛ *¼ teaspoon salt*

*STREUSEL MIXTURE*
3/4 *1½ cups chopped nuts*
¼ *½ cup sugar* BROWN
½ *1 teaspoon cinnamon*

Preheat oven to 350F (175C). Grease 2 (8-inch-round) cake pans. Prepare streusel mixture and set aside.

In a medium bowl, beat together shortening and sugar until creamy. Beat in eggs, bananas and vanilla and fold in sour cream. In a small bowl, combine flour, soda, baking powder and salt. Fold into creamed mixture, stirring only enough to blend ingredients.

Sprinkle prepared pans with ⅓ of the streusel mixture. Carefully spread ½ the batter over the streusel mixture. Sprinkle with another ⅓ of the streusel mixture. Spread the remaining batter over the streusel. Sprinkle the remaining streusel mixture over the top.

Bake about 40 minutes or until a wooden pick inserted in the center comes out clean. Cool in pans on a wire rack 10 minutes; turn out onto serving plates or wire rack. Serve warm or at room temperature.

Makes 2 (8-inch-round) coffee cakes.

### STREUSEL MIXTURE
In a small bowl, combine all ingredients.

### Sour Cream Basics
In most baked foods, like this quick coffee cake, fat-free or light sour cream can be used in place of regular sour cream. The flavor and consistency are close enough to make a good substitute.

JOYCE DUBOIS      WOLSEY, SOUTH DAKOTA      SOUTH DAKOTA STATE FAIR

# Country Apple Coffee Cake

Lucille Cline is a home economist who was first a teacher and then an extension home economist in Kansas for twenty years. Now retired and a widow, she has more time to do the baking she enjoys. Known as "the cookie lady" to neighborhood children, she wins blue ribbons for baking at the fair and prizes in other recipe contests. This tasty quick coffee cake is different because it is topped with a generous amount of dried apples, which have been simmered in orange juice.

*1½ cups (8 oz.) dried apples,*
  *coarsely chopped*
*¾ cup orange juice*
*1 cup all-purpose flour*
*1 teaspoon baking powder*
*¼ teaspoon baking soda*
*⅛ teaspoon salt*

*¼ cup butter or margarine, softened*
*½ cup granulated sugar*
*1 egg*
*1 teaspoon vanilla extract*
*3 tablespoons low-fat plain yogurt*
*Powdered sugar*

In a medium saucepan, combine apples and orange juice. Bring to a boil over medium heat. Reduce heat, cover and simmer, stirring occasionally, about 15 minutes or until apples are tender and liquid is absorbed. Set aside.

Preheat oven to 350F (175C). Grease an 8-inch-square baking pan. In a small bowl, stir together flour, baking powder, soda and salt. In a medium bowl, beat butter and sugar until light and fluffy. Beat in egg and vanilla. Stir in half the flour mixture, the yogurt and the remaining flour, mixing just enough to blend thoroughly.

Spread batter in the prepared pan. Top evenly with apples. Bake 30 to 35 minutes or until a wooden pick inserted in the center comes out clean. Cool in pan on a wire rack 10 minutes. Sprinkle with powdered sugar. Serve warm.

Makes 1 (8-inch-square) coffee cake.

### Buying Dried Fruit

Eight ounces used to be the standard weight for packages of dried apples and apricots. An old recipe may call for an 8-ounce package without a cup measurement. Now you need to check the weight of the package, as package sizes will vary. If you buy dried fruit at a co-op, packages may come in an even wider variety of sizes. Home-dried apples usually are not as moist as commercial varieties, so it takes more fruit to match the commercial weight, and they need longer cooking time to soften.

Commercially dried fruit will keep up to 6 months at room temperature, if tightly wrapped. After opening a package, transfer the fruit to a tightly closed container. Dried fruit can be frozen for longer storage.

LUCILLE CLINE    WICHITA, KANSAS    KANSAS STATE FAIR

# Basic Yeast Breads

*Without wishing in the slightest degree to disparage the skill and labour of breadmakers by trade, truth compels us to assert our conviction of the superior wholesomeness of bread made in our own homes.*

Eliza Acton, *Modern Cookery,* 1855

Of entries in the major state and regional fairs are any indication, the art of bread baking is thriving. Even the enthusiasm for bread machines hasn't affected the number of conventionally made breads entered in this most competitive category.

The major difference I have observed between bread winners now and a decade ago, when the first *Blue Ribbon Winners* was published, is the interest in whole-grain breads. More than half the breads and rolls in this chapter demonstrate imaginative ways of combining whole-wheat and rye flours, rolled oats, cornmeal, muesli and wheat germ in various combinations, from savory beer bread to a maple-sweetened oatmeal bread.

White flour recipes also are noteworthy, from an herb-scented dinner bread made with pureed tomatoes to a French bread beaten with a wooden spoon instead of being kneaded.

This range of recipes points up one of the things I have learned from testing these and other blue ribbon winners: unconventional methods and unusual ingredients can create a winning product. So I test the recipe exactly as submitted. If the technique is really unusual, I note that and might suggest an alternate method.

But finding interesting new recipes and learning the secrets of blue ribbon winners is one of the most satisfying aspects of putting together a collection of recipes like this.

## About Flour

The one change often made in these bread recipes as submitted and as published is the addition of a range in the amount of white flour.

Flour may be a commodity, but that doesn't mean all flour is alike. Even among those labeled "all purpose," there's a difference in protein content. Even a small variation can mean a difference in the amount of flour needed in a recipe.

The same brand of flour will vary slightly from year to year because of the characteristics of the wheat grown that year. Even weather plays a part. Flour will pick up moisture during the hot, humid weather that is often typical at state fair time. During dry winter weather, when the thermometer drops below zero, flour will be drier.

## Protein Content

Thanks to the Food and Drug Administration's 1994 labeling law, it's now impossible to tell from the label on a sack of flour what the protein content is.

With the old labeling, we knew that those which showed 12 to 14 grams of protein per cup of flour would be excellent for kneaded breads. The range in all-purpose flour would be 8 to 11 grams per cup. You could choose one in the high range for bread and pick one in the low range for cookies and pie crust, where you don't want to develop the gluten.

Now labeling is based on ¼ cup of flour, rather than 1 cup. The result: all flour shows 3 grams per ¼ cup. Since the food company is allowed to round figures up or down, the protein content actually could range from 2.5 to about 4 grams per ¼ cup and still be considered accurate for labeling.

With the more accurate original labeling, based on 1 cup, the protein level could be anywhere from 10 to 16 grams of protein.

Here are a few guidelines to help determine protein levels:

- Flour labeled "bread flour" will be high-protein flour.
- Other flours that are labeled "all purpose" but state on the label that the flour is made entirely from hard wheat will be higher in protein.
- Unbleached flour has a little more protein than bleached flour, because of the bleaching process.

One other change in the past decade is the elimination of bromate from bread flour. Bromate was added to strengthen the dough and to make it more tolerant. If you overproofed your rolls or loaves of bread, for example, they were less likely to collapse in the oven.

Because of some concerns about bromate being a carcinogen, it no longer is added. If you have been using bread flour and have been accustomed to that extra level of tolerance, it's important now not to overproof bread.

Our recipe directions now say until "just doubled." It's better to slightly underproof the loaves, since they will continue to rise in the oven until the yeast is killed by the heat.

# Honey Whole-Wheat Bread

Louise Schneiderman has been exhibiting at the North Dakota State Fair for more than thirty years and has more than two thousand ribbons to show for it. A busy child-care provider, she still manages to do her own baking and canning. Her blue ribbon whole-wheat bread is light textured with a wonderful whole-wheat flavor. It's the kind of classic whole-wheat bread you'll want to make again and again.

*2 (¼-oz.) packages active dry yeast*
   *(5 teaspoons)*
*1¼ cups warm (105 to 115F; 40 to 45C)*
   *water*
*⅓ cup honey*
*¼ cup butter, melted*

*1 tablespoon salt*
*1 cup milk, scalded and cooled to*
   *lukewarm*
*3 cups whole-wheat flour*
*2¾ to 3½ cups bread flour*
*Melted butter*

In a large bowl, sprinkle yeast on warm water and stir to dissolve. Add honey, ¼ cup butter, salt, milk and whole-wheat flour. Blend at low speed with mixer or stir until flour is moistened. Gradually stir in bread flour to make a stiff dough.

Turn out dough onto floured surface. Knead 10 minutes or until dough is smooth and elastic, adding a little more flour, if necessary. Wash and grease large bowl. Place dough in greased bowl, cover and let rise in a warm space until doubled in size, about 1 hour. Grease 2 (8½ × 4½-inch) loaf pans.

Punch down dough. Divide dough in half, shape into balls. Turn out on lightly floured surface. Cover and let rest 10 minutes. Shape dough into 2 loaves. Place in greased pans and lightly brush tops with melted butter. Cover and let rise in a warm place until loaves are light and just doubled in size, about 40 to 45 minutes.

Preheat oven to 375F (190C). Bake 40 to 45 minutes or until loaves sound hollow when lightly tapped. Remove from pans to wire rack to cool.

**Makes 2 (1½-lb.) loaves.**

### Using Bread Flour
Bread flour has more gluten strength than all-purpose flour because it is milled from hard (high-protein) wheat. The sturdier doughs made from bread flour feel more elastic and require a longer kneading time (about 10 minutes) to develop the gluten.

If you substitute all-purpose flour for bread flour, you may need to add a little more flour. Kneading time for all-purpose flour is shorter (6 to 8 minutes) because there is less gluten.

LOUISE SCHNEIDERMAN    BOTTINEAU, NORTH DAKOTA    NORTH DAKOTA STATE FAIR

# Muesli Bread

Brenda Gray makes this hearty bread with a special Swiss muesli available only in her area, but any European-style granola will do. The bread has a nutty texture and makes exceptionally good toast. The dough rises in less time than some hearty whole-grain breads, so watch that it doesn't overproof. You may need to cover the loaves with foil during the end of the baking time, so the granola topping doesn't overbrown.

| | |
|---|---|
| ¼ cup warm (105 to 115F; 40 to 45C) water | 2 teaspoons salt |
| 3 tablespoons honey | ½ cup raisins (optional) |
| 1 (¼-oz.) package active dry yeast (scant 1 tablespoon) | 1½ cups Swiss muesli or granola |
| 2 tablespoons vegetable oil | 1½ cups boiling water |
| 2 tablespoons butter | ⅓ cup plus 3 tablespoons buttermilk |
| 1 teaspoon ground cinnamon | ½ cup whole-wheat flour |
| | 4 to 4½ cups all-purpose flour |

In a small bowl, combine warm water, 1 tablespoon honey and yeast. Let stand until bubbly, about 10 minutes. In a large bowl, combine remaining 2 tablespoons honey, oil, butter, cinnamon, salt, raisins, if using, and 1 cup muesli. Add boiling water and stir until moistened. Let stand until cereal is softened, about 5 minutes.

Stir in ⅓ cup buttermilk, whole-wheat flour and yeast mixture. [If temperature of dough is more than 115F (45C) after adding flour, let mixture cool before adding yeast.] Gradually beat in all-purpose flour to make a stiff dough that pulls away from the sides of the bowl.

Turn dough out on lightly floured surface and knead 5 to 8 minutes or until dough is smooth and elastic, adding additional flour if needed. Wash and grease large bowl. Place dough in greased bowl, and turn dough to grease top. Cover with plastic wrap and let rise in a warm place until doubled, about 30 to 40 minutes. Grease 2 (8½ × 4½-inch) loaf pans.

Punch down dough. Turn out on lightly floured surface and knead briefly to release air bubbles. Divide dough in half. Shape dough into 2 loaves and place in prepared pans. Cover and let rise in a warm place until just doubled, about 30 minutes.

Preheat oven to 350F (175C). Soften remaining ½ cup muesli in the 3 tablespoons buttermilk. Spoon over loaves. Bake about 45 minutes or until loaves are deep golden brown and sound hollow when tapped on the bottom. If necessary, cover tops with foil to prevent muesli from overbrowning. Remove from pans and let cool on wire rack.

Makes 2 (1½-lb.) loaves.

### Testing the Temperature of Liquids

Many blue ribbon bakers depend on a thermometer rather than testing the temperature of the liquids by touch. If the liquid is too cool, it will slow or stop the action of the yeast. If it's too hot, it will kill the yeast.

When yeast is dissolved directly in water, the method used in most of these recipes, the temperature range is 105 to 115F (40 to 45C), often described as "warm." When the undissolved yeast is added to the dry ingredients, liquids should be hotter, 120 to 130F (50 to 55C).

BRENDA GRAY     CLAREMONT, CALIFORNIA     LOS ANGELES COUNTY FAIR

# Whole-Grain & Honey Bread

In sixteen years of fair exhibiting, Elaine Klempay has won more than one hundred ribbons in areas as diverse as cross-stitch to cookies, but her great love is yeast baking. She added soy flour, wheat germ and whole-wheat flour to an oatmeal bread. The result is a nutritious loaf with a pleasing, slightly sweet whole-grain flavor.

*2 cups water*
*1¼ cup rolled oats, preferably old-fashioned*
*2 (¼-oz.) packages active dry yeast*
  *(5 teaspoons)*
*½ cup warm (105 to 115F; 40 to 45C)*
  *water*
*2 teaspoons salt*
*1 cup whole-wheat flour*

*3 tablespoons soy flour*
*1 tablespoon wheat germ*
*3 tablespoons dry milk powder*
*4 to 5 cups bread flour*
*¼ cup vegetable oil*
*½ cup honey*
*1 egg white lightly beaten with*
  *1 tablespoon water*

In a medium saucepan, heat 1 cup of the water to boiling. Stir in 1 cup of the rolled oats, cover and let rest 5 to 10 minutes. Dissolve yeast in ½ cup warm water. In food processor or blender, chop remaining ¼ cup oatmeal. Set aside for topping.

In a medium bowl, combine salt, whole-wheat flour, soy flour, wheat germ, dry milk, and 1 cup bread flour. In a large bowl, combine vegetable oil, honey, remaining 1 cup water and oat mixture. Stir in yeast mixture and beat well. Gradually add remaining bread flour to make a slightly soft dough that begins to pull away from the sides of the bowl.

Turn out onto floured surface and knead 8 to 10 minutes until dough is smooth and elastic, adding more flour if necessary. Wash and grease large bowl. Place dough in large bowl, and turn dough to coat top. Cover with plastic wrap and let rise in a warm place about 40 minutes or until light and doubled in size. Spray 2 (8½ × 4½-inch) loaf pans with vegetable spray or grease.

Punch down dough. Turn out onto floured surface. Divide in half and shape into balls. Shape each dough ball into a 12 × 10-inch rectangle. Roll into a 10-inch cylinder and pinch the loose edge to seal. Fold in the ends. Place in prepared pans, seam side down, cover with plastic wrap and let rise until dough is just doubled, about 30 minutes.

Preheat oven to 375F (190C). Brush bread with egg white mixture. Sprinkle the loaves with finely chopped oats. Bake 30 to 40 minutes or until bread is a deep golden brown and the loaf sounds hollow when tapped on the bottom. Remove from pans and let cool on wire racks.

**Makes 2 (1½-lb.) loaves.**

## 🎗 *Oatmeal in Bread*

Oatmeal is a popular ingredient in these whole-grain breads, where it adds a pleasanty mild nutty flavor. You can use either uncooked, quick-cooking or regular rolled oats in most recipes, but not instant oatmeal. Oats have very little gluten so they must be combined with wheat flour.

If a recipe calls for cooked oatmeal, expect a very smooth-textured loaf. But don't substitute cooked for uncooked oatmeal unless you make an adjustment for the extra liquid in the cooked oatmeal.

ELAINE KLEMPAY    CANFIELD, OHIO    CANFIELD FAIR

# Nut-Brown Beer Bread

Cooking is Roy Struve's hobby and he estimates he has a collection of ten thousand recipes. Beer adds a tangy flavor, but no alcohol remains in the nutritious, low-fat loaf. He recommends using a dark beer to get the characteristic flavor of a prize-winning beer bread.

2 (¼-oz.) packages active dry yeast
   (5 teaspoons)
⅓ cup brown sugar
1 cup warm (105 to 115F; 40 to 45C)
   water
1 (12-oz.) can dark beer, warmed
   (105 to 115F; 40 to 45C)

3 tablespoons margarine, melted
1 cup toasted wheat germ
5 to 6 cups unbleached all-purpose flour
2 teaspoons salt
1 cup whole-wheat flour

Dissolve yeast with 1 teaspoon brown sugar in ½ cup warm water in large bowl of electric mixer. Stir in warm beer, remaining ½ cup water and margarine. Add wheat germ, 3½ cups all-purpose flour and salt. Beat at medium speed until smooth and elastic. Stir in whole-wheat flour and all-purpose flour to make a soft dough that pulls away from the sides of the bowl.

Turn out onto floured surface and knead about 5 minutes or until dough feels springy, adding flour if needed. Wash and grease large bowl. Transfer dough to greased bowl and turn once to coat top surface. Cover with plastic wrap and let rise in a warm spot until double in bulk, 45 to 60 minutes.

Punch down dough, turn out onto floured surface and divide in half. Cover with bowl and let rest 5 minutes. Grease 2 (8½ × 4½-inch) loaf pans. Form dough into 2 loaves and place in prepared pans. Cover with plastic wrap and let rise until just double, 35 to 40 minutes.

Preheat oven to 375F (190C). Bake 40 to 45 minutes until loaves are deep brown and the bottom sounds hollow when tapped. Remove from pans and let cool on wire rack.

Makes 2 (1½-lb.) loaves.

ROY STRUVE    ANKENY, IOWA    IOWA STATE FAIR

# Onion Sesame Bread

Lee Rathbone is a grandmother who has been baking her own bread since her children were preschoolers. She scorns bread machines and dough hooks, preferring to "vent my frustrations by slapping the dough around." Now retired as a technical editor, she has time to travel and learn about the food of other countries. Then she comes home and entertains friends at dinner. She likes to serve this hearty, flavorful bread to accompany sauerkraut and sausages.

| | |
|---|---|
| *1½ cups beer* | *1 tablespoon salt* |
| *2 (¼-oz.) packages active dry yeast* | *½ cup vegetable oil* |
| *(5 teaspoons)* | *1 cup finely chopped yellow onion* |
| *1 cup whole-wheat flour* | *¾ cup sesame seeds* |
| *1 cup medium rye flour* | *1 egg* |
| *2½ to 3 cups unbleached all-purpose flour* | *2 teaspoons water* |
| *2 tablespoons sugar* | *Fresh or dried rosemary, finely chopped* |

In a small saucepan, heat beer to 105F (40C). Pour ½ cup into a small bowl. Stir in yeast and let proof 10 minutes. In a large bowl, mix together wheat and rye flours, 2 cups all-purpose flour, sugar and salt. Make a well in the center. Pour in yeast mixture, remaining beer and oil. Stir until well blended, adding all-purpose flour if needed to make a dough that pulls away from the sides of the bowl.

Turn out on lightly floured surface and knead until smooth and elastic, about 10 minutes. Wash and grease bowl. Place dough in bowl and turn dough to grease top. Cover with plastic wrap and let rise in a warm place until double, about 1 hour. Let onion drain in a strainer while dough is proofing. Grease 1 large or 2 medium baking sheets.

Punch down dough. Knead in drained onion and sesame seeds. Turn dough out onto lightly floured surface, form into a ball and divide in half. Shape dough into braids or round loaves. Place on baking sheet, cover and let rise until just doubled, about 45 to 60 minutes.

Preheat oven to 375F (190C). Lightly beat together egg and water. Brush loaves lightly with egg wash. Sprinkle with rosemary. Carefully brush again with egg wash. Bake until well browned and crusty, 45 to 50 minutes. Turn out on wire racks to cool.

**Makes 2 braids or round loaves.**

### Storing Sesame Seeds
Sesame seeds are high in oil and become rancid quickly. Unless the seeds are fresh, the bread can take on a slightly bitter flavor. Store sesame seeds tightly covered in the refrigerator or freeze them.

LEE RATHBONE    SAN DIEGO, CALIFORNIA    LOS ANGELES COUNTY FAIR

# Good Health Bread

John Chovan, who has a Ph.D. in engineering, combines his methodical and logical side with a creative side, which includes a music degree and a love of cooking. Making this robust bread may require a trip to a co-op for the seeds it calls for, but the blend of flavors they add makes it worth the effort. He starts the loaf baking in a cold oven, which he has found produces a better shaped loaf. Include the sour dough starter if you have it (page 45). If not, add an extra ¼ cup warm water. Either way, the resulting bread is exceptionally good tasting.

*1 (¼-oz.) package active dry yeast*
  *(scant 1 tablespoon)*
*1¼ cups warm (105 to 115F; 40 to 45C)*
  *water*
*¼ cup Sourdough Starter (page 45)*
  *or your own*
*2 tablespoons honey*
*1½ teaspoons salt, preferably kosher*
*¼ cup rolled oats*
*2 tablespoons unhulled sesame seeds*

*2 tablespoons flax seeds*
*2 tablespoons sunflower kernels*
*2 tablespoons millet*
*2 tablespoons pine nuts, roasted and*
  *chopped*
*1½ cups whole-wheat flour, preferably*
  *freshly ground*
*2¼ to 2½ cups bread flour*
*1 egg yolk mixed with 2 teaspoons water*

In a large bowl, dissolve yeast in warm water. Add sourdough starter, honey, salt, rolled oats, sesame seeds, flax seeds, sunflower kernels, millet and pine nuts; mix thoroughly. Add whole-wheat flour and mix well. Add bread flour a little at a time to make a soft dough that pulls away from the sides of the bowl.

Turn dough out on a floured surface and knead 10 minutes or until dough is smooth and elastic. Wash and oil bowl. If desired, cover dough and let rest 5 minutes, then knead again for about 25 minutes (or knead with dough hook for entire time). Form dough into a ball, place in bowl and turn dough to coat top. Cover with plastic wrap and let rise in a warm place until doubled in bulk, 40 to 60 minutes. Grease a darkened 9 × 5-inch or 8½ × 4½-inch aluminum pan.

Punch down dough. Form into a loaf and place in prepared pan. Brush with egg yolk mixture. Place pan in a cold oven.

Heat oven to 350F (175C). Bake about 50 minutes or until a deep golden brown, 200F (95C) on instant-read thermometer. Remove from pan and cool on wire rack.

Makes 1 (2-lb.) loaf.

**VARIATION**

Bake in a preheated 375F (190C) oven.

### 🏅 *Oven Spring*

When bread goes into a preheated oven, steam from the moisture in the bread causes the dough to swell before the heat finally stops the action of the yeast. This is called oven spring. Although this is usually considered desirable, John Chovan decided his bread had better shape when he started in a cold oven, avoiding oven spring.

However, you must be careful not to overproof the dough. The loaf will continue to rise in the oven until the internal temperature of the bread reaches 140F (60C). If the bread is overproofed, it may collapse and you will have a dense loaf with a heavy texture.

JOHN CHOVAN   COLUMBUS, OHIO   OHIO STATE FAIR

# Anadama Bread

The Iowa State Fair unquestionably has the widest variety of food entry categories of any fair. One of the more unusual is for Anadama Bread. Although there are many variations of this American heritage recipe, Norma Herring's big, hearty loaf deserved to be a winner. It was one of fifty entries she took to the state fair, although she had had heart surgery earlier in the year. She suggests that a thick slice of this bread toasted and spread with homemade apple butter makes a wonderful breakfast treat. Who could resist?

*2 cups water*
*½ cup cornmeal*
*½ cup molasses, preferably dark*
*⅓ cup solid vegetable shortening*
*1½ teaspoons salt*

*5½ cups bread flour*
*2 (¼-oz.) packages quick-rising active*
  *dry yeast (5 teaspoons)*
*2 eggs*
*½ teaspoon shortening, melted*

In a medium saucepan, bring the 2 cups of water to a boil. Very gradually stir in cornmeal. Add molasses, shortening and salt. Cool to warm (120 to 130F; 50 to 55C). In a large bowl, combine 3 cups flour and yeast. With an electric mixer at low speed, beat in cornmeal mixture and eggs until well mixed. Beat 3 minutes on high speed. By hand, stir in remaining flour to make a stiff dough that pulls away from the sides of the bowl.

Turn out on lightly floured surface and knead until smooth and elastic, about 10 minutes. Wash and grease large bowl. Place dough in bowl, and turn dough to grease top. Cover and let rise in a warm place until doubled in size, about 30 minutes.

Punch down dough, turn out on lightly floured surface. Divide dough into 2 pieces. Cover with a large bowl and let rest 10 minutes. Grease 2 (8½ × 4½-inch) loaf pans. Shape dough into loaves. Place in prepared pans. Cover and let rise until just doubled, about 30 minutes.

Preheat oven to 375F (190C). Brush loaves with melted shortening. Bake about 45 to 50 minutes, covering tops with foil after 30 minutes to keep from becoming too brown. Turn out onto wire rack to cool.

Makes 2 (1¾-lb.) loaves.

NORMA HERRING     DEXTER, IOWA     IOWA STATE FAIR

# Refrigerator Oatmeal Bread

Linda Hemond says she and her family have a mutually satisfactory arrangement: she loves to bake and they love to eat. A busy financial analyst, she especially appreciates this no-knead recipe, which won the sweepstakes in bread, in addition to a blue ribbon. She refrigerates the rich dough overnight and in the morning shapes and bakes the loaves.

*2 (¼-oz.) packages active dry yeast*
*(5 teaspoons)*
*½ cup warm (105 to 115F; 40 to 45C)*
*water*
*1½ cups boiling water*
*1 cup quick-cooking rolled oats*

*½ cup light molasses*
*⅓ cup solid vegetable shortening*
*1 teaspoon salt*
*6¼ cups sifted all-purpose flour*
*2 eggs, slightly beaten*

In a small bowl, dissolve yeast in lukewarm water. In a large bowl, combine 1½ cups boiling water, rolled oats, molasses, shortening and salt. Mix well. Cool to lukewarm. Add yeast mixture and 2 cups flour. Add eggs and mix well. Add remaining flour, 2 cups at a time, to make a moderately stiff dough. Mix vigorously until smooth. Grease top of dough lightly. Cover tightly with plastic wrap and refrigerate at least 2 hours or overnight.

Grease 2 (8½ × 4½-inch) loaf pans. Punch down dough. Turn out dough on lightly floured surface, shape into 2 loaves and place in prepared pans. Cover with plastic wrap and let rise in a warm place until just doubled in size, 1½ to 2 hours.

Preheat oven to 375F (190C). Bake 40 minutes or until loaves sound hollow when tapped. Cover loaves with foil the last 10 to 15 minutes if crusts are getting too brown. Remove from pan to wire rack to cool.

Makes 2 (1½-lb.) loaves.

### Refrigerated Doughs

While any yeast dough can be refrigerated briefly, you need a specially formulated, enriched dough for longer refrigeration. Although refrigerated dough most often is used in roll recipes, Linda Hemond's recipe shows that even whole-grain breads can be mixed one day and baked later.

If a recipe is made with milk and ¼ cup or more sugar, three days is the limit. A dough like this, made with water, can be refrigerated a few days longer.

LINDA HEMOND     WILLISTON, VERMONT     CHAMPLAIN VALLEY EXPOSITION

# Maple Oatmeal Bread

Blue ribbon winner, sweepstakes and best of show were the accolades heaped on Marian Tobin's Maple Oatmeal Bread. It's hearty country-style bread—big loaves with a rich brown color, a sturdy crust and a rich, slightly sweet flavor from the maple syrup used as the sweetening. As a Vermont expert on maple syrup, she recommends using Grade A Dark Amber for its heartier flavor.

| | |
|---|---|
| *¾ cup water* | *2 (¼-oz.) packages active dry yeast* |
| *1 cup brewed coffee* | *(5 teaspoons)* |
| *1 cup regular or quick-cooking rolled oats* | *¼ cup lukewarm (105 to 115F; 40 to 45C)* |
| *⅓ cup solid vegetable shortening* | *water* |
| *½ cup pure maple syrup* | *2 eggs* |
| *½ cup sugar* | *4¾ to 5 cups bread flour* |
| *2 teaspoons salt* | |

In a small saucepan, heat water and coffee just to boiling. Pour over rolled oats in a large bowl. Stir in shortening, maple syrup, sugar and salt. Cool mixture to lukewarm.

In small bowl, dissolve yeast in warm water and let stand 5 minutes. Blend oat mixture, yeast mixture, eggs and 2 cups flour at low speed with mixer until flour is moistened. Gradually stir in enough flour to make a stiff dough that pulls away from the sides of the bowl.

Turn out dough on floured surface. Cover with an inverted bowl and let stand 15 minutes. Knead 10 minutes or until smooth and elastic, adding additional flour if needed. Wash and grease large bowl. Place dough in greased bowl, cover and let rise in a warm place until doubled, 45 to 60 minutes. Grease 2 (8½ × 4½-inch) or 2 (9 × 5-inch) loaf pans.

Punch down dough. Divide into 2 parts. Shape into loaves and place in prepared loaf pans. Cover and let rise in a warm place until just doubled in size, about 45 minutes.

Preheat oven to 350F (175C). Bake about 45 to 50 minutes until loaves sound hollow when tapped. If loaves are getting too brown, cover with aluminum foil. Remove from pan to wire rack to cool.

Makes 2 (2-lb.) loaves.

### Maple Syrup

The use of pure maple syrup as a sweetener in bread is a New England tradition that deserves to be expanded. Save the milder, light-colored syrup for pancakes. Take advantage of the fuller flavor of the less-expensive darker grades for bread. Don't substitute maple-flavored syrups, which are very sweet with less maple flavor, for pure maple syrup.

After opening, maple syrup will keep about a year in the refrigerator.

MARIAN TOBIN     UNDERHILL, VERMONT     CHAMPLAIN VALLEY EXPOSITION

# Oatmeal Cinnamon Bread

Being a home-schooling mom for the past fourteen years has given Debra "Cookie" Burk an opportunity to experiment with ways to provide wholesome, healthy meals for her family. Baking her own bread, starting with grinding her own wheat, is an important part of her strategy. In this recipe, she sprinkles just a little cinnamon sugar on the rolled-out dough, adding a touch of sweetness that makes the nutritious whole-grain bread more attractive to her six children. Her Old Timey Cinnamon Bread variation is an easy and economical way to turn the bread into a breakfast treat.

*1½ cups rolled oats, preferably old-fashioned*
*1 cup whole-wheat flour*
*½ cup packed light brown sugar*
*1 tablespoon salt*
*2 tablespoons margarine*
*2 cups boiling water*
*1 (¼-oz.) package active dry yeast (scant 1 tablespoon)*

*½ cup warm (105 to 115F; 40 to 45C) water*
*3½ to 4½ cups all-purpose flour*
*¼ cup granulated sugar*
*2 teaspoons ground cinnamon*
*1 egg lightly beaten with 1 tablespoon water*

In a large bowl, combine rolled oats, whole-wheat flour, brown sugar, salt, margarine and boiling water. Stir to combine and let cool to warm (115F, 45C). Dissolve yeast in warm water. Stir into warm flour mixture. Gradually add all-purpose flour to make a stiff dough that pulls away from the sides of the bowl.

Turn out dough onto floured surface. Knead 5 to 8 minutes until dough is smooth and elastic, adding additional flour as necessary. Wash and grease large bowl. Place dough in bowl, and turn dough to grease top. Cover with plastic wrap and let rise in a warm place until light and doubled in bulk, about 1 hour. Grease 2 (9 × 5-inch) or 2 (8½ × 4½-inch) loaf pans.

Punch down dough and turn out on floured surface. Divide dough in half and form each piece into a ball. Roll out each ball into a 12 × 8-inch rectangle. In a small bowl, combine granulated sugar and cinnamon. Sprinkle half on each rectangle. Starting from the 8-inch side, roll up jelly-roll style. Pinch edges together to seal. Place in prepared pans. Cover and let rise in a warm place about 1 hour or until just doubled in size.

Preheat oven to 350F (175C). Brush loaves with egg mixture. Bake 40 to 45 minutes or until loaves are light brown and sound hollow when tapped on the bottom. Remove from pans to wire rack to cool. If you like a soft crust, place bread in a plastic bag while still warm.

Makes 2 (1½-lb.) loaves.

### VARIATION

**OLD TIMEY CINNAMON BREAD** Sprinkle each rectangle of dough with ½ cup raisins along with cinnamon-sugar mixture. Glaze baked loaves with a mixture of 1 cup powdered sugar, 1 tablespoon milk and ¼ teaspoon vanilla.

DEBRA BURK    RANSOM CANYON, TEXAS    PANHANDLE SOUTH PLAINS FAIR

# Irlene's Rye Bread

When a Minnesotan called her orange- and fennel-flavored blue ribbon winner "limpa bread," Irlene Yarbrough said she had never heard of this Scandinavian specialty. She always thought of this old recipe as her best rye bread. A hearty, rich-flavored country bread, it is dark-colored and moist, so it may appear to look baked before it is. For more accurate results, use an instant-read thermometer inserted in the center; it should read 200F (95C).

| | |
|---|---|
| 2 (¼-oz.) packages active dry yeast (5 teaspoons) | 3 tablespoons solid vegetable shortening |
| 1½ cups warm (105 to 115F; 40 to 45C) water | 3 tablespoons grated orange peel (from 3 large oranges) |
| ¼ cup molasses | 1 teaspoon fennel seeds |
| ⅓ cup sugar | 2½ cups medium rye flour |
| 1 tablespoon salt | 2¼ to 2¾ cups all-purpose flour |
| | Cornmeal |

In a large bowl, dissolve yeast in warm water and let stand until bubbly. Stir in molasses, sugar, salt, shortening, orange peel and fennel seeds. Blend in rye flour with an electric mixer at low speed or with a wooden spoon. Stir in all-purpose flour to make a stiff dough that pulls away from the sides of the bowl.

Turn out on lightly floured surface, cover and let rest 15 minutes. Knead 5 to 8 minutes or until smooth and elastic, adding additional flour if needed. Wash and grease a large bowl. Place dough in greased bowl, cover and let rise in a warm place until doubled in size, about 1 hour.

Punch dough down and turn over. Cover and let rise again until double, about 40 minutes. Generously grease a large baking sheet and sprinkle with cornmeal.

Punch down dough and divide in half. Shape into 2 round, slightly flattened loaves. Place loaves at opposite corners of baking sheet. Cover and let rise until just doubled, about 45 minutes.

Preheat oven to 375F (190C). Bake 40 to 45 minutes, covering the loaves with foil if they begin to get too brown.

Makes 2 (1¼-lb.) round loaves.

### ⍟ Determining When Bread Is Done

One fact became evident in testing several dozen basic bread recipes for this book: with dark whole-grain bread, color is not a good indication of doneness. Tapping the bottom of the loaf and getting a hollow sound is usually, but not always, an accurate method.

Dark, moist breads like Irlene's Rye Bread are the most difficult to judge. I learned that the most accurate method is to use an instant-read thermometer inserted through the center of the loaf. When it reaches 200F (95C), the bread is baked. The test applies to all yeast bread, not just whole-grain.

IRLENE YARBROUGH          STRAFFORD, MISSOURI          OZARK EMPIRE FAIR

# Bohemian Beer Bread

After a state fair judge challenged Geraldine Sandoval to develop a true beer bread, she researched bread books until she learned the secrets. The result won a blue ribbon, and the same judge said it was the best beer bread he had ever tasted. Using a dark stout (like Guinness) and rye and whole-wheat flour were two of her discoveries. Another secret ingredient is her own Bohemian flour. In making the bread, be careful not to use too much flour. The dough should feel slightly sticky, but very workable.

*¾ cup stout or dark beer*
*2 tablespoons solid vegetable shortening*
*2 tablespoons brown sugar*
*2 tablespoons molasses*
*1 (¼-oz.) package active dry yeast*
*(scant 1 tablespoon)*
*¼ cup warm (105 to 115F; 40 to 45C)*
*water*

*3½ cups Bohemian flour (see Note below)*
*1 teaspoon salt*
*2 teaspoons caraway seeds*
*1 egg*
*1 tablespoon water*

In a small saucepan, heat beer, shortening, brown sugar and molasses until shortening is nearly melted. Remove from heat. In a small bowl, dissolve yeast in warm water and let stand until bubbly, about 5 minutes. In a large bowl, stir together 3 cups Bohemian flour, salt and caraway seeds. Stir in yeast mixture and warm beer mixture by hand (dough will be very stiff).

Turn out onto floured surface and knead until dough is smooth and elastic and begins to feel slightly moist, about 5 minutes, adding Bohemian flour, if needed. Wash and grease bowl. Place dough in greased bowl and cover with plastic wrap. Let rise in a warm place until an indentation remains when you push a finger ½ inch into the dough, about 1 hour. (The dough may not look doubled in size.) Grease a baking sheet.

Turn dough out on lightly floured surface. Knead a few times to remove air bubbles. Shape into a round loaf. Place on greased baking sheet. Cover and let rise in a warm place until an impression remains when you push a finger into the side of the dough.

Preheat oven to 350F (175C). With a sharp knife, slash a ½-inch-deep lattice design on top of loaf. With a fork, in a small bowl, beat egg with water until well mixed. Brush top of loaf with a thin layer of egg glaze. Bake 45 to 60 minutes until top is deep brown and the bottom sounds hollow when tapped.

Makes 1 (1¾-lb.) round loaf.

**NOTE**

**BOHEMIAN FLOUR** Use equal parts bread flour, whole-wheat flour and medium rye flour. Leftover Bohemian flour can be used in any whole-grain bread recipe.

GERALDINE SANDOVAL    ALBUQUERQUE, NEW MEXICO    NEW MEXICO STATE FAIR

# Finnish Farmers' Sourdough Rye Bread

If you are a sourdough baker, you'll welcome this interesting way to use your starter. If you are new to sourdough baking, you'll find Geraldine Sandoval's starter, which contains some yeast, an easy one to make successfully and to keep on hand. Her blue ribbon winner is an authentic Finnish country rye bread. It has a mildly tangy sourdough rye flavor and is characterized by its unusual shaping. The result is a show-off loaf you'll enjoy serving to guests.

*1 (¼-oz.) package active dry yeast*
*  (scant 1 tablespoon)*
*1½ teaspoons sugar*
*1 cup warm (105 to 115F; 40 to 45C)*
*  water*
*1½ teaspoons salt*

*2 teaspoons vegetable oil*
*2 tablespoons caraway seeds*
*¾ cup Sourdough Starter (see opposite)*
*1½ cups medium rye flour*
*2 to 2¼ cups all-purpose flour*
*Melted butter for brushing*

In a large bowl, combine yeast, sugar and warm water. Let stand 10 minutes. With wooden spoon or mixer at low speed, stir in salt, oil, caraway seeds and sourdough starter. Beat in ½ cup each rye flour and all-purpose flour. Add 1 cup rye flour and beat well. Gradually stir in all but 1 cup all-purpose flour.

Turn dough out on floured surface and knead 10 minutes, adding remaining flour as needed to make a stiff dough. Wash and grease large bowl. Place dough in greased bowl, cover and let rise in a warm place until double in size, about 1 hour. Grease a large baking sheet.

Punch down dough and divide in half. Turn out onto lightly floured surface. Knead each portion and shape into smooth balls. Place on opposite ends of prepared baking sheet, cover and let rise in a warm place until loaves are doubled in size, about 45 minutes.

Preheat oven to 375F (190C). Press the long handle of a wooden spoon across the middle of each loaf, almost to the bottom of the loaf. Make 2 more indentations on either side. Loaves will flatten out. Brush loaves with melted butter. Bake 35 minutes or until loaves are golden brown and sound hollow when tapped. Remove from baking sheet and cool on wire rack.

Makes 2 (1-lb.) round loaves.

**VARIATION**

Dough can be made into 1 large loaf. Bake 45 minutes or until it sounds hollow when tapped on bottom.

**SOURDOUGH STARTER**

The starter is best if you use it once a week. If you do not use it for two or three weeks, discard half and replenish.

*2 cups all-purpose flour*
*3 tablespoons sugar*
*1 (¼-oz.) package (scant 1 tablespoon)*
  *active dry yeast*

*2 cups warm water (105F to 115F;*
  *40 to 45C)*

In a 4- to 6-cup plastic pitcher or large nonmetallic bowl, combine all ingredients. Beat with a wooden or plastic spoon until blended. Fermentation will dissolve small lumps. Cover with a cloth. Set in a warm place free from drafts and let ferment 2 to 3 days. Stir mixture several times a day.

To use, remove starter needed for recipe. Refrigerate remaining starter in a plastic pitcher or plastic container with a lid that has an air vent or hole in it. Label container with contents.

After using some starter, replenish by stirring in equal amounts of water and all-purpose flour (such as ½ cup water and ½ cup flour). Let starter stand at room temperature until full of bubbles. Refrigerate. If a clear liquid forms on top, stir back into starter.

Makes 3 to 4 cups.

GERALDINE SANDOVAL     ALBUQUERQUE, NEW MEXICO     NEW MEXICO STATE FAIR

# Country Sesame Seed Egg Bread

Denise Turnbull has won the grand championship as well as blue ribbons for this impressive, rich braided loaf. For a well-shaped braid, it's important not to overproof it. The large, deep golden brown loaf can look baked before it is. The instant-read thermometer test (200F, 95C) is good to use here. In addition to being extremely good eating, this rich bread stays fresh for several days and makes superb toast.

*5 to 5½ cups bread flour*
*1 (¼-oz.) package active dry yeast*
*   (scant 1 tablespoon)*
*1 cup milk*
*⅓ cup packed light brown sugar*

*⅓ cup butter*
*1 teaspoon salt*
*3 eggs*
*1 egg white mixed with 1 teaspoon water*
*Sesame seeds*

In a large bowl, combine 1½ cups flour and yeast. In a medium saucepan, combine milk, brown sugar, butter and salt. Heat over medium heat to 120F (50C), stirring constantly. Add to flour mixture and beat with an electric mixer at low speed until well blended, scraping the sides of the bowl. Beat at high speed 2 minutes. Add eggs, one at a time, and beat thoroughly. Add 2 cups flour and mix well. With a wooden spoon, mix in enough flour to make a soft dough that pulls away from the sides of the bowl.

Turn dough out on lightly floured surface and knead until smooth and elastic, 8 to 10 minutes. Wash and grease large bowl. Add dough to bowl, turning dough to coat all sides. Cover with plastic wrap and let rise at warm room temperature until doubled, about 1 hour. Grease a large baking sheet.

Punch down dough and turn out on lightly floured surface. Divide dough into 3 equal pieces. Roll each piece of dough into a rope about 15 inches long. Arrange the ropes side by side, slightly apart, on prepared baking sheet. Pinch ends firmly to seal. Braid the ropes together. Pinch ends together and tuck under both ends. Cover and let rise 25 minutes; braid will not double.

Preheat oven to 350F (175C). Brush braid with egg white mixture and sprinkle generously with sesame seeds. Bake 30 to 45 minutes or until bread is a deep golden brown and loaves sound hollow when tapped. Cool on wire rack.

Makes 1 (2-lb.) loaf.

DENISE TURNBULL      MONMOUTH, ILLINOIS      ILLINOIS STATE FAIR

# New Orleans French Bread

Anyone who has tried to duplicate a true French bread knows the crackly crust and open texture are difficult to achieve at home. For more satisfactory results, try Shirley Roberson's recipe from New Orleans for a superb loaf of an American-style French bread. It has a more tender crumb, lighter crust and exceptionally good flavor. As a bonus, it tastes as good on the second day. Note that the dough rises twice before it's made into loaves.

*1 cup boiling water*
*2 tablespoons butter-flavored solid*
*    vegetable shortening*
*2 tablespoons sugar*
*1 tablespoon salt*
*1 cup cold water*

*2 (¼-oz.) packages active dry yeast*
*    (5 teaspoons)*
*5½ to 6½ cups sifted all-purpose flour*
*Cornmeal*
*1 egg white lightly beaten with*
*    1 tablespoon water*

In a large bowl, combine boiling water, shortening, sugar and salt and stir to melt shortening. Stir in cold water and let mixture cool to 105 to 115F (40 to 45C). Sprinkle yeast over mixture and let stand 15 minutes. Stir to dissolve. With an electric mixer, beat in 4 cups flour at medium speed 3 minutes. Stir in enough flour to make a stiff dough.

Turn dough out on a floured surface. Wash and grease large bowl. Knead dough until it is smooth and elastic, about 5 minutes. Place dough in greased bowl, turning dough greased side up. Cover and let rise in a warm place until double, about 45 minutes.

Punch down dough, cover and let rise again until almost double, about 30 minutes. Grease a large baking sheet and sprinkle with cornmeal. Turn dough out onto lightly floured surface. Knead dough briefly until it forms a ball. Divide into 2 equal pieces. Shape into 2 long loaves, tapering the ends. Place on prepared baking sheet. With a sharp knife, cut ¼-inch-deep diagonal slices in dough. Brush with egg white mixture. Cover and let rise in a warm place until just double, about 20 minutes.

Preheat oven to 375F (190C). Bake 25 to 35 minutes or until golden brown and bottom of bread sounds hollow when tapped.

**Makes 2 (1½-lb.) loaves.**

SHIRLEY STAFFORD ROBERSON     LUBBOCK, TEXAS     PANHANDLE SOUTH PLAINS FAIR

# Wooden Spoon French Bread

Brenda Gray had never baked bread when a friend gave her this recipe. It proved to be the start of a quarter century of making bread for family and friends. At the time, Brenda didn't realize the technique of beating rather than kneading the dough was unusual, but it works. This is a good bread to make when you have to spend a couple of hours in the kitchen. Although the recipe is somewhat similar to New Orleans French Bread, this makes a more open-textured, rustic-style loaf.

*2 (¼-oz.) packages active dry yeast
  (5 teaspoons)
½ cup warm (105 to 115F; 40 to 45C)
  water
2 cups hot water
3 tablespoons sugar*

*1 teaspoon salt
⅓ cup vegetable shortening, melted
6 to 6½ cups all-purpose flour
1 egg white lightly beaten with
  2 teaspoons water*

In small bowl, dissolve yeast in warm water. In a large bowl, combine hot water, sugar, salt and shortening. When mixture has cooled to warm (105 to 115F; 40 to 45C), add yeast and 3 cups flour; beat until smooth. Beat in 1 cup flour, then with large wooden spoon, stir in about 2 cups of flour to make a soft dough that pulls away from the sides of the bowl. Leaving spoon in bowl, cover bowl loosely with plastic wrap and let dough rest 10 minutes, then beat. Repeat resting and beating 5 times.

Turn dough out onto lightly floured surface. Knead enough to work out air bubbles. Grease a large baking sheet. Divide dough in half. Roll each part out into a 12 × 9-inch rectangle. Shape into long narrow loaves, tapering ends. Carefully transfer to baking sheet, leaving 3 to 4 inches between loaves. Brush with egg white mixture and cut 3 diagonal slices across each loaf with a sharp knife. Cover loosely with plastic wrap sprayed with nonstick cooking spray. Let rise 30 minutes.

Preheat oven to 400F (205C). Bake 35 minutes or until bread is a deep golden brown and sounds hollow when tapped on the bottom.

**Makes 2 (1½-lb.) loaves.**

### Using Plastic Wrap
Covering dough with a kitchen towel while it rises is a thing of the past for almost anyone who tries using plastic wrap instead. The plastic fits tightly over the bowl or loaves, keeping the dough warm and moist. If the shaped dough is soft, spray the underside of the wrap with nonstick cooking spray, so it doesn't stick to the dough and pull it out of shape.

BRENDA GRAY    CLAREMONT, CALIFORNIA    LOS ANGELES COUNTY FAIR

# Focaccia

After Mary Ann Ferguson-Rich won a blue ribbon the first time she entered fair competition in 1981, she was hooked. Many blue ribbons later, she still bakes her prize-winning recipes in an electric oven that is the same model used in the *Bewitched* television show in the 1960s. The shaping and thickness of focaccia varies depending on the region of Italy where it is made. Mary Ann's own recipe has the full flavor, open light crumb and thin crust characteristic of good homemade focaccia. If fresh sage isn't available, use a smaller amount of fresh or dried rosemary.

*1 (¼-oz.) package active dry yeast*
*(scant 1 tablespoon)*
*1 cup warm (105 to 115F; 40 to 45C)*
*water*
*3 to 3½ cups all-purpose flour*

*2 teaspoons salt*
*¼ cup plus 1 tablespoon olive oil*
*¼ cup fresh sage leaves, chopped*
*Cornmeal*
*Whole sage leaves*

In a small bowl, dissolve yeast in warm water. Place 3 cups of flour and salt in a large bowl. Add yeast mixture and ¼ cup olive oil and mix until a stiff dough forms that pulls away from the sides of the bowl, adding flour 1 tablespoon at a time, if needed.

Turn out on lightly floured surface and knead 5 to 10 minutes until dough is very smooth and satiny. Wash and grease bowl. Place dough in bowl, cover with plastic wrap and let rise in a warm place until doubled, about 1 hour.

Punch down dough. Turn out onto floured surface and knead in chopped sage leaves. On waxed paper, roll out into a 10-inch circle about ½ inch thick. Cover dough with another sheet of waxed paper. Let rise 45 to 60 minutes or until puffy.

Preheat oven to 375F (190C). When focaccia is ready, place baking sheet in the oven for a few minutes to heat. Remove sheet from oven and sprinkle with cornmeal. Slip focaccia onto baking sheet. With your finger, poke ½-inch-deep holes in the surface of the bread, brush with the remaining 1 tablespoon olive oil and decorate with sage leaves. Bake 25 to 35 minutes or until golden. Cool on wire rack.

Makes 1 round loaf.

### Freezing Bread
Some breads such as focaccia are best the day they're baked, but they can be frozen for that just-baked flavor. Wrap the cooled loaf tightly in heavy freezer foil, making sure it is airtight. Then slip the loaf into a heavy plastic bag or double wrap with freezer paper and seal. Thaw the loaf before unwrapping. If desired, heat unwrapped loaf before serving.

MARY ANN FERGUSON-RICH     TALLMADGE, OHIO     CANFIELD FAIR

# Italian Tomato & Onion Herb Bread

You may shed a few tears as you chop the onions for Tina Brown's great tasting bread. But once you try it, you'll agree it's worth a tear or two. Even the dough has a rich herb aroma, and the smell of the bread baking is irresistible. You can mix the dough with a heavy-duty mixer, but it is too stiff to knead with a dough hook. The texture of the dough is unusual, but a few minutes of kneading by hand makes it smooth and satiny.

*1 (16-oz.) can tomatoes*
*2 (¼-oz.) packages active dry yeast*
   *(5 teaspoons)*
*1 tablespoon sugar*
*6 cups all-purpose flour*
*2 cups finely chopped onion, drained*
*1½ teaspoons salt*

*2 tablespoons Italian herb seasoning*
*1 teaspoon celery seeds*
*¼ teaspoon freshly ground black pepper*
*6 tablespoons butter, melted*
*1 egg white mixed with 2 teaspoons water*
*Fresh sage, basil or rosemary (optional)*

Puree undrained tomatoes in blender or food processor. Pour into a medium saucepan and heat to 105 to 115F (40 to 45C). Stir in yeast and sugar. Let stand 8 to 10 minutes or until foamy. In a large bowl, combine 5 cups of flour, chopped onion, salt, herb seasoning, celery seeds and pepper. Beat in tomato mixture and melted butter until thoroughly combined with flour; dough will be stiff and in coarse shreds.

Turn dough out onto floured surface and knead in enough remaining flour to make a smooth, elastic dough that feels slightly moist, about 5 minutes. Wash and grease large bowl. Place dough in greased bowl and turn dough to coat top. Cover with plastic wrap and let rise in a warm place about 1 to 1½ hours or until doubled. Grease a large baking sheet.

Punch down dough. Divide dough in half. Form into round loaves. Place on opposite corners of prepared baking sheet. Brush loaves with egg white mixture. If desired, arrange herb leaves on top of loaves, first dipping them in egg white mixture. Cover and let rise about 45 minutes or until just doubled.

Preheat oven to 375F (190C). Bake loaves 40 to 45 minutes or until bottoms sound hollow when tapped or instant-read thermometer reaches 200F (95C).

Makes 2 (1½-lb.) loaves.

**NOTE**

If you have a 14½-ounce can of tomatoes, add a scant ¼ cup water after pureeing.

TINA BROWN    MONTCLAIR, CALIFORNIA    LOS ANGELES COUNTY FAIR

# Dilly Casserole Bread

The recipe that won the $25,000 grand prize in Pillsbury's twelfth Bake-Off contest again proved to be a big winner for Ruth Taylor. Her Dilly Casserole Bread not only was awarded the blue ribbon in the dill bread category, but it beat out the top winners in the twenty-four bread classes as overall bread winner. Delicious flavor and easy preparation of the open-textured, no-knead casserole bread have made it a classic.

2¼ to 2½ cups all-purpose or
    unbleached flour
2 tablespoons sugar
2 to 3 teaspoons instant minced onion
2 teaspoons dill seeds
1 teaspoon salt
¼ teaspoon baking soda
1 (¼-oz.) package active dry yeast
    (scant 1 tablespoon)

1 (8-oz.) carton (1 cup) creamed
    cottage cheese
¼ cup water
1 tablespoon margarine or butter
1 egg
Margarine or butter, melted
Coarse salt (optional)

Generously grease a 1½- or 2-quart casserole dish. In a large bowl, combine 1 cup flour, sugar, onion, dill seeds, salt, baking soda and yeast; blend well. In a small saucepan, heat cottage cheese, water and 1 tablespoon margarine until very warm (120 to 130F; 50 to 55C). Add warm liquid and egg to flour mixture. Blend with an electric mixer at low speed until moistened. Beat 3 minutes at medium speed. Stir in remaining 1¼ to 1½ cups flour to form a stiff batter.

Cover loosely with plastic wrap and cloth towel. Let rise in warm place until light and doubled in size, about 45 to 60 minutes.

Stir down dough. Place in prepared casserole dish. Cover and let rise in a warm place until light and doubled in size, 30 to 45 minutes.

Preheat oven to 350F (175C). Bake 30 to 40 minutes or until deep golden brown and loaf sounds hollow when lightly tapped. Immediately remove from casserole dish and place on wire rack. Brush warm loaf with melted margarine and sprinkle with coarse salt, if desired. Cool completely.

Makes 1 (20-oz.) loaf.

**NOTE**

Amount of flour will vary with the amount of liquid in the creamed cottage cheese.

RUTH TAYLOR     DES MOINES, IOWA     IOWA STATE FAIR

# Whole-Wheat Cloverleaf Rolls

Marjorie Johnson has won a blue ribbon for this recipe so often that she had to drop out of the competition for two years after she had won three times in a row. Her goal is to make each baking experience a learning experience. She says she spends as much time writing up the results of her experimenting as she does in baking. For others who use a heavy-duty mixer with dough hook, she has included precise instructions for this recipe. Her method of mixing the dough for this recipe is unusual, but it definitely works.

| | |
|---|---|
| 2 (¼-oz.) packages active dry yeast (5 teaspoons) | 2 eggs |
| 1 cup warm (105 to 115F; 40 to 45C) water | ⅓ cup dry milk powder |
| ¼ cup butter | 1 teaspoon salt |
| ¼ cup honey | 2¼ cups whole-wheat flour |
| | 2¼ to 2¾ cups bread flour |
| | Melted butter |

In a large mixer bowl, dissolve yeast in warm water. In a small bowl, beat together butter and honey until creamy. Beat in eggs, one at a time. Add dry milk and salt to dissolved yeast. Beat in creamed mixture, the whole-wheat flour and 1 cup bread flour. Beat 3 minutes at medium speed. Beat in 1 cup bread flour. Stir in remaining flour to make a dough that pulls away from the sides of the bowl.

Turn out dough on floured surface and knead 8 to 10 minutes or until dough feels springy and smooth. Wash and grease large bowl. Place dough in bowl and turn dough to grease top. Cover with plastic wrap and let rise in a warm place until double, about 1 hour.

Punch down dough and let rise again until double, about 30 minutes. Turn dough out on lightly floured surface. For cloverleaf rolls, grease 24 medium muffin cups. Cut dough in half. Cut each half into 36 pieces. Shape into balls. Place 3 balls in each greased muffin cup. Cover with plastic wrap and let rise until just double.

Preheat oven to 350F (175C). Bake rolls 12 to 15 minutes or until golden brown. Time will depend on size and shape of the rolls.

**Makes 24 cloverleaf rolls. (Half of dough will make 24 pan rolls or 16 crescent rolls.)**

### NOTE

Marjorie gives these directions for kneading with a dough hook:

- Use the paddle at speed 4 until you have added the whole-wheat and 1 cup bread flour.
- Exchange the paddle for the dough hook. Add 1 cup flour and knead at speed 2 for 3 minutes with dough hook.
- Add flour as needed to make a dough that leaves the side of the bowl, while kneading with dough hook for 3 minutes more.
- Then turn the dough out on a lightly floured surface and knead briefly to make sure "the dough is a perfect consistency."

MARJORIE JOHNSON      ROBBINSDALE, MINNESOTA      MINNESOTA STATE FAIR

# Bread Sticks

Keeping up her golf game and preparing for the Iowa State Fair means Thelma Huston has an especially complicated schedule every August. A gourmet cook, she makes her own ravioli, Chinese pot stickers and noodles. In addition, she's also an enthusiastic yeast baker. Her bread sticks recipe is a good one for anyone who is not an experienced yeast baker. The small amount of dough is easy to knead and rises quickly. If you like crisp bread sticks, eliminate the final rise after they are formed.

| | |
|---|---|
| 1 (¼-oz.) package active dry yeast (scant 1 tablespoon) | 1 teaspoon salt |
| | 1 tablespoon sugar |
| ⅔ cup warm (105 to 115F; 40 to 45C) water | 1¾ to 2 cups all-purpose flour |
| | 1 egg beaten with 1 tablespoon water |
| ¼ cup soft solid vegetable shortening | Sesame seeds or poppy seeds |

In a medium bowl, dissolve yeast in warm water. Stir in shortening, salt, sugar and 1 cup flour and beat until well blended. Stir in flour to make a stiff dough that pulls away from the sides of the bowl.

Turn out dough on lightly floured surface. Knead 3 to 5 minutes or until dough is smooth and elastic. Wash and grease bowl. Place dough in greased bowl, cover and let rise in a warm place until doubled in size, about 40 minutes. Grease a 13 × 11-inch baking sheet.

Punch down dough. Turn out onto lightly floured surface. Form dough into a long roll and cut into 10 equal pieces. Roll each piece into a rope 8 inches long. Place about 1 inch apart on prepared baking sheet. Brush bread sticks with egg mixture and sprinkle with sesame or poppy seeds. Cover and let rise about 20 minutes or until light but not doubled.

Preheat oven to 400F (205C). Bake about 20 minutes or until bread sticks are deep golden brown.

Makes 10 bread sticks.

### Using an Egg Wash
Blue ribbon winners know that eye appeal is important in a field as competitive as yeast breads. So many recipes like these bread sticks include an egg glaze. A little water is combined with whole egg, egg yolk or egg white and the mixture brushed on before baking.

Whole egg or egg yolk adds a rich, golden glaze. Egg white gives the crispest crust. If you are adding a topping of seeds, the glaze also helps them adhere to the crust. For best results, brush on two light coats of egg wash, rather than one heavy one.

THELMA HUSTON      DES MOINES, IOWA      IOWA STATE FAIR

# Potato Rolls

When you taste Lola Jean's old-fashioned potato rolls, you aren't surprised to learn the recipe came from a church cookbook. This is the kind of special heritage recipe that is passed down in families and shared with friends. She also uses the versatile dough for cinnamon rolls. Cut with a 3-inch biscuit cutter, the dough would make superb hamburger buns. This is a big recipe. Part of the dough could be refrigerated for a few days, and the baked rolls freeze well.

| | |
|---|---|
| *1 cup water* | *1 cup warm (105 to 115F; 40 to 45C)* |
| *½ cup margarine* | *water* |
| *½ cup sugar* | *2 eggs* |
| *2 teaspoons salt* | *1 cup mashed potatoes* |
| *2 (¼-oz.) packages active dry yeast* | *6½ to 7½ cups all-purpose flour* |
| *(5 teaspoons)* | |

In a medium saucepan, heat the 1 cup water, margarine, sugar and salt until margarine is nearly melted (or heat mixture in microwave on HIGH 1 minute). Set aside to cool to warm (105 to 115F; 40 to 45C). In a large bowl, dissolve yeast in the warm water. Stir in eggs, mashed potatoes, warm margarine mixture and 3 cups flour. Beat until smooth. Add enough additional flour to make a soft dough that pulls away from the sides of the bowl.

Turn out on floured surface and knead 5 to 8 minutes or until dough is smooth and elastic, adding additional flour as needed. Wash and grease large bowl. Place dough in greased bowl and turn dough to grease top. Cover with plastic wrap and let rise in a warm place until doubled in bulk, about 45 minutes. Grease a large baking sheet.

Punch down dough. Turn out onto lightly floured surface. Divide dough in half and form each piece into a ball. Roll out 1 ball to about ½-inch thickness. Using a medium glass or round cutter, cut out rolls. Place on prepared baking sheet 1 inch apart. Repeat with remaining dough. Cover and let rise until almost doubled, about 30 minutes.

Preheat oven to 350F (175C). Bake about 20 minutes or until rolls are golden brown.

**Makes about 4 dozen medium rolls.**

LOLA JEAN     FOUNTAIN VALLEY, CALIFORNIA     LOS ANGELES COUNTY FAIR

# Muffins & Quick Breads

*You don't get tired of muffins, but you don't find inspiration in them.*
George Bernard Shaw, *Man and Superman*

George Bernard Shaw was referring, of course, to the yeast-raised bread we call English muffins. Muffins, as we know them, are uniquely American. If Shaw could have sampled the variety of muffins in this chapter, he might have found inspiration in the creativity revealed in these recipes.

In this century, muffins probably have changed the most of any of the quick breads. Low-fat, low-sugar basic muffins were the norm for decades. Now the most popular ones are sweet and rich and can be eaten as a light dessert or sweet snack, as well as a breakfast bread.

These rich, cakelike muffins first gained popularity after office workers started buying them in bakeries to enjoy with coffee at work. They were good eaten at room temperature and stayed fresh-tasting longer than the old basic breakfast muffins.

Soon people began to realize that they could make the same kind of expensive muffins at home for a fraction of the cost. They could freeze them and bring an even better-tasting fresh treat to eat at work every day. Articles about making these popular new muffins at home appeared in magazines and on newspaper food pages. Recipes were exchanged and new ones created. Now this cake-type muffin has become the choice for many.

State fairs have picked up on this trend. Instead of having entry categories just for the traditional plain muffins, many have expanded to include this popular cake-type muffin. The Iowa State Fair even has a category just for Morning Glory Muffins, because they are so well liked there.

Scones also have become much better known, partly because of the proliferation of coffee bars. People like them as an accompaniment to strong-flavored coffees. As with muffins, customers discovered it's not difficult to make even better-tasting scones at home.

Making fruit and nut loaf breads for the holidays has long been a tradition in many homes. Despite the fact that they are not as quick to bake, we are discovering that making them can fit into busy schedules. We no longer need to save them for special occasions.

All fruit and nut breads keep well for up to a week. Some are even better made one day and stored overnight before cutting. Although they take about an hour to bake, they are relatively quick to mix. Several recipes in this chapter make two loaves, so you can have one to eat now and one to freeze.

At the Pillsbury Company, during the big movement of women into the work force in the 1980s, we knew that making quick breads at home had become something of a lost art. As we sent out food-page releases about the economy of making muffins at home to carry to work, we debated about whether consumers still understood what we meant if we used the term "quick bread."

The name goes back to the late 1800s, when housewives were liberated from their dependence on bread made with unreliable yeast when the first commercial baking powder came on the market. Finally home bakers had a reliable chemical leavening that could be used to make a variety of breads, an essential part of every meal in those days.

Yeast bread had to be made by a slow sponge method to compensate for the poor-quality yeasts. So the biscuits and cornbread they could whip up with the new baking powder and, later, with reliable baking soda, were indeed quick breads.

It appears that we are seeing a trend back to making and enjoying the great variety of breads possible using baking powder and baking soda as the leavening. These blue ribbon recipes range from simple biscuits and cornbread to special fruit- and nut-filled loaves. You may want to bake your way through the chapter!

# Banana Bran Muffins

As a young bride Mary Ann Hildreth started exhibiting her baking and preserving entries at the county fair. She soon graduated to the big Ohio State Fair. For more than a quarter century she has been such a consistent winner there that she has been featured in articles in local and metropolitan newspapers.

Bran muffins are the favorite breakfast bread for many. Her tasty fruit version is a little richer and sweeter than the basic recipe. Be sure to use very ripe bananas and mash them well. They furnish most of the liquid in this recipe.

*½ cup butter or margarine, softened*
*1 cup sugar*
*2 eggs*
*1½ cups mashed ripe bananas*
   *(3 medium or 2 large)*
*1 teaspoon orange extract*

*1¼ cups sifted all-purpose flour*
*½ cup bran cereal*
*¾ teaspoon soda*
*½ teaspoon salt*
*½ cup raisins*
*½ cup finely chopped nuts*

Preheat oven to 350F (175C). Line 12 (2½-inch) muffin cups with paper liners or grease.

In a large bowl, beat butter and sugar together with an electric mixer until well blended. Beat in eggs, bananas and orange extract. In a medium bowl, stir together flour, bran cereal, soda and salt. Stir flour mixture, raisins and nuts into butter mixture, mixing just enough to blend ingredients.

Spoon batter into prepared muffin cups, filling about three-fourths full. Bake 20 to 30 minutes or until deep golden brown and a wooden pick inserted in the center of a muffin comes out clean.

**Makes 12 muffins.**

### Muffin Method

Older bakers will remember that muffins nearly always were made by combining the wet ingredients with the dry ingredients, mixing only until they were blended. This was known as the "muffin method." This way of making a basic muffin was so well established that "muffin method" was used as a shorthand way to describe any baked product mixed that way.

Now, with the enthusiasm for rich, sweet muffins, many are made by creaming the fat and sugar together, then adding the eggs. While this creaming method sounds like the start of a cake, it's still important when you make muffins not to overmix when you add the flour, or the muffins may be tough.

MARY ANN HILDRETH    FAIRHORN, OHIO    OHIO STATE FAIR

# Helen's Banana Bread Muffins

Helen Lambert took her old family recipe for banana bread and turned it into a blue rib-bon muffin. Because she has learned that appearance is nearly as important as great fla-vor in this competitive category, she added a topping of raw sugar and sliced almonds when she exhibited them.

Her family always requests these rich, sweet muffins as a snack when they visit, so she usually has a supply in her freezer.

*2 cups all-purpose flour*
*1 teaspoon baking soda*
*½ teaspoon salt*
*¾ cup butter or margarine, softened*
*1½ cups sugar*
*2 eggs*
*1½ cups mashed ripe banana*
  *(3 medium or 2 large)*

*1 teaspoon vanilla extract*
*½ cup buttermilk*
*½ cup sliced almonds*
*¼ cup sliced almonds, for topping*
  *(optional)*
*¼ cup raw or coarse granulated sugar,*
  *for topping (optional)*

Preheat oven to 350F (175C). Grease 18 (2½-inch) muffin cups or coat with cooking spray.

In a small bowl, stir together flour, soda and salt. In a medium bowl, beat butter and sugar together until fluffy. Add eggs, mashed banana and vanilla. Beat 2 minutes, until well blended. Add flour mixture alternately with the buttermilk, stirring after each addition. Fold in ½ cup sliced almonds.

Spoon batter into prepared muffin cups, filling about three-fourths full. If desired, sprinkle tops with a few sliced almonds and raw sugar. Bake 20 minutes or until tops are slightly browned and a wooden pick inserted in the center of a muffin comes out clean.

Makes 18 muffins.

### Freezing Muffins
Muffins are best served fresh. Because almost any muffin freezes well, if the recipe makes more than you can use, freeze extras. As soon as they have cooled, arrange them in a single layer in a plastic freezer bag. Place the bag on its side in the freezer so the muffins keep their shape. A plastic or metal container with a tight lid also works well.

Label the muffins and mark the date. Muffins can be frozen up to 3 months. Reheat them in a 350F (175C) oven 5 to 10 minutes, until they are thawed and warm.

HELEN LAMBERT     NEW HOPE, MINNESOTA     MINNESOTA STATE FAIR

# Oatmeal Muffins

With cakelike muffins now the norm, state fair judges welcomed Marjorie Johnson's less-rich, breakfast-type oatmeal muffins. Soaking the oatmeal in buttermilk gives them a smooth texture, and the flavor combination of oats and brown sugar is outstanding. Best served warm, they can be frozen and reheated.

*1 cup quick-cooking rolled oats*
*1 cup buttermilk*
*1 cup all-purpose flour*
*1 teaspoon baking powder*
*½ teaspoon baking soda*

*¼ teaspoon salt*
*⅓ cup vegetable oil*
*½ cup packed light brown sugar*
*1 egg*

Combine the rolled oats and buttermilk in a medium bowl. Cover the bowl and let stand 30 minutes. Preheat oven to 375F (190C). Line 12 (2½-inch) muffin cups with paper baking cups or grease bottoms only.

Sift flour, baking powder, soda and salt together. In a small bowl, beat oil, brown sugar and egg until thoroughly blended; add to oatmeal mixture. Stir in flour mixture just enough to moisten dry ingredients.

Spoon batter into prepared muffin cups, filling two-thirds full. Bake 20 to 22 minutes or until a wooden pick inserted in the center of a muffin comes out clean. Serve warm.

**Makes 12 muffins.**

### Muffin Pan Sizes

Muffin pans come in a variety of sizes, from mini to jumbo. For those in the middle range, the pans specified in these recipes, the cups are about 2½ inches across the top and 2 inches across the bottom. However, the capacity of the cups varies, depending on the manufacturer.

Since muffin recipes are quite tolerant, this variation doesn't make a difference in quality. But you may get a different yield or have to bake the muffins a few minutes more or less than the recipe specifies.

Unless the recipe says otherwise, fill the muffin cups about two-thirds full (richer muffins with added ingredients do not rise as much). If this leaves you with some empty muffin cups, put a little water in them to distribute the heat evenly throughout the pan.

MARJORIE JOHNSON      ROBBINSDALE, MINNESOTA      MINNESOTA STATE FAIR

# Orange Blueberry Muffins

Blueberry muffins are so popular that in Minnesota they've been named the official state muffin. Down in the Ozarks good cooks improve on the basic recipe, as Nancy Johnson shows with her orange-flavored oatmeal variation. When she has lots of blueberries, she adds up to 3 cupfuls. This is a big recipe, but they freeze well.

*1 cup quick-cooking or regular rolled oats*
*1 cup orange juice*
*½ cup finely chopped nuts*
*1⅓ cups sugar*
*1 teaspoon ground cinnamon*
*3 cups all-purpose flour*
*4 teaspoons baking powder*

*½ teaspoon baking soda*
*1 teaspoon salt*
*1 cup vegetable oil*
*3 eggs, beaten*
*1½ cups fresh or frozen blueberries*
*1 tablespoon grated orange peel*

In a medium bowl, combine rolled oats and orange juice. Prepare topping by mixing together nuts, ⅓ cup sugar and cinnamon. Preheat oven to 400F (205C). Grease 24 (2½-inch) muffin cups or coat with cooking spray.

In a large bowl, mix together flour, baking powder, soda, salt and remaining 1 cup sugar. Make a well in the center of the dry ingredients and add the oatmeal mixture, vegetable oil and eggs. Mix together, stirring only until dry ingredients are moistened. Carefully fold in blueberries and orange peel.

Spoon batter into prepared muffin cups, filling about three-fourths full. Sprinkle with topping mixture. Bake about 15 minutes, until tops are golden and a wooden pick inserted in the center of a muffin comes out clean. Serve warm or at room temperature.

Makes 24 muffins.

### Measuring Flour

Flour packs down in the sack or in a canister. While few quick bread recipes specify sifted flour, for accurate measurement, you should gently spoon the flour into the dry measuring cup and level it off with the straight edge of a knife.

If you measure by dipping the measuring cup into the flour, you may add too much flour. This can be significant in a recipe like Orange Blueberry Muffins, which calls for 3 cups of flour.

NANCY JOHNSON     CLEVER, MISSOURI     OZARK EMPIRE FAIR

# Morning Glory Muffins

Morning Glory Muffins apparently originated as a popular upscale bakery item during the height of the muffin mania in the 1980s. When people tasted these cake-type muffins loaded with added ingredients, they were eager to make them at home. Food editors ferreted out the recipes and soon variations appeared in newspapers and magazines.

The muffins were so popular in Iowa that the state fair set up a separate Morning Glory Muffin category. Louise Piper's blue ribbon recipe was judged best among the many in this highly competitive group.

The tasty muffins won't rise quite as high as muffins with fewer added ingredients, so fill the muffin cups three-fourths full. The standard wooden pick test isn't as accurate for this muffin, so also look for golden brown color.

| | |
|---|---|
| *3 eggs, beaten* | *½ teaspoon salt* |
| *1 cup vegetable oil* | *2 teaspoons ground cinnamon* |
| *1 teaspoon vanilla extract* | *1½ cups shredded carrots* |
| *2 cups all-purpose flour* | *1¼ cups peeled, grated apple* |
| *1¼ cups sugar* | *¾ cup flaked coconut* |
| *2 teaspoons baking soda* | *½ cup chopped walnuts* |

Preheat oven to 375F (190C). Grease 18 (2½-inch) muffin cups or coat with cooking spray.

In a medium bowl, mix together eggs, oil and vanilla. In a medium bowl, stir together flour, sugar, baking soda, salt and cinnamon. Make a well in the center of the dry ingredients and add the egg mixture. Mix just until the ingredients are combined. Gently fold in the carrots, apple, coconut and walnuts.

Spoon batter into prepared muffin cups, filling about three-fourths full. Bake about 20 minutes, until the top springs back when lightly touched and muffins are golden. Let muffins cool in the pans on a wire rack about 5 minutes. Remove from pans and cool completely before serving. They freeze well.

Makes 18 muffins.

## 🏅 *Using Cooking Spray*

Using cooking spray is a quick, tidy method for greasing muffin cups or loaf pans. It works at least as well as solid shortening or butter and is especially good for a recipe that has many added ingredients. These are more likely to stick than a plain muffin or bread. Vegetable oil is never the best choice, however, because it can be absorbed by the product during baking.

LOUISE PIPER     ROLFE, IOWA     IOWA STATE FAIR

# Maple Pecan Muffins

Charlene Reardon's supervisor at the hospital where she works describes her as "a talented baker with a Texas-sized heart who has been transplanted to California." Charlene and her husband bake quick breads for events to support the Children's Miracle Network, and she was a major contributor to her hospital's fund-raising cookbook.

She says her muffins can be made with maple-flavored pancake syrup, but for the tastiest product, she recommends pure maple syrup. Although the ingredient list looks long, the batter is mixed together quickly.

*1 egg, beaten*
*¾ cup milk*
*⅓ cup vegetable oil*
*⅓ cup pure maple syrup*
*1 teaspoon maple flavoring*
*2 tablespoons sugar*
*1½ cups sifted all-purpose flour*
*¼ cup whole-wheat flour*
*¼ cup wheat germ*
*1½ teaspoons baking powder*

*½ teaspoon baking soda*
*¼ teaspoon salt*
*½ cup chopped pecans*

*GLAZE*
*½ cup powdered sugar, sifted*
*2 tablespoons very finely chopped pecans*
*1 tablespoon pure maple syrup*
*About 1 teaspoon water*

Preheat oven to 400F (205C). Grease 12 (2½-inch) muffin cups.

In a medium bowl, stir together egg, milk, oil, maple syrup, maple flavoring and sugar. In a medium bowl, stir together flours, wheat germ, baking powder, soda and salt. Make a well in the center of the dry ingredients and pour in the milk mixture. Mix just until the flour is moistened (mixture will be lumpy). Fold in pecans.

Spoon batter into prepared muffin cups, filling about two-thirds full. Bake 18 to 20 minutes or until a wooden pick inserted in the center of a muffin comes out clean.

Let muffins cool in the pans on a wire rack for a few minutes while preparing glaze. Remove muffins from pans and finish cooling on the wire rack. Drizzle glaze over the tops. Let it set before serving.

Makes 12 muffins.

**GLAZE**

In a small bowl, mix powdered sugar, pecans, maple syrup and enough water to make a glaze that can be drizzled over the muffins from a spoon.

### Tips for Cake-Type Muffins

Rich cake-type muffins are better served after they have cooled. They may break apart if you try to remove them from the muffin cups too soon. Let the pan of muffins cool on a wire rack for a few minutes. Steam will condense around the muffins and help loosen them. This also gives the muffins time to "set up," so they are easier to handle.

Blue ribbon bakers treasure their older, well-used muffin pans. These develop a well-seasoned surface, which releases the muffins easily. Even nonstick pans should be greased.

CHARLENE REARDON     SHAFTER, CALIFORNIA     KERN COUNTY FAIR

# Texan Corn Muffins

Michelle Keim adapted her Texas Skillet Cornbread (page 65) for muffins, using an unusual method of heating the muffin cups. This gives a sturdier crust and rich color and made the blue ribbon difference for her corn muffins entry. The muffins are best served warm from the oven. Her recipe is easily halved to make six muffins.

*About ¼ cup vegetable shortening*
*2 eggs*
*1 cup milk*
*½ cup margarine, melted*
*1 cup yellow cornmeal*

*1 cup unbleached all-purpose flour*
*4 teaspoons baking powder*
*½ teaspoon salt*
*3 tablespoons sugar*

Preheat oven to 425F (220C). Put a scant teaspoonful of solid vegetable shortening in 12 muffin cups. Place muffin pan in the oven to heat.

In a medium bowl, mix together eggs, milk and margarine. In a large bowl, stir together cornmeal, flour, baking powder, salt and sugar. Pour in egg mixture and stir just until mixture is smooth and blended thoroughly.

Remove muffin pan from the oven. Carefully spoon batter into the muffin cups, filling two-thirds full. Immediately return the pan to the oven and bake about 20 minutes or until the tops are golden brown and a wooden pick inserted in the middle of a muffin comes out clean. Cool in the pan on a wire rack for a few minutes before removing. Serve hot.

**Makes 12 muffins.**

MICHELLE KEIM     LUBBOCK, TEXAS     SOUTH PLAINS FAIR

# Mexican Cornbread

Cornbread baked in a cast-iron skillet is the ultimate in old-time Southern bread. But the surprise element here is the decidedly south-of-the-border accent in Nancy Johnson's Mexican Cornbread. With the addition of cream-style corn, cheese and chiles, this rich, moist cornbread is one of the best-tasting versions you'll ever eat. Because it is made with all cornmeal, no flour, it has a rather coarse texture and doesn't freeze well.

*1½ cups yellow cornmeal*
*3 teaspoons baking powder*
*1 teaspoon salt*
*1 cup cream-style corn*
*⅔ cup vegetable oil*

*2 eggs, slightly beaten*
*2 jalepeño chiles, seeded and*
*    finely chopped*
*2 tablespoons chopped bell pepper*
*1 cup (4 oz.) grated mild cheese*

Preheat oven to 375F (190C). Grease a 9- to 10-inch cast-iron skillet or a 9-inch-square baking pan. Place in the oven to heat.

In a large bowl, stir together cornmeal, baking powder and salt. Add cream-style corn, oil, eggs, chiles and chopped peppers. Stir just enough to blend ingredients.

Pour half the batter into the greased, heated skillet or pan. Sprinkle half the cheese over the batter. Carefully top with remaining batter and sprinkle on the rest of the cheese. Bake about 35 minutes or until golden brown and a wooden pick inserted in the center comes out clean.

Makes 9 to 12 servings.

### Using Hot Chiles

With the interest in Tex-Mex cooking, it's become relatively easy to find fresh jalepeño chiles. The small green chiles are very hot, but the heat will vary in intensity even among chiles from the same plant. They're most flavorful when freshly picked and lose flavor during storage. The oil that gives all chiles in the capsicum family their fiery flavor is concentrated in the ribs and can cause burns. Wear thin surgical or rubber gloves when you handle jalepeño chiles. Be especially careful not to touch your face or eyes when working with them.

If you prefer less heat, substitute the milder fresh Anaheim chiles or use about ¼ cup chopped well-drained canned green chiles, either hot or mild. Canned jalepeño chiles also are available. They are easier to use, but the flavor won't be quite the same.

NANCY JOHNSON    CLEVER, MISSOURI    OZARK EMPIRE FAIR

# Texas Skillet Cornbread

Michelle Keim bakes cornbread in a cast-iron skillet, but she heats the skillet on the stove-top, pours the cornbread batter in and heats that briefly before putting it in the hot oven. This gives the cornbread a good brown crust on the bottom and sides. Her recipe uses equal parts of flour and cornmeal, so it has a soft, light texture and isn't crumbly.

*2 eggs, slightly beaten*
*1 cup milk*
*½ cup margarine, melted*
*1 cup yellow cornmeal*
*1 cup unbleached all-purpose flour*

*4 teaspoons baking powder*
*½ teaspoon salt*
*3 tablespoons sugar*
*1 tablespoon vegetable shortening*

Preheat oven to 425F (220C).

In a medium bowl, mix together eggs, milk and margarine. In a large bowl, stir together corn-meal, flour, baking powder, salt and sugar. Pour in egg mixture and stir just until mixture is smooth and blended thoroughly.

Put vegetable shortening in a 10-inch cast-iron skillet. Heat on stovetop until shortening has melted and covers the bottom of the skillet. Pour cornbread mixture into the fat and heat on the stovetop 30 seconds. Then bake about 20 minutes, until edges are brown and center is golden.

To bake in an 8-inch-square pan, put 1 tablespoon of shortening in the pan and heat in the oven until shortening melts. Grease bottom and sides of pan. Pour cornbread mixture into the pan and bake about 25 minutes or until golden brown.

Makes 10 servings.

### Baking in a Cast-Iron Skillet

Baking cornbread in a cast-iron skillet goes back to early pioneer days when coals in the fire-place substituted for oven heat.

The earliest covered frying pans were called "spiders." They had three legs, each about 3 inches long, to raise the pan above the level of the coals, and so were thought to resemble spi-ders. With a few coals placed on the lid the spider could bake wonderful hearty, crusty corn-bread.

As ovens became more common, the spiders lost their legs. But the crusty cornbread they produced was difficult to achieve in ordinary baking pans. So a well-cared-for, old cast-iron skil-let remains the pan of choice for many cornbread bakers.

If a recipe is called "spider bread" or "spider cornbread," you can be sure it is a heritage recipe, baked in a heated cast-iron skillet.

MICHELLE KEIM    LUBBOCK, TEXAS    SOUTH PLAINS FAIR

# Irish Soda Bread

Watching the movie *State Fair* years ago made Jo Ellen Hall want to enter and win a ribbon. After winning other cooking contests, she finally took the plunge. On her first try she brought home a blue ribbon for her Irish Soda Bread. The bread, which uses both baking soda and baking powder, has a velvety texture and delicious flavor and is best eaten the day it is made. Leftovers are good toasted.

| | |
|---|---|
| *4 cups all-purpose flour* | *1 tablespoon caraway seeds* |
| *¼ cup sugar* | *⅓ cup solid vegetable shortening* |
| *1 tablespoon baking powder* | *1 cup raisins or currants* |
| *1 teaspoon baking soda* | *1 egg* |
| *1 teaspoon salt* | *1¾ cups buttermilk* |

Preheat oven to 350F (175C). Grease a large baking sheet.

In a large bowl, sift flour, sugar, baking powder, baking soda and salt. Stir in caraway seeds. Cut in shortening with a pastry blender or two knifes until mixture resembles coarse crumbs. Stir in raisins.

In a medium bowl, beat egg with a fork until just mixed. Stir in buttermilk until well combined. Add buttermilk mixture to flour mixture. Stir just until mixture forms a soft dough that clings together and forms a ball.

Turn dough out on a floured surface. Knead gently 10 or 12 times. Place dough on prepared baking sheet. Pat dough into a 7-inch round. Score top of dough with a sharp knife making an X about 4 inches long and ¼ inch deep. Bake 55 to 60 minutes or until a wooden pick inserted in the center comes out clean. Immediately remove from baking sheet and cool on a wire rack.

**Makes 1 large loaf, 12 servings.**

### VARIATION

For a sweet crust, combine 1 tablespoon sugar and 1 tablespoon water in custard cup. Brush over hot loaf.

### The Evolution of Baking Powder

For American bread bakers, 1886 was a significant year. For the first time they could make a loaf of bread using a reliable chemical leavening. Finally they were able to buy a combination of cream of tartar and soda that was factory-blended and sealed in cans so it kept its leavening power for months.

This was the first commercial baking powder. Before that, cooks had had to depend on *saleratus,* a crude form of baking soda, which gave an off-color and flavor to foods, or a homemade concoction of baking soda and cream of tartar. Unless perfectly blended, the results were most uncertain.

Soon other manufacturers came up with formulations that used different kinds of acids. But they all shared one characteristic—when liquid was added, the gases that raised the dough or batter were released immediately, so baking couldn't be delayed.

The most popular baking powder now is double-acting. Only part of the gas is released right away. The rest is released in the oven, so a short delay in baking the batter won't result in a failure.

JO ELLEN HALL      DES MOINES, IOWA      IOWA STATE FAIR

# Steamed Brown Bread

Steamed brown bread is one of our earliest American recipes. Made with three grains, Mary Linda Horn's version is typical of pioneer recipes from a time when white flour was a precious commodity used sparingly.

Making steamed brown bread may require improvisation (see Improvising a Steamer, below). Baking it in cans is traditional, but any combination of containers that fit in the steamer and hold the equivalent of 6 cups will do. Steaming time is not very precise. Start testing it about 15 minutes before you think it might be done. As Mary Linda advises, "Just pay attention and don't fret."

|  |  |
|---|---|
| *1 cup all-purpose flour* | *1 teaspoon salt* |
| *1 cup cornmeal* | *2 cups buttermilk* |
| *1 cup whole-wheat flour* | *¾ cup molasses* |
| *2 teaspoons soda* | *1 cup raisins* |

Grease 4 (1-lb.) fruit or vegetable cans or a 7-inch tube mold.

In a large bowl, beat all the ingredients together 30 seconds or just until batter is well blended, scraping bowl often. Fill greased cans or mold two-thirds full. Cover tightly with foil.

Using a steamer or a rack in a Dutch oven, place rack in pan and pour boiling water up to the level of the rack. Place covered containers on the rack. Cover pan.

Keep water boiling over low heat and steam bread about 3 hours or until a wooden pick inserted in the center comes out clean. (Add boiling water during steaming, if necessary.)

Cool in the cans 15 minutes on a wire rack. Then remove from cans. Serve at room temperature or wrap in foil and warm before serving.

**Makes 4 small loaves or a 7-inch mold.**

### Improvising a Steamer
If you don't have a regular steamer, you can improvise one easily using a canner, a Dutch oven or a large saucepan with tight-fitting cover. Place a wire rack in the pan at least an inch from the bottom. If the rack is not adjustable, balance it on inverted custard cups.

Do not use a double boiler; it doesn't allow the steam to circulate around the mold.

MARY LINDA HORN      DELAWARE, OHIO      OHIO STATE FAIR

# Maple Pecan Scones

Louise Piper is a registered nurse, but her greatest enjoyment is being in the kitchen baking and preserving. Although most people would point to her as the expert, she says competing at the fair is still a great learning experience for her. Using real maple syrup and butter for outstanding flavor and handling the scone dough as little as possible are her secrets for blue ribbon results.

*3 cups all-purpose flour*  
*1 cup finely chopped pecans*  
*4 teaspoons baking powder*  
*¼ teaspoon salt*

*¾ cup butter (no substitutes)*  
*½ cup pure maple syrup*  
*½ cup milk*

Preheat oven to 375F (190C). Lightly grease a large baking sheet.

In a large bowl, stir flour, pecans, baking powder and salt until thoroughly mixed. Cut in butter until mixture resembles cornmeal. Combine maple syrup and milk in a measuring cup. Add to dry ingredients and stir until just blended.

Turn dough out onto a lightly floured surface. Knead gently 6 times. Divide dough in half. Pat or roll each half into a circle about 6 inches in diameter and ¾ inch thick. Place on prepared baking sheet. Cut each circle into 6 or 8 wedges; separate slightly. Bake about 15 minutes or until a wooden pick inserted near the center of a wedge comes out clean. Serve warm.

**Makes 12 to 16 scones.**

### About Scones

Home-baked scones have become a popular treat in this country for tea, coffee or for a special breakfast. Whether you do as most people and pronounce the name to rhyme with "own" or prefer the Scottish pronunciation that rhymes with "gone," we have taken this import to our hearts.

Although the English and Scots have had several centuries of making these tea breads at home, they still are most likely to serve traditional currant scones. Creative Americans, on the other hand, are coming up with almost as many flavor variations as we have for muffins.

Plain scones usually are split, buttered and served with a sweet spread. More flavorful ones, like these Maple Pecan Scones, need no enhancement, except perhaps a little butter.

LOUISE PIPER     ROLFE, IOWA     IOWA STATE FAIR

# Shirley's Baking Powder Biscuits

You might expect a blue ribbon baking powder biscuit from Texas to be Texas-sized, soft, and made with self-rising flour. Instead, Shirley Stafford Roberson's tasty quick bread could be the pride of any midwestern baker.

She and Orville Lawson (page 70) both add sugar and extra shortening to a basic recipe, with winning results. She bakes her biscuits an inch apart, so they are a rich golden brown on the sides as well as the top. She bakes them in her electric range, but she insists they're really best baked in a wood stove.

| | |
|---|---|
| *2 cups all-purpose flour* | *½ cup butter-flavored solid vegetable* |
| *3 teaspoons baking powder* | *shortening* |
| *4 teaspoons sugar* | *¾ cup milk* |
| *1 teaspoon salt* | *½ teaspoon butter flavoring (optional)* |
| | *Olive oil to brush biscuits* |

Preheat oven to 450F (230C). In a large bowl, combine flour, baking powder, sugar and salt. Cut in shortening until mixture resembles fine crumbs. Add milk and butter flavoring, if using, and stir until the dough leaves the sides of the bowl (dough will be soft and slightly sticky).

Turn dough out onto a floured surface. Knead until dough holds its shape, about 30 seconds. Roll dough ½ to ¾ inch thick. Cut into rounds with a floured 2½-inch cutter. Place on an ungreased baking sheet about 1 inch apart. Brush the tops and sides with olive oil. Bake 12 to 14 minutes or until golden brown.

Makes 10 biscuits.

### Understanding Chemical Leavenings

Baking powder and baking soda make quick breads possible. These chemical leavenings eliminate the time-consuming element of yeast.

Biscuits and other quick breads that are made with acidic buttermilk use the neutralizing baking soda, which releases gas bubbles and makes the biscuits rise. Baking soda works quickly, so any product using only baking soda must go into a heated oven right away. If the batter is stirred too much after it is added, the gas is released before it has a chance to raise the batter.

Biscuits made with "sweet" milk and no other acids use baking powder. Modern baking powder is a complex combination of acids and alkalis. With the commonly used double-acting baking powder, part of the chemicals in it produce fine gas bubbles immediately. The rest produce more gas as the biscuits are baked. For this reason baking powder biscuits are more tolerant than buttermilk biscuits and can wait for a while before they are baked, if necessary.

Many quick breads use both baking soda, to neutralize a variety of acid ingredients, and baking powder, for more reliable results.

SHIRLEY STAFFORD ROBERSON    LUBBOCK, TEXAS    PANHANDLE SOUTH PLAINS FAIR

# Caterer's Baking Powder Biscuits

Two rather similar recipes for baking powder biscuits demonstrate clearly how small changes in ingredients and slightly different baking techniques can result in products that have equally good eating qualities but are noticeably different in appearance, texture and even flavor.

Orville Lawson's recipe was given to him by a Chicago caterer. He considers it a midwestern biscuit. He brings an engineer's precision to his baking and his exact instructions are included in the recipe. The dough is very soft, and he bakes the biscuits close together so they are high and very light.

*2 cups sifted all-purpose flour*
*4 teaspoons baking powder*
*1 tablespoon sugar*
*1 teaspoon salt*

*⅓ cup solid vegetable shortening*
*1 cup minus 2 tablespoons milk*
*Milk to brush biscuits*

Preheat oven to 450F (230C).

Sift flour, baking powder, sugar and salt together two times onto waxed paper. Then sift into a medium bowl. With a pastry blender, cut in shortening until mixture resembles fine meal. Add milk all at once and stir vigorously with a fork 30 seconds or until dough is thoroughly blended.

Turn dough out on a well-floured surface and knead 30 seconds (dough should be soft). Pat or roll to ⅔ inch thick. Let stand 1 minute, then cut into rounds with a 2-inch cutter.

Place biscuits on an ungreased baking sheet about ¼ inch apart. Then knead the scraps of dough a few times and roll out ⅔ inch thick. Let stand 1 minute. Cut into rounds. Brush tops of biscuits with milk. Bake 10 to 15 minutes or until golden brown. Serve immediately.

**Makes 12 biscuits.**

### Sifting Flour for Quick Breads

Most quick breads call for unsifted flour, but an older recipe may call for sifted flour. While quick breads are more tolerant than cakes, meaning you can use a little more or a little less of an ingredient without a failure, it's best to follow the recipe. There can be as much as ¼ cup difference between 1 cup of sifted and 1 cup of unsifted flour, if you use the method of dipping the cup into the flour and sweeping off the excess (see Measuring Flour, page 60).

ORVILLE LAWSON      ALBUQUERQUE, NEW MEXICO      NEW MEXICO STATE FAIR

# Honeyed Date-Nut Bread

Cynthia Clarke includes California honey and oranges along with the dates from the Imperial Valley in her prize-winning version of date-nut bread. Like many date breads, this one is even better tasting and easier to slice after it has been stored for a day. Wrapped in foil and refrigerated, the richly flavored loaf will keep well for a week.

You can use an 8½ × 4½-inch loaf pan for this big recipe if it holds 7 cups. Otherwise, if you don't have a 9 × 5-inch pan, bake the extra batter in well-greased muffin cups.

| | |
|---|---|
| *2 cups pitted dates, cut into small pieces* | *¾ cup hot water* |
| *2 tablespoons solid vegetable shortening* | *2 cups all-purpose flour* |
| *⅔ cup packed light brown sugar* | *1 teaspoon baking soda* |
| *½ cup honey* | *1 teaspoon salt* |
| *¾ teaspoon vanilla extract* | *1 egg, beaten* |
| *¾ teaspoon grated orange peel* | *¾ cup pecans, chopped* |
| *¼ cup fresh orange juice* | *¼ cup black or California walnuts, chopped* |

In a medium bowl, combine dates, shortening, brown sugar, honey, vanilla, orange peel, juice and hot water. Let stand 15 minutes.

Preheat oven to 325F (165C). Grease a 9 × 5-inch loaf pan.

In a small bowl, stir flour, baking soda and salt together. Add egg to date mixture and mix well. Stir in flour, soda and salt just enough to moisten dry ingredients. Fold in pecans and walnuts. Turn batter into prepared pan.

Bake about 1 hour or until a wooden pick inserted in the center of the loaf comes out clean. Cool in the pan on a wire rack 10 minutes, then turn out on a wire rack to cool completely. Wrap in foil or plastic wrap and store in the refrigerator or other cool place overnight or longer before slicing.

Makes 1 large loaf.

### Loaf Pan Sizes

The correct pan size is very important for having well-shaped loaves. See page 2 for more information.

CYNTHIA CLARKE     LAKEWOOD, CALIFORNIA     LOS ANGELES COUNTY FAIR

# Apricot Walnut Bread

After Linda Shaw's children were grown, her coworkers at California State Polytechnic University suggested she turn her considerable baking talents to entering the Los Angeles County Fair. She won a blue ribbon with her first entry in 1982 and has been winning with breads and preserves ever since. Her husband and coworkers are enthusiastic testers as she perfects the recipes she wants to enter.

Soaking the dried apricots in brandy adds an extra subtle flavor to this attractive fruit-filled bread.

| | |
|---|---|
| *1 cup dried apricots* | *2 teaspoons baking powder* |
| *¼ cup brandy or orange juice* | *¼ teaspoon baking soda* |
| *1 egg* | *½ teaspoon salt* |
| *⅔ cup sugar* | *½ cup orange juice* |
| *2 tablespoons vegetable oil* | *½ cup water* |
| *2 cups all-purpose flour* | *1 cup chopped walnuts* |

Preheat oven to 350F (175C). Grease and flour bottom and bottom half of the sides of an 8½ × 4½-inch loaf pan.

Cut apricots into ¼-inch squares with a sharp knife or kitchen scissors. Place apricots in a small bowl, add brandy and toss to moisten apricots. Soak while you prepare the batter.

In a large bowl, beat egg until light. Beat in sugar and oil. In a medium bowl, stir together flour, baking powder, soda and salt. Drain apricots, using liquid to replace an equivalent amount of water, if desired. Add flour mixture to batter alternately with orange juice and water, beginning and ending with flour. Mix only enough to blend ingredients. Fold in apricots and walnuts.

Pour batter into prepared pan and bake about 1 hour or until a wooden pick inserted in the center of the loaf comes out clean. Cool in pan on a wire rack 10 minutes. Remove from pan and finish cooling on waxed paper–covered rack. For richer flavor, wrap the loaf in foil and store in a cool place for a day before serving.

Makes 1 loaf.

### Bamboo Skewers

Most recipes call for testing for doneness by inserting a wooden pick in the center of the baked product. For quick breads and other products that are more than 2 inches thick, a long thin bamboo skewer is even better. It is long enough so that you can be sure the product is baked all the way through. These handy kitchen helpers are available in packages in larger supermarkets, kitchen supply stores or Oriental food or gift shops.

LINDA SHAW     UPLAND, CALIFORNIA     LOS ANGELES COUNTY FAIR

# Spicy Apple Raisin Bread

Jacqueline Core took a zucchini bread recipe and substituted chopped apples to make a deliciously spicy bread that's loaded with fruit and nuts. She has always enjoyed trying new recipes. Since she retired she's had time to turn her talents to fair competition, where she quickly showed her blue ribbon baking talents. Her apple bread is a great favorite at potlucks.

| | |
|---|---|
| 3 cups all-purpose flour | 1¼ cups vegetable oil |
| 1½ teaspoons baking soda | 4 eggs, beaten |
| ½ teaspoon baking powder | 4 teaspoons vanilla extract |
| 1½ teaspoons salt | 3 cups chopped, peeled apple |
| 2 teaspoons ground cinnamon | ⅔ cup raisins |
| 1 teaspoon ground cloves | ½ cup chopped walnuts |
| 2½ cups sugar | |

Preheat oven to 325F (165C). Grease bottoms only of 2 (9 × 5-inch) or 2 (8½ × 4½-inch) loaf pans.

In a large bowl, stir together flour, soda, baking powder, salt, cinnamon and cloves. Add sugar, oil, eggs and vanilla. Beat at low speed or by hand 2 minutes. Add apples, raisins and walnuts and stir together for 1 minute, until well blended.

Divide batter evenly between prepared baking pans. Bake about 1 hour or until bread begins to shrink from the edges of the pan. (The wooden pick test may not be accurate because of the amount of apples.)

Cool in pans on a wire rack 10 minutes. Remove from pans and cool completely before cutting. Loaves are easier to cut after wrapping in foil and refrigerating 1 day. Store well wrapped in the refrigerator.

Makes 2 loaves.

### Choosing Cooking Apples

Because fruit quick breads are sweet, the apple varieties that will add the best flavor are tart, juicy cooking apples. Three widely available choices are Granny Smith, McIntosh and Winesap. Or, check with the produce manager of your supermarket for other locally grown varieties.

JACQUELINE CORE    SAN JUAN CAPISTRANO, CALIFORNIA    LOS ANGELES COUNTY FAIR

# Orange-Raisin Nut Bread

Anyone with an abundant supply of oranges will particularly welcome this recipe for a great-tasting quick bread. Charlene Reardon makes her versatile recipe with a variety of fresh, canned or frozen fruit. But it was this version, which used fresh orange puree, that brought her a blue ribbon. The flavor is a well-balanced blend of spice and orange. Crunchy pecans and raisins give it an interesting texture.

*6 medium oranges*
*2½ cups all-purpose flour*
*1 teaspoon baking soda*
*½ teaspoon salt*
*1 tablespoon ground cinnamon*
*2 cups sugar*

*1 cup vegetable oil*
*4 eggs*
*½ teaspoon pure orange extract*
*1½ cups chopped pecans*
*1 cup raisins*

Preheat oven to 350F (175C). Grease 2 (9 × 5-inch) or 2 (8½ × 4½-inch) loaf pans.

Prepare orange puree by peeling oranges. Over a 2-cup glass measure, cut between the membranes to release orange sections. Drop seeded orange sections and all their juice into the measuring cup. You need 2 cups orange sections with juice. Pour orange sections with juice into a blender and process about 15 seconds or until pureed.

In a small bowl, thoroughly mix flour, soda, salt and cinnamon. In a large bowl, beat together sugar, oil, eggs and orange extract. Pour in orange puree and blend. Stir in dry ingredients until just combined. Fold in pecans and raisins.

Pour batter evenly into prepared pans. Bake about 55 minutes, until a wooden pick inserted in the center of a loaf comes out clean. Cover the loaves with foil if they brown too quickly.

Cool in pans on a wire rack 5 minutes. Remove from pans and cool on rack. Loaves can be sliced when cooled or wrapped in foil and refrigerated overnight before serving.

**Makes 2 loaves.**

### Choosing Oranges for Recipes

Navel oranges, available from November to June, are considered eating oranges, while the later Valencias are the juice oranges. However, either will work in this recipe.

A medium orange will yield about ⅓ cup of sections and 4 teaspoons of shredded peel. The amount of juice depends on the variety, ranging from ¼ to ⅓ cup.

Oranges should be washed well before cutting. Remove the peel by cutting a thin slice off each end, then cut strips from top to bottom or around the orange, removing all the white membrane with the peel. A greenish tinge on the skin doesn't affect the flavor, but brightly colored oranges give the most attractive peel.

CHARLENE REARDON        SHAFTER, CALIFORNIA        KERN COUNTY FAIR

# Praline Pumpkin Date Bread

Like many southern Californians, Cynthia Clarke uses lots of California dates when she bakes. She took a traditional pumpkin bread, added dates and then made it special with a baked-on streusel topping. The spicy, moist loaves can be cut as soon as they are cool. They also keep well wrapped in foil and refrigerated or frozen. Bake the bread in an 8½-inch pan for a tall loaf or in a 9-inch pan for a country look.

*½ cup packed light brown sugar*　　　*½ teaspoon ground cloves*
*½ cup chopped pecans*　　　　　　　*1⅔ cups sugar*
*2 tablespoons butter, softened*　　　　*⅔ cup vegetable oil*
*3 cups all-purpose flour*　　　　　　*2 teaspoons vanilla extract*
*2 teaspoons baking soda*　　　　　　*4 eggs*
*½ teaspoon baking powder*　　　　　*1 (15- or 16-oz.) can pumpkin*
*¼ teaspoon salt*　　　　　　　　　*1 cup chopped dates*
*1 teaspoon ground cinnamon*

Preheat oven to 350F (175C). Grease and flour 2 (8½ × 4½-inch) or 2 (9 × 5-inch) loaf pans.

In a small bowl, combine brown sugar, pecans and butter; reserve for topping.

Into a medium bowl, sift together flour, soda, baking powder, salt, cinnamon and cloves. In another medium bowl, beat together sugar, oil, vanilla, eggs and pumpkin until well blended. Stir in flour mixture, just until well blended. Fold in dates.

Pour batter evenly into prepared pans. Sprinkle with topping mixture. Bake 50 to 55 minutes or until a wooden pick inserted in the center of a loaf comes out clean. If the loaves are browning too fast, cover with foil for the last 10 to 15 minutes.

Cool in the pans on a wire rack 15 minutes. Remove from pans and cool completely before slicing. Loaves freeze well.

Makes 2 loaves.

### Sifting or Stirring Dry Ingredients
Some recipes in this book, especially those that call for several spices or a large number of dry ingredients, call for sifting dry ingredients together. Others say to mix the dry ingredients together in a bowl. Either method works, as long as they are completely blended before adding them to the wet ingredients.

It's especially important in quick breads and muffins that the baking powder and baking soda are well distributed. If they aren't, it can affect the flavor and texture.

CYNTHIA CLARKE　　　LAKEWOOD, CALIFORNIA　　　LOS ANGELES COUNTY FAIR

# Orange Walnut Bread

Kathy Klass and her mother share their recipes and baking experiments during the year and then both enter the ones they think might rate a ribbon.

Orange Walnut Bread is one that Kathy says was developed by trial and error. It has a lovely fresh orange flavor, enhanced by the orange glaze. The loaf can be sliced as soon as it has cooled, and it also keeps well wrapped in foil and refrigerated.

| | |
|---|---|
| *1½ cups all-purpose flour* | *Grated peel of 1 large orange* |
| *1½ teaspoons baking powder* | *½ cup orange juice* |
| *¼ teaspoon baking soda* | *1 cup chopped walnuts* |
| *¼ teaspoon salt* | |
| *½ cup butter, softened* | *ORANGE GLAZE* |
| *¾ cup sugar* | *¼ cup orange juice* |
| *2 eggs, separated* | *¼ cup powdered sugar* |

Preheat oven to 350F (175C). Grease an 8½ × 4½-inch loaf pan.

In a small bowl, stir together flour, baking powder, soda and salt. In a medium bowl, beat butter and sugar together until fluffy. Add egg yolks one at a time, beating after each addition. Add grated orange peel. Add flour mixture and ½ cup orange juice alternately, stirring to blend.

In a small bowl, beat egg whites until stiff. Gently fold in egg whites and walnuts. Pour batter into prepared pan. Bake 50 to 60 minutes or until a wooden pick inserted in the center of loaf comes out clean.

Prepare glaze and spoon over loaf as soon as it comes out of the oven. Cool in pan on a wire rack 10 minutes. Remove bread from pan. Cool completely on rack before slicing.

Makes 1 loaf.

**ORANGE GLAZE**

In a small bowl, combine ¼ cup orange juice and powdered sugar.

### The California Orange Industry's Modest Start

The important navel orange growing and marketing business in California had a modest beginning in the backyard of Mrs. Eliza Tibbets, Riverside, CA. She received two seedless orange trees from the USDA in Washington, DC. These winter-ripening oranges originally had been introduced in Brazil.

Despite the fact that Mrs. Tibbets irrigated her trees with dishwater because water was scarce, the trees thrived. The fruit was of such excellent eating quality that it attracted widespread attention. Soon other pioneer colonists in the area also planted the navel orange and eventually a new business was born.

Summer-ripening Valencias were introduced later. These trees came from Spain by way of the Moors and Arabs. With the two varieties available, California eventually was able to offer a year-round supply of oranges to the country.

KATHY KLASS    NORWALK, CALIFORNIA    LOS ANGELES COUNTY FAIR

# Pies & Pastries

*The whole business of making a pie crust is artistry and skill, and honor goes to the fingers of the deft.*

Della T. Lutes, *Home Grown*

The earliest pies we know about are those mentioned in ancient Roman literature, where they describe eating meats encased in a baked paste. This crust was used primarily to hold in the meat juices and not served with the meat.

Pies baked in a "coffin" (an edible pie crust) turn up later in medieval manuscripts. These usually were mixtures of meat or fish, fruit and spices. One of those recipes from the fifteenth century *Noble Boke of Cookery* describes a pie filled with spiced river lamprey, not likely to win any blue ribbons today.

Even in the earliest American cookbooks, the English-influenced recipes were more likely to be meat or fish pies rather than desserts. But by the nineteenth century, when agriculture was thriving and food was abundant, dessert pies began to come into their own.

Fruit pies have always been a favorite way for families who raised some fruit or berries to use up a bumper crop. However, we don't find many early cookbook recipes for plain fruit pies. It was assumed that the directions were passed by word of mouth from mother to daughter, so everyone would know how to make them.

In colonial times, communal brick ovens in the northeast colonies were rated in terms of the number of pies they held. Ten-pie ovens were common and there were even twenty-pie ovens.

In cold weather, fruit pies were turned out by mass production and stored in cold closets or frozen in the snow. Pie often was eaten for breakfast as well as for dinner and supper, so any good-sized family could go through a number of pies in a week.

For many, pies typify honest country cooking, but we know that today fair winners are as likely to come from metropolitan areas as from the country.

Fruit pies prevail among our blue ribbon winners, possibly because most fairs take place in late summer, when fresh fruit is most abundant. They also are easier to transport in perfect condition than the more delicate and perishable meringue-topped and cream pies.

But along with the fresh cherry and peach pies that showcase locally grown produce, in this chapter we also have pies that pair fruit and a creamy filling, fruit pie with a soufflélike topping and fruit tarts.

A retired engineer tells how he made the lemon meringue pie that was named Best of Show, competing with 104 other entries. Or, if you prefer a different kind of lemon pie, you can discover a treasured heritage recipe for a lemon sponge pie or one for a two-layer citrus chiffon pie.

Because of food safety concerns, we tell you how to safely adapt a recipe that originally used raw beaten egg whites. This is a tip you can use for other favorite recipes you may have thought you could never use again. We also tell you how to make sure meringue is baked to a safe temperature.

Chocolate lovers can satisfy their cravings with one of three ultrarich, absolutely delicious pies and tartlets. For coconut lovers we have an unusual and unusually good coconut macaroon pie. Some fairs include a category for cheesecake along with pies, so we also are able to offer a wonderful orange cheesecake.

Research on pie baking tells us that many people don't bake pies because they think it is too difficult to make a good crust. Pie-judging criteria at a number of state fairs counts the crust as 40 percent of the total score, and it never counts for less than 25 percent. These are make-or-break numbers for anyone who wants to take home a blue ribbon.

Many of our blue ribbon winners have signature additions to their basic pie crust recipe or a technique that they think is important. Since crust counts so much in the enjoyment of pie as well as in judging, we wanted you to know exactly how these blue ribbon winners prepared theirs. The tips they share have been included in the recipes and in the blue ribbon tips.

In addition, in the decade between the publication of the first *Blue Ribbon Winners* and this cookbook, a number of pie bakers started using a basic pastry richer than the long-time standard. At first it looked like we might have to include a dozen pie crust recipes to take care of all the variations we found. But by the time all the recipes were analyzed, it turned out we had two basic recipes, with small but important individual variations, plus three other recipes that were basic enough to be used for other pies.

Each recipe now indicates the pie crust recipe used, with a note at the end of the recipe with any variations. You may want to duplicate the winner's recipe exactly, or mix and match.

With these pie crust recipes and the winners' tips for success, you need never fear making pie crust again.

# Blackberry Pie

For her state fair entries Denise Turnbull chooses the kind of food her family likes to eat. They prefer uncomplicated desserts like a pie with a tender, flaky crust, bursting with fresh fruit or berries. Her one concession to judges for her blackberry pie is to thicken the juice a bit more than she does for her family. Her husband, particularly, likes a rather runny fruit pie, but judges don't. They awarded this pie the grand championship, so obviously they approved of her changes.

Testers thought her version of the richer basic pie crust was particularly good.

*Basic Rich Pie Crust (page 109)* | *1½ cups sugar plus extra for sprinkling*
*(see Note, below)* | *¾ teaspoon ground cinnamon*
*4 cups fresh blackberries* | *⅛ teaspoon salt*
*¼ cup quick-cooking tapioca* | *2 tablespoons butter, cut into small pieces*

Prepare dough for crust and chill. In a medium bowl, gently combine blackberries and tapioca. Let stand 15 minutes. Preheat oven to 450F (230C).

In a small bowl, combine sugar, cinnamon and salt. On a floured surface roll out one piece of chilled dough to a 13-inch-diameter circle. Ease into a 9-inch pie plate and refrigerate. Roll out second piece of dough for the top crust.

Toss the sugar mixture with the blackberries. Spoon filling into chilled crust; dot with the butter. Cover with top crust. Seal and flute edges. Sprinkle crust lightly with sugar and cover edges with foil.

Bake 15 minutes, reduce heat to 375F (190C) and bake 30 to 40 minutes or until crust is golden brown and juices bubble up. Remove foil the last 15 minutes of baking. Cool pie on a wire rack.

Makes 1 (9-inch) pie, 8 servings.

### VARIATION

Substitute 4 cups dry-pack frozen blackberries, partially thawed. Drain off any liquid.

### NOTE

Denise uses chilled butter-flavored solid vegetable shortening, adds 1 tablespoon lemon juice and chills the dough for half an hour before rolling out.

### *Using Tapioca as a Thickener*

Tapioca is a starch from the roots of the tropical cassava plant. The quick-cooking form can be used as a thickener in fruit pies instead of flour or cornstarch. The tiny particles become clear when they are cooked, but they may not dissolve completely. If that is objectionable, first grind the tapioca in the blender until it is as fine as cornmeal.

To substitute tapioca for cornstarch, use an equal amount. Replace flour with a little less tapioca.

DENISE TURNBULL    MONMOUTH, ILLINOIS    ILLINOIS STATE FAIR

# Strawberry-Rhubarb Pie

Orville Lawson's first cooking experience came as a teenager, over a campfire. Although he occasionally prepared a meal as an adult, his serious interest in cooking came after he retired and he and his wife Virginia moved to New Mexico. He decided to join her in state fair competitions, where his specialties are pies and candy.

His engineering background shows in the precision of his directions. Since he has perfected the art of making a lattice crust, we asked him to describe how he does it. His own directions follow in the blue ribbon tip.

| | |
|---|---|
| *Basic Pie Crust for Double Crusts* | *½ teaspoon ground nutmeg* |
| *(page 110)* | *2 cups ½-inch pieces rhubarb* |
| *1¼ cups sugar* | *2 cups halved strawberries* |
| *5 tablespoons all-purpose flour* | *2 tablespoons butter* |

Prepare dough for crust and chill. Preheat oven to 400F (205C).

Roll out bottom crust as directed for a 9-inch pie and use to line a 9-inch pie pan. In a medium bowl, combine sugar, flour and nutmeg. Add rhubarb and strawberries and toss gently to mix. Spoon filling into lined pie pan. Dot with butter.

Use remaining dough for a lattice top (see below). Cover pie with lattice top. Seal and flute edges. Bake about 50 minutes or until pastry is golden brown and juice bubbles up through the lattice top. Cool on a wire rack.

Makes 1 (9-inch) pie, 8 servings.

### Making a Perfect Lattice Crust

Orville Lawson says two words describe how to make a lattice crust: "Very carefully." His directions follow:

- Roll the dough for the bottom crust at least 1-inch larger than the rim of the pie pan.
- Roll the dough for the top crust. Using a ½-inch-wide metal straightedge, cut the dough into strips with a pastry wheel to give a pleasing scalloped edge.
- Weave the lattice on the pie rather than forming it on a piece of waxed paper and transferring it to the pie.
- To start the lattice, take a strip of dough from the center of the cut strips and place it across the pie, crossing the center point. Place the second strip at right angles to the first strip, crossing the center of the pie. Continue adding strips, using a basket weave, spacing the strips ½ inch apart.
- Fold the overhang from the bottom crust up and over the ends of the lattice. Press it together gently and finish with a decorative edge of your choice.

ORVILLE LAWSON      ALBUQUERQUE, NEW MEXICO      NEW MEXICO STATE FAIR

# Fresh Cherry Pie

If, like Nancy Johnson, you are lucky enough to live in an area where sour pie cherries grow, you can take advantage of the brief period they are available. Since the bright red fruit is too tart to eat out-of-hand, there is no better way to use it than in a rich-tasting pie with a tender, flaky crust.

If you can get tree-ripened fruit, add a minimum amount of sugar for the best fruit flavor. Shipped-in pie cherries are picked before they are fully ripe, so you may need to add a little more sugar.

| | |
|---|---|
| *Never-Fail Pie Crust (page 111)* | *2 teaspoons lemon juice* |
| *4 cups pitted, tart cherries* | *¼ teaspoon almond extract* |
| *¾ cup sugar plus extra for sprinkling* | *2 tablespoons butter* |
| *2¾ tablespoons tapioca* | *1 tablespoon melted butter, for brushing* |

Prepare dough for crust. Preheat oven to 425F (220C).

In a medium bowl, gently stir together cherries, sugar, tapioca, lemon juice and almond extract. Roll out dough as directed for a double-crust 9-inch pie. Line a 9-inch pie pan with dough.

Spoon cherry filling into lined pie pan. Dot filling with 2 tablespoons butter. Place top crust on filling. Seal and flute edges. Cut slits in the top crust for steam to escape. Brush with the melted butter and sprinkle with sugar.

Bake 10 minutes, reduce the heat to 350F (175C) and bake about 30 minutes or until crust is golden and juices bubble up through the slits in the crust. Cool pie on a wire rack before serving.

Makes 1 (9-inch) pie, 8 servings.

## VARIATION

If fresh cherries are not available, use 2 (16-oz.) cans pitted tart red cherries, drained.

## Choosing a Pie Pan

Blue ribbon winners stick with old reliable pie pans, glass or dull metal. They know that crust will not brown properly in shiny metal pans, which reflect the heat.

Where to use a shiny pie pan? Use for pies with crumb crusts, which do not need to brown.

NANCY JOHNSON        CLEVER, MISSOURI        OZARK EMPIRE FAIR

# Peach Pie

Linda Pauls suggests tasting the peaches and then adjusting the amount of sugar in this pie filling. If you can get tree-ripened fruit, the peaches will be much sweeter. She wisely lets the pure peach flavor come through and uses just enough thickening for a slightly juicy filling.

To prevent the edges of the pie from getting too brown, she tents the crust with foil (see blue ribbon tip, below).

| | |
|---|---|
| *Basic Pie Crust for Double Crusts* | *1 tablespoon cornstarch* |
| *(page 110) (see Note below)* | *4 cups sliced peaches, preferably Elbertas* |
| *1¼ cups sugar* | *1 tablespoon butter* |
| *1 tablespoon all-purpose flour* | *Sugar* |

Prepare dough for crust. Preheat oven to 450F (230C).

In a medium bowl, combine sugar, flour and cornstarch; add peaches and toss gently to mix. Roll out bottom crust as directed for a 9-inch pie and use to line an 8- or 9-inch pie pan. Spoon peach filling into lined pie pan; dot with butter.

Roll out top crust; cut a decorative design in the crust for vents. Moisten edges of bottom crust and ease top crust over filling. Seal and trim crusts; crimp edges. Sprinkle the crust with a little water and sprinkle lightly with sugar.

Bake 10 minutes, then reduce heat to 375F (190C) for 35 to 40 minutes, until golden brown and juices bubble up through the vents. Cool on a wire rack.

**Makes 1 (8- or 9-inch) pie, 6 to 8 servings.**

### VARIATION

Substitute 4 cups sugar-pack peaches (frozen without syrup), partially thawed. Reduce sugar slightly.

### NOTE

Linda uses Basic Pie Crust for Double Crusts but uses butter-flavored solid shortening plus 1 extra tablespoon.

### *Preventing Overbrown Pie Crust Edges*

A high stand-up rim on pie crust will brown faster than the rest of the pie. For a perfect golden-brown crust, blue ribbon winners often cover the crust in one of two easy ways:

To "tent" the crust, take a 12-inch square of foil, fold it into quarters and cut out a 7-inch opening in the center. Open the square and loosely encase the edge of the crust in the foil rim. Remove this about halfway through the baking process.

Or, cover the edge loosely with a 1½-inch strip of foil. Remove this at least 15 minutes before the pie is finished baking.

When you remove the foil depends partly on the temperature you are using to bake the pie. Note that, for pies, the crust is covered at the beginning of the baking rather than at the end. Some of the pie recipes include specific directions from the winners about covering the edge of the crust.

LINDA PAULS    BUHLER, KANSAS    KANSAS STATE FAIR

# Golden Apple Pie

Virginia Lawson's first state fair entry was African violets. It took nearly twenty years for her to move into the foods area, where she now excels in baking. Pies are her favorite. When she makes apple pie, the Golden Delicious apple is her choice. She uses spice with a light hand to let the apple flavor come through.

Golden Delicious apples are tangy-sweet in the fall, but become more mellow in the winter. If they aren't tart enough, add a little lemon juice to the filling.

As Best of Show winner for a decorated gum-paste candy box, it's not surprising that this artist with food uses pastry apples and leaves to decorate her apple pie.

*Basic Rich Pie Crust*
*(page 109)*
*¾ cup sugar*
*¾ teaspoon ground cinnamon*
*¼ teaspoon ground nutmeg*
*2 tablespoons all-purpose flour*

*⅛ teaspoon salt*
*5 large or 8 medium Golden Delicious*
*apples (2½ to 3 pounds) peeled,*
*quartered, cored and thinly sliced*
*crosswise*
*2 tablespoons butter*

Prepare dough for crust. Preheat oven to 450F (230C).

In a large bowl, thoroughly blend together sugar, cinnamon, nutmeg, flour and salt. Add apples and toss to combine.

Roll half the prepared dough on a floured surface to a 13-inch round; ease into a 9-inch pie plate. Pile apples into pastry shell, mounding them slightly in the center; dot with butter.

Roll the second half of the dough into a 12-inch round; ease over apples. Trim crust to a 1-inch overhang. Roll overhang under pie plate rim; crimp to seal. Cut steam vents in the top crust. Garnish with apples and leaves cut from leftover dough, brushing bottoms with water if dough is dry.

Bake 15 minutes. Reduce heat to 400F (205C) and bake about 45 minutes or until crust is golden and filling juices bubble up through the vents. Cool on a wire rack.

**Makes 1 (9-inch) pie, 8 servings.**

### Freezing Apple & Other Fruit Pies

Although many varieties of apples, including Golden Delicious, are available all year, they have the best flavor for pies before long storage.

Apple pies, as well as most other fruit pies, freeze well. Make as usual, except dip the apple slices in a mixture of ascorbic acid or commercial anti-darkening agent and water, so they won't darken during freezer storage. (Look for ascorbic acid or anti-darkening agent with canning and freezing supplies in the supermarket. Follow package directions.)

Do not cut vents in the top crust.

Freeze the unbaked pie in its pan, covering it with an inverted paper plate for protection. Wrap in freezer paper or place in a freezer-weight plastic bag. Mark with a "use by" date of up to 4 months.

To bake, unwrap the pie, cut vent holes in the top crust and bake without thawing 15 to 20 minutes in a preheated 450F (230C) oven, then reduce heat to 375F (190C) and bake 20 to 30 minutes or until crust is golden brown and juices begin to bubble up.

VIRGINIA LAWSON    ALBUQUERQUE, NEW MEXICO    NEW MEXICO STATE FAIR

# Lattice-Crust Pineapple Pie

Like many blue ribbon bakers, Emily Lewis worked her way up from county fair to state fair, learning what makes a winner. Her specialty is pies. She will bake all night if that's what it takes to get them to the fair as fresh as possible.

Her tasty pineapple pie with its pretty lattice crust is easily made any time of year from ingredients you can keep on hand. With help from a pie crust expert, she developed a richer basic pie crust that is tender and flaky. This contributed to the Award of Excellence she received, in addition to the blue ribbon for this pie.

*Basic Pie Crust for Double Crusts
  (page 110) (see Note, below)
2 (15¼-oz.) cans sweetened crushed
  pineapple
¾ cup sugar plus extra for sprinkling
4½ tablespoons cornstarch*

*⅛ teaspoon salt
4½ tablespoons butter
2 tablespoons orange juice
½ teaspoon grated orange peel
1 tablespoon milk*

Prepare crust and chill at least 15 minutes. Drain pineapple, reserving 1½ cups of juice.

In a medium saucepan, mix together ¾ cup sugar, cornstarch and salt. Stir in reserved juice. Bring to a boil over medium heat, stirring constantly. Cook 3 minutes, stirring constantly. Remove from heat. Add drained pineapple, butter, orange juice and peel. Cool to room temperature.

Preheat oven to 425F (220C). Roll out bottom crust as directed for a 9-inch pie. Line a deep 9-inch pie pan with dough. Use remaining dough for lattice topping (see page 80). Pour filling into lined pie pan; top with lattice crust. Trim crust and flute edges. Brush with milk and sprinkle lightly with sugar. Cover edges of crust with foil.

Bake 15 minutes. Reduce temperature to 350F (175C) and bake 20 to 25 minutes or until the crust is golden and juices bubble up. Remove foil for the last 15 minutes. Cool on a wire rack before serving.

**Makes 1 (9-inch) pie, 8 servings.**

## VARIATION

If only 20-oz. cans of crushed pineapple are available, use 1½ cans.

## NOTE

Emily chills the shortening, adds ¼ cup butter, forms the dough into 2 rounds and refrigerates them for a minimum of 15 minutes before rolling out the crusts.

### Pie Pan Sizes

The lack of standardization in baking pan sizes also is apparent in pie pan sizes. A standard 9-inch pie pan holds about 3¾ cups of liquid, but a 2-inch-deep 9-inch pan holds about 5 cups of liquid. If you use a decorative pottery or ceramic pie plate for your home baking, the only way to know how much it holds is to measure its liquid capacity.

For smaller families, an 8-inch pie pan is often the choice. These hold 2¾ to 3 cups of liquid, roughly one-fourth less than a standard 9-inch pan.

It's a good idea to mark the capacity of your pie pans on the bottom with nail polish. Then, when you are trying a new recipe it will be easier to know which of your pans to use.

EMILY LEWIS     WAUSEON, OHIO     OHIO STATE FAIR

# Sour Cream Pear Pie

Denise Turnbull says she enjoys winning ribbons, but the best part of the Illinois State Fair is the friendships she makes. Besides entering her baking in the open competition, her recipes often are chosen for a "bake-off," in which contestants have to prepare their baked products before an audience, as well as the judges. The contestants use that time to renew friendships and to share experiences with other excellent cooks.

Her one-crust Sour Cream Pear Pie, using sliced canned pears, is an adaptation of an apple sour cream pie recipe. The contrasts between the sweet pears, the slightly tangy cream filling and the crunchy topping give this pie lots of taste appeal.

*Basic Rich Pie Crust (page 109)*
  *(see Note, below)*
*3 cups sliced, canned pears*
*½ cup sugar*
*1 tablespoon cornstarch*
*⅛ teaspoon salt*
*1 cup sour cream*

*1 teaspoon vanilla extract*
*½ teaspoon almond extract*

*TOPPING*
*½ cup all-purpose flour*
*⅓ cup sugar*
*¼ cup butter*

Prepare dough for crust and chill. Preheat oven to 375F (190C). Drain pear slices thoroughly.

In a medium bowl, combine sugar, cornstarch and salt. Blend in sour cream, vanilla and almond extracts. Add pears and gently toss, using a rubber spatula, to coat pears.

On a floured surface roll out 1 piece of chilled dough into a 13-inch round. Ease into a 9-inch pie pan. Flute pie edges. Arrange pears and sour cream mixture in the pie shell. Cover pie edges with foil. Bake 25 minutes.

While pie is baking, make topping. Remove foil from pie. Sprinkle topping evenly over filling. Return to the oven and bake 25 to 30 minutes or until the topping is very lightly browned and juices from the filling just begin to bubble up. Cool pie on a wire rack. Serve slightly warm or chilled. Store in the refrigerator.

Makes 1 (9-inch) pie, 8 servings.

**TOPPING**

In a small bowl, combine flour and sugar; cut in butter until mixture is crumbly.

**NOTE**

Denise uses chilled butter-flavored shortening, adds 1 tablespoon lemon juice and chills the dough 30 minutes before rolling out. The single-crust pie will use a little more than half the recipe. Remaining dough can be frozen for future use.

### Making Decorative Edges

Eye appeal is important in judging pies. Two easy edgings give pies a more attractive, finished look:

For either, make a stand-up, outside edge on the pie crust. For a scalloped edge, place your thumb against the outside edge of the pie crust and press the dough around it with the thumb and index finger of your other hand.

For a rope edge, place the thumb on the pastry edge at an angle. Press the pastry against the thumb with the knuckle of the index finger.

DENISE TURNBULL     MONMOUTH, ILLINOIS     ILLINOIS STATE FAIR

# Lemon Meringue Pie

Orville Lawson was the first man ever to win Best of Show in the pie contest at the New Mexico State Fair. Competing with 104 other entries, he triumphed with this Lemon Meringue Pie.

Many consider lemon meringue the true test of an excellent pie baker: you must cook the filling at a medium heat and stir constantly to prevent scorching. If you add the hot mixture to the egg yolks too fast, you'll get flecks of cooked egg in the filling. However, if you follow his pie directions, you, too, can make a prize-worthy pie.

The meringue also takes special care. See opposite for directions on how to make a perfect meringue.

This pie is best eaten soon after it has cooled enough to cut. Any leftovers should be refrigerated.

*Basic Rich Pie Crust (page 109)*
*1 cup sugar*
*4 tablespoons cornstarch*
*1½ cups warm water*
*3 egg yolks, slightly beaten*
*3 tablespoons butter*
*½ cup lemon juice*
*2 tablespoons grated lemon peel*

*MERINGUE*
*4 egg whites, at room temperature*
*¼ teaspoon cream of tartar*
*¼ cup sugar*

Prepare and bake pie crust in a 9-inch pie pan.

Preheat oven to 350F (175C).

In a heavy saucepan, thoroughly mix sugar and cornstarch. Gradually stir in warm water. Cook over medium heat, stirring constantly, until the mixture thickens and comes to a boil. Boil gently 2 minutes, stirring constantly. Remove from heat.

Slowly drizzle half the hot mixture into the egg yolks, stirring constantly. Then, slowly pour the egg yolk mixture into the mixture in the saucepan. Return saucepan to medium heat and boil gently 2 minutes, stirring constantly.

Remove pan from heat; stir in butter, lemon juice and lemon peel. Place cooled baked crust on a wire rack. Pour in filling and let stand at room temperature while making the meringue.

Prepare meringue. Spoon onto pie filling taking care to seal the meringue onto the edge of the crust to prevent shrinking.

Bake 15 minutes or until meringue is golden. Cool on a wire rack for 2½ to 3 hours before serving. Refrigerate leftovers.

Makes 1 (9-inch) pie, 8 servings.

**MERINGUE**

In a medium bowl, with an electric mixer, beat egg whites with cream of tartar until foamy. Gradually add sugar, continuing to beat until egg whites are stiff but still glossy.

 *Tips for a Perfect Meringue*

- Wait to make the meringue until the hot filling has been poured into the crust. Then work quickly so the filling is still hot when you spread the meringue.
- Be sure the bowl and beaters are clean and free from any grease or oil. Use a small, deep glass or metal (not plastic) bowl.
- Beat the egg whites and cream of tartar at high speed until foamy. Then beat at medium speed while adding sugar, so it will be completely dissolved. Return to high speed to complete beating.
- Getting just the right stiffness is critical. The peaks should be somewhat stiff, but they should bend over when the beaters are withdrawn and should still be glossy.
- Swirl the meringue in mounds, not peaks. Peaks will overbrown. Bake the meringue at 350F (175C) 12 to 15 minutes to make sure that the raw egg white is cooked to a safe temperature.
- To cut the meringue neatly, use a sharp knife and dip it into hot water after each cut.

ORVILLE LAWSON    ALBUQUERQUE, NEW MEXICO    NEW MEXICO STATE FAIR

# Lemon-Lime Daiquiri Pie

Julie Dilleshaw-Canada says she has made this recipe for so many years she can't remember where it originated. Like many pies that date back to a time when we considered the inside of an egg to be almost sterile, her original recipe includes raw beaten egg whites.

This lovely, light pie is a recipe to treasure and to adapt. If pasteurized eggs are available in your area, we suggest you use them. Or, use the method described in the blue ribbon tip to make the meringue.

Lemon and lime juice are nearly the same color, so to get the pretty two-layer effect, add a few drops of yellow food color to the lemon filling. The fluffy lime layer is a very pale green, and the toasted coconut adds a nice contrast in texture.

*COCONUT CRUST*
*2 cups flaked coconut*
*3 to 4 tablespoons butter, melted*

*½ cup flaked coconut, lightly toasted*

*LIME FILLING*
*⅔ cup sugar*
*1 envelope unflavored gelatin*
*¼ teaspoon salt*
*⅓ cup lime juice*
*⅓ cup water*
*3 egg yolks, slightly beaten*
*½ teaspoon grated lime peel*

*¼ cup light rum*
*3 egg whites*
*6 tablespoons sugar*

*LEMON FILLING*
*¾ cup sugar*
*3 tablespoons cornstarch*
*¼ teaspoon salt*
*¾ cup water*
*1 tablespoon butter*
*⅓ cup lemon juice*
*1 teaspoon grated lemon peel*
*4 drops yellow food coloring*

Preheat oven to 325F (165C). Prepare Coconut Crust. Cool the crust while making the fillings.

Prepare Lime Filling. Prepare Lemon Filling and spoon into cooled pie shell. Cover with Lime Filling and sprinkle with toasted coconut. Chill several hours or overnight before serving. Refrigerate leftovers.

Makes 1 (9-inch) pie, 8 servings.

**COCONUT CRUST**

Combine the coconut and melted butter in a small bowl. Press into the bottom and up the sides of a 9-inch pie plate. Bake until the coconut is lightly browned, about 15 minutes. (At the same time, on a baking sheet, toast ½ cup coconut to garnish the pie).

### LIME FILLING

Combine sugar, gelatin and salt in a medium saucepan. In a small bowl, stir together lime juice, water and egg yolks just enough to mix. Stir into sugar mixture. Cook on low heat, stirring constantly, until the mixture bubbles, thickens slightly and coats a silver spoon.

Remove pan from heat; stir in lime peel and rum. Chill until it has the consistency of corn syrup, stirring occasionally.

When mixture has thickened, if using pasteurized egg whites, in a small bowl, beat egg whites until soft peaks form; gradually beat in sugar and beat until stiff peaks form but egg whites are still glossy. (If using regular eggs, follow directions in blue ribbon tip, below.) Fold into gelatin mixture. Chill until the mixture mounds.

### LEMON FILLING

Combine sugar, cornstarch and salt in a medium saucepan. Gradually stir in water. Cook over medium-low heat, stirring constantly, until mixture boils and thickens. Boil 1 minute.

Remove from heat. Add butter, stirring until it melts. Add lemon juice, grated lemon peel and food coloring and stir until smooth. Refrigerate until mixture has cooled.

### *Using Raw Beaten Egg Whites Safely*

The American Egg Board understood that many favorite old recipes such as chiffon pies called for folding raw beaten egg whites into the mixture, so they developed this method of heating the whites to a safe temperature while making the meringue.

While egg yolks are much more likely than egg whites to carry the *salmonella enteritis* bacterial organism, it still is prudent to take every precaution, particularly if there have been outbreaks of *salmonellosis* in your area.

Use only clean, unbroken eggs. Don't wash them; they were sanitized before they were packed.

Combine the 3 egg whites with 6 tablespoons sugar in the top of a double boiler. (Always use a minimum of 2 tablespoons sugar per white or the egg will coagulate too rapidly, and you won't get a meringue.) Over simmering water, beat the whites with a hand-held electric mixer, first at medium speed to combine the sugar and egg whites, and then at high speed. Beat until the egg whites stand in stiff peaks but are still moist. (This takes only a short time; don't overbeat.) Remove the meringue from the heat. Mix a big spoonful of meringue into the lime mixture to blend; then fold the lime mixture into the meringue. Chill the pie as soon as assembled and keep it refrigerated.

You can use the same method for making cold soufflés, seven-minute frosting and royal icing. If a recipe calls for cream of tartar (this one does not), leave it out if your only choice is an unlined aluminum pan. The acid will react with the pan and turn the beaten whites an unattractive gray color.

JULIE DILLESHAW-CANADA     BAKERSFIELD, CALIFORNIA     KERN COUNTY FAIR

# Sweet Summer Pie

After taking cooking classes and experimenting with interesting new recipes, Bonnie Orlando says she eventually learned that a winning recipe is one that tastes great. In this case, her blue ribbon pie also is unusual and very attractive.

The baked open-faced nectarine and strawberry pie is covered with a soufflélike topping instead of meringue, then returned to the oven just long enough to bake and brown the topping. While the pie is best eaten within a few hours after it is baked, the soufflé topping holds up better than meringue.

*Basic Rich Pie Crust (page 109)*
  *(see Note, opposite)*
*⅓ cup all-purpose flour*
*⅔ cup sugar*
*5 cups peeled, thinly sliced nectarines*
*1 cup sliced strawberries*
*4 egg yolks*
*⅛ teaspoon salt*

*⅓ cup sugar*
*⅓ cup fresh orange juice*
*3 tablespoons fresh lemon juice*
*2 teaspoons grated orange peel*
*1½ teaspoons grated lemon peel*
*4 egg whites*
*½ cup sugar*

Preheat oven to 425F (220C). Prepare dough for crust and roll out dough to a 13-inch circle. Ease into a 9-inch pie pan, making a high fluted edge.

In a medium bowl, mix flour and ⅔ cup sugar. Add nectarines and strawberries and toss gently to coat fruit. Spoon evenly into pie shell.

Cover rim of dough with a strip of foil. Bake 30 minutes and remove foil. Bake 10 to 15 minutes or until fruit is tender and juices are just beginning to bubble up.

Meanwhile, in the top of a double boiler over simmering water, beat egg yolks, salt and ⅓ cup sugar with a hand-held electric mixer about 3 minutes or until egg yolks are thick and light lemon-colored. Add orange and lemon juices and mix until smooth. Cook over simmering water, stirring constantly, until mixture begins to thicken. Cook 8 to 10 minutes, stirring constantly, until mixture is thick. Remove from heat; add orange and lemon peels and refrigerate, stirring once or twice.

When fruit is baked, remove pie from the oven and reduce the heat to 350F (175C).

In a medium bowl, beat the egg whites with a mixer at medium speed until foamy. Gradually beat in sugar, then beat at high speed until stiff peaks form but egg whites are still glossy. Fold into cooled egg yolk mixture. Spread over the hot fruit filling, making sure meringue touches the edge of the crust to seal the filling.

Bake 15 minutes or until the topping is puffy and golden brown. Cool pie on a wire rack. Serve slightly warm or at room temperature. Refrigerate leftovers.

**Makes 1 (9-inch) pie, 8 servings.**

**NOTE**

The pie shell will use a little more than half the recipe. Freeze the rest for future use.

### *About Nectarines*

Although nectarines are sold under their generic label, they are developed to suit the customers' desires. More than eighty major varieties are raised commercially, each with a season of only about two weeks.

Color is an important factor. White-fleshed varieties are firmer and more resistant to bruising, an advantage for the grower. They are particularly prized in Asia but have had a less enthusiastic reception in this country.

Golden skin color on nectarines used to be prized. Now we look for a high-red blush. The only problem is that the red color, which we equate with ripeness, comes on early. It's actually more difficult to tell when this fruit is ready to use.

Current fashion also favors crispness rather than the melting ripe peach texture we cherished in past years. This can be an advantage when you bake nectarines in a recipe like Sweet Summer Pie, but they may not be everyone's choice for eating the nectarines out of hand.

How to sort out the confusion? Get to know your grocery store produce manager. These knowledgeable people can guide you to make the best choices.

BONNIE ORLANDO     SYRACUSE, NEW YORK     NEW YORK STATE FAIR

# Oregon Pear Tart

Dee Hansen (her "formal" name is DeLoris) likes to use the fruit and nuts Oregon is famous for in her baking. Bartlett pears are her choice for this lovely tart in the summer and early fall and Anjou or Comice pears in the winter. Instead of the more traditional French apricot jam or currant jelly glaze, she likes to make a glaze with Oregon raspberries for the color and flavor combination. Oregon hazelnuts (filberts) add richness and texture to the filling. (See All About Hazelnuts, page 173, for directions for toasting.)

The recipe looks involved, but no step is difficult. Make and partially bake the crust first. Prepare the pears next, so they will be ready as soon as you've mixed the filling. Make the raspberry glaze while the tart is baking. If you don't have a tart pan with a removable bottom, use a 9- or 10-inch pie pan.

*1 (10-inch) Tart Shell (page 112)*
*1½ cups sugar*
*¾ cup water*
*1 teaspoon vanilla extract*
*3 to 4 medium pears, peeled, halved and*
  *cored*
*⅓ cup butter, softened*
*1 egg*
*1 tablespoon kirsch or rum*
*½ cup toasted hazelnuts (page 173),*
  *finely ground*
*1 tablespoon all-purpose flour*

*RASPBERRY GLAZE*
*2 cups raspberries, fresh or frozen*
  *without syrup*
*¼ cup water*
*1 tablespoon lemon juice*
*⅛ teaspoon salt*
*2 tablespoons cornstarch*
*⅔ cup sugar*

Partially bake and cool crust. Preheat oven to 375F (190C).

In a medium saucepan, bring ¾ cup of the sugar and the water to a boil, stirring to dissolve sugar. Boil, stirring until mixture is clear; stir in vanilla. Reduce heat to a simmer. Drop pear halves into the hot syrup. Keeping liquid just below a simmer, cook pears 3 to 5 minutes, until just tender. Do not overcook; pears must hold their shape. With a slotted spoon, remove from syrup and drain well.

In a small bowl, cream butter and remaining ¾ cup sugar. Beat in egg, kirsch, hazelnuts and flour. Spread the filling over the partially baked crust.

Carefully cut the pears crosswise into ⅓-inch-thick slices, keeping them assembled in halves. Arrange them in the shell with the stem ends pointing toward the center of the tart. Bake about 25 minutes or until the filling is set and golden brown. Cool on a wire rack.

While tart is baking, prepare Raspberry Glaze. When tart has cooled, spoon cooled glaze over the top of the tart. Serve the tart at room temperature or chilled.

Makes 1 (10-inch) tart, 8 servings.

**RASPBERRY GLAZE**

In a medium saucepan, crush raspberries with a potato masher. Add water and simmer over low heat for 5 minutes. Strain through a sieve; measure 1 cup of juice. Return juice to pan. Stir in lemon juice and salt.

In a small bowl, mix together cornstarch and sugar. Add to warm raspberry juice. Cook, stirring constantly, until mixture is thick and clear. Cool before using to glaze tart.

## When Tarts Served as Plates

Tarts are of ancient origin. One theory about the name goes back to the Middle Ages, when plates were scarce. To supply enough plates for their grand feasts, large households used the undercrust of bread, usually a kind of bread the French then called *tourte* or tarte. After one ate dinner, one ate the plate.

As life became more refined, these "plates" were specially prepared. They were more cakelike, filled with dainty food and called tarts or tartlets, depending on their size.

The strict meaning of *tart,* then, is an open crust in the nature of a plate.

DEE HANSEN   KEIZER, OREGON   OREGON STATE FAIR

# Orange-Glazed Apple Tart

When the summer Gravensteins are ready to pick, Oregonians know its prime apple pie time. Because these tangy apples are so prized and don't store well, many people freeze enough to use in pies all year.

Gravensteins are Fran Neavoll's choice for her elegant lattice-topped tart. Since Gravensteins don't ship well, they are only available where they are grown. Good substitutes are juicy, slightly tart apples like Cortland, McIntosh or Granny Smith. Use ¾ cup sugar if the apples are tart. The orange glaze will add extra sweetness.

*Basic Rich Pie Crust (page 109)*
*(see Notes, below)*
*½ to ¾ cup granulated sugar*
*2 tablespoons cornstarch*
*½ teaspoon apple pie spice*
*5 to 6 cups peeled, cored and thinly*
*sliced apples, preferably Gravenstein*
*(6 medium apples)*

*2 tablespoons golden raisins*
*½ teaspoon grated orange peel*
*1 teaspoon lemon juice*
*2 teaspoons butter, cut in small pieces*
*1 cup powdered sugar, sifted*
*1 tablespoon orange juice*

Preheat oven to 425F (220C). Prepare dough for crust and roll out for a 9-inch pan. Lightly flour a 9-inch tart pan with removable bottom or a 9-inch pie pan. Line with dough.

In a large bowl, combine granulated sugar, cornstarch and apple pie spice. Add apples, raisins, orange peel and lemon juice. Gently toss to coat apples.

Layer apples in the lined tart pan. Dot with butter. Use remaining dough for lattice top (see page 80). Trim and seal edges. Cover edge of crust with foil.

Bake about 35 minutes and remove foil. Bake 15 minutes or until crust is golden and juices bubble up.

Cool tart on a wire rack about 10 minutes. In a small bowl, combine powdered sugar and orange juice until smooth. Drizzle sugar mixture over the slightly cooled tart. Finish cooling tart on a wire rack before serving.

**Makes 1 (9-inch) tart, 8 servings.**

### NOTES

Fran uses butter-flavored solid shortening and adds 2 teaspoons grated orange peel.

Fran decorates her tart with apple and leaf shapes cut from dough trimmings. She colors them by pouring 1 tablespoon of water into each of two small bowls and stirring in 1 drop of red coloring to one and 1 drop of green to the other.

She dips the apples and leaves into the colored water, pricks them with a fork and bakes them in the 425F (220C) oven about 6 minutes, just until lightly brown. When cool, she arranges them on the tart after she has drizzled on the icing.

### *Freezing Apple Slices*

When you have a favorite cooking apple that is available only for a relatively short time, you can freeze containers of apple slices for up to 8 months.

Freezing in a sugar syrup will give you the best shape and flavor, but a simple sugar pack works well for pie apples. Choose ripe but firm unblemished fruit. Peel, core and slice the apples into a shallow pan. Toss the apples gently with a commercial anti-darkening agent or ½ teaspoon ascorbic acid powder and ½ cup sugar per quart. (Look for anti-darkening agents with other canning and freezing supplies at your supermarket. Drugstores carry pure ascorbic acid powder. Check package directions.)

Package apples in rigid plastic containers, wide-mouthed glass canning jars or heavy plastic bags. Store in the freezer at 0F ($-$20C). If your freezer temperature is above 10F ($-$10C), plan to use the apples within 2 months.

FRAN NEAVOLL    SALEM, OREGON    OREGON STATE FAIR

# Dream Peach Pie

When an expert baker like Marge Cuff says this is her favorite pie, you know it's a recipe to cherish. She makes it with a variety of fresh fruits or berries, but she won her blue ribbon with this peach version. A light, fluffy cream cheese filling is covered with sliced fresh fruit and a topping of lightly thickened fresh fruit puree.

Whether she's baking for her family or for the fair, Marge says she always uses the freshest and the best-quality ingredients she can obtain. She's making sure the tradition of fine cooking continues in her family by teaching her four grandchildren to bake.

*Basic Pie Crust for Single Crusts*  
*(page 111) (see Note, below)*  
*1 cup sugar*  
*6 tablespoons cornstarch*  
*2 cups mashed fresh peaches*  
*1 cup water*

*1 (3-oz.) package cream cheese, softened*  
*¼ cup powdered sugar*  
*¾ cup frozen whipped topping, thawed*  
*1 cup peeled sliced fresh peaches*  
*Whipped cream (optional)*

Prepare and bake pie crust in a 9-inch pie pan.

In a heavy saucepan, stir together sugar and cornstarch. Stir in mashed peaches and water. Cook over medium heat, stirring constantly, until the mixture comes to a boil and begins to thicken. Reduce heat to low and simmer, stirring constantly, 1 minute. Cool mixture while making the rest of the filling.

In a medium bowl, beat the cream cheese and powdered sugar with an electric mixer until fluffy. Fold in whipped topping.

Spread cream cheese mixture in cooled pie shell. Arrange fresh peach slices over the cream cheese mixture. Spoon on cooled peach mixture.

Refrigerate 3 hours or longer. Serve with whipped cream, if desired.

**Makes 1 (9-inch) pie, 8 servings.**

### Note

Marge adds ½ teaspoon sugar to the basic recipe.

### About Peaches

Most of the fresh peaches available in the market are freestone or semi-freestone, where the flesh does not cling to the fruit. Cling peaches are used by food processors and seldom sold fresh. The color of ripe peaches varies from golden to dark reddish-brown, depending on the variety. Choose peaches without green tinges for the best flavor.

Ripen firm fruit at room temperature. Fully ripe fruit can be stored for a few days in the refrigerator.

To peel peaches, dip them in boiling water 20 to 25 seconds. The skin should peel off easily.

Three medium freestone peaches will weigh about 1 pound and will give you 2 cups of slices. Two cups of mashed peaches will require 4 peaches.

MARGE CUFF        KEIZER, OREGON        OREGON STATE FAIR

# Raisin Pie

Early Pennsylvania Dutch called lemon-accented raisin pie "funeral pie" because it was always one that neighbors brought to a bereaved family. Raisins were one fruit that was available all year, probably the reason the custom began. Nancy Johnson's version of this heritage recipe was Grand Champion Pie, beating out all the other expert pie bakers at the Ozark Empire Fair.

*Never-Fail Pie Crust (page 111)*
*1½ cups sugar plus extra for sprinkling*
*¼ cup all-purpose flour*
*1 egg, well beaten*
*3 tablespoons lemon juice*

*2 teaspoons grated lemon peel*
*⅛ teaspoon salt*
*3 cups raisins*
*1¾ cups water*
*1 tablespoon butter, melted*

In the top of a double boiler, mix 1½ cups sugar and flour; stir in egg. Mix in lemon juice, peel, salt, raisins and water. Cook over simmering water 15 minutes, stirring occasionally, until thickened. Remove filling from heat.

Preheat oven to 450F (230C). Prepare dough for crust and roll out dough for top and bottom crusts. Line a 9-inch pie pan with dough. Pour filling into lined pie plate. Place top crust on filling. Seal and flute edges. Cut slits in the top crust for steam to escape. Brush with melted butter and sprinkle with sugar.

Bake in a preheated oven 10 minutes; lower heat to 350F (175C) and bake 20 minutes longer, or until crust is golden brown and juices bubble up through the slits in the crust. Cool pie on a wire rack before serving.

Makes 1 (9-inch) pie, 8 servings.

### History of Dessert Pies in America
By the nineteenth century, American agriculture was thriving and the country had an abundant food supply. With little labor-saving equipment available, daily life for most men and women involved hard physical work. Three or more hearty meals a day was the rule. Pie was a favorite dessert because it satisfied their hearty appetites and helped provide the energy they needed.

The Pennsylvania Dutch, America's champion pie bakers, probably created raisin pie. It certainly was one of the fifty different dessert pies social chroniclers attribute to them at this time. Because the dried fruit was available even in remote areas, the popularity of raisin pie spread. Old cookbooks have recipes for sour cream raisin and a meringue-topped version as well as a two-crust pie.

NANCY JOHNSON    CLEVER, MISSOURI    OZARK EMPIRE FAIR

# Chocolate Tartlets with Buttery Pastry

Tracy Penn Liberatore comes from a long line of outstanding cooks and bakers. She had heard so many stories about these talented women that she wanted to keep the tradition alive. When her mother thought she was ready to enter a competition, Tracy started with an "historical peach pie" contest at the local historical society. Soon she moved on to Ohio's very competitive state fair.

Eating her tarts is rather like enjoying a delectable truffle encased in pastry. The bite size is appropriate for this rich treat, but it may be difficult to stop with just one. Tracy arranges them on an antique platter, an attractive idea for a dessert buffet.

She has made the recipe with milk instead of heavy cream, but she says "go for the cream. It's worth it!" Roll the dough as thinly as possible, so it will be crisp.

| | |
|---|---|
| *Buttery Pastry (see opposite)* | *BUTTERY PASTRY* |
| *1⅓ cups (8 oz.) semisweet chocolate chips* | *2½ cups all-purpose flour* |
| *⅓ cup sugar* | *1 teaspoon sugar* |
| *2 cups whipping cream* | *1 teaspoon salt* |
| *White chocolate shavings, if desired* | *1 cup butter, chilled, cut into small pieces* |
| | *¼ to ½ cup ice water* |

Preheat oven to 400F (205C). Prepare dough for crust and bake.

In a medium saucepan over low heat, or in the top of a double boiler over simmering water, melt chocolate chips with sugar, stirring constantly. Slowly pour in cream, stirring to make a smooth mixture. Cook over low heat or simmering water, stirring constantly, until the mixture bubbles around the edges and begins to thicken. Cook, stirring constantly, for 8 to 10 minutes or until mixture is thick.

Cool mixture to room temperature, but do not let it set. (To cool quickly, set pan in a pan of iced water, stirring occasionally.)

Spoon filling into baked shells (about 1 tablespoonful for a 2½-inch tart). Refrigerate 2 hours to set filling. Keep refrigerated until shortly before serving.

Makes about 2 dozen 2½-inch tarts.

**BUTTERY PASTRY**

Combine flour, sugar and salt in a medium bowl. Cut in butter until dough resembles coarse meal. Add water, a spoonful at a time, just until dough sticks together.

On a floured surface, roll out half the dough to no more than ⅛-inch thickness, keeping remaining dough refrigerated. Using a tartlet pan as a measure, cut dough into circles ¼ inch larger than the pan. Press the pastry circles into the pans; run a sharp knife over the top edges.

Place the tart pans on a baking sheet. To keep the pastry from puffing up, press a tart pan of the same size into the pastry-lined pan or prick the dough with a fork, and bake. Repeat with the remaining dough. Re-rolled scraps of dough will be less tender and can be reserved for another use.

Bake 10 to 12 minutes or until golden. Cool tarts on wire racks 1 to 2 minutes; carefully remove from the pans.

### *Improvising Tiny Tart Pans*

No tiny tart pans? Use miniature muffin or cupcake pans instead. These usually measure about 1¾ inches across the top and 1¼ inches across the bottom. You can bake the tart shells in the cups or turn the pan upside down and fit the dough over the bottoms.

Cut the tart pastry with a 2-inch cookie cutter or glass. Fit the pastry in or over the muffin cup and prick it with a fork so it won't puff out of shape in the oven. Place the muffin pans on a cookie sheet for easier handling, and bake according to recipe directions.

Tracy Penn Liberatore    Columbus, Ohio    Ohio State Fair

# Banana-Split Pie

You'll be reminded of a soda fountain banana split when you taste Cheryl Christiansen's no-bake pie. Crushed pineapple, sliced strawberries and banana slices are layered over a sweet, creamy filling. The pie is topped with whipped cream or topping and a sprinkling of nuts. Since you only have to bake a pie crust, this make-ahead refrigerator dessert is a good choice in hot weather.

*Basic Pie Crust for Single Crusts (page 111)*
*1 (3-oz.) package cream cheese, softened*
*½ cup margarine, softened*
*2 cups powdered sugar, sifted*
*½ cup (8-oz. can) crushed pineapple,*
  *well drained*

*½ cup sliced strawberries*
*2 medium bananas, thinly sliced*
*8 ounces frozen whipped topping, thawed,*
  *or 1 cup heavy cream, whipped and*
  *sweetened*
*¼ cup chopped walnuts*

Prepare and bake pie crust in a 9-inch pie pan.

In a mixer bowl, with an electric mixer, beat cream cheese, margarine and powdered sugar until very light and fluffy, about 10 minutes. Spoon into baked pie shell and spread to cover evenly.

Spoon pineapple evenly over cream cheese layer; arrange strawberry slices and banana slices over pineapple.

Cover with whipped topping, making sure fruit is completely covered. Sprinkle with walnuts. Cover and refrigerate until serving time.

Makes 1 (9-inch) pie, 8 servings.

### About Cream Cheese

Cream cheese is the largest-selling packaged cheese in the world. Its popularity as a dessert ingredient has contributed to this wide use. Although cream cheese was introduced in 1872, it wasn't until about 1930 that it became so widely used.

The first cream cheese was made in New York State. Because at that time Philadelphia was considered a home of fine food, it was named Philadelphia Brand, to indicate high quality. If the birthplace of this white, fresh cheese had been honored instead, we might know it now as Chester cheese.

Fresh cream cheese has a shorter shelf life than aged cheese and must be refrigerated. Once the package is opened it should be used within 2 weeks.

CHERYL CHRISTIANSEN      MCPHERSON, KANSAS      KANSAS STATE FAIR

# Lemon Sponge Pie

If making lemon meringue pie seems too challenging, you can get the same sweet-tart lemony flavor from Shirley Casity's Lemon Sponge Pie. Probably one of the many pie recipes first created in early Pennsylvania Dutch kitchens, this recipe isn't found in many cookbooks. In Shirley's case, it was handed down through at least three generations.

The stiffly beaten egg whites are folded into the filling, instead of being used as a meringue topping. Using milk instead of water in the filling also contributes to the texture that gives the pie its name. Use a deep 9-inch pie pan or else build up a high edge on the crust in a regular pie pan to hold the generous amount of filling.

*Basic Pie Crust for Single Crusts*
  *(page 111) (see Note, below)*
*3 tablespoons butter, softened*
*1½ cups sugar*
*4 egg yolks*
*3 tablespoons all-purpose flour*

*⅛ teaspoon salt*
*1¼ cups milk*
*2 tablespoons grated lemon peel*
*⅓ cup fresh lemon juice*
*4 egg whites, at room temperature*

Prepare dough for crust and use to line a 9-inch pie pan. Preheat oven to 375F (190C).

In a large mixer bowl, beat butter and sugar until well mixed. Beat in egg yolks, flour, salt, milk, grated lemon peel and juice until well blended.

In a medium bowl, with clean beaters, beat egg whites until stiff but still moist. Gently fold into filling mixture. Pour into unbaked pie shell.

Bake 15 minutes. Reduce heat to 300F (150C) and bake 45 minutes or until top is golden and a wooden pick inserted near the center comes out clean.

Cool on a wire rack, then refrigerate until served. Refrigerate leftovers.

Makes 1 (9-inch) pie, 8 servings.

**NOTE**

Shirley uses milk instead of water.

### The Oral Tradition Still Exists

For the Amish and Mennonite people, bountiful meals and rich baking are an important part of life. In the old Pennsylvania Dutch tradition, pies were a favorite dessert. While they no longer are served three times a day, pie baking still takes place at least once a week.

These experienced pie bakers know their recipes by heart, and they are passed along as mothers and daughters work together. Lemon Sponge Pie is one of several out-of-the-ordinary lemon pies that are tried-and-true favorites in Amish and Mennonite homes but seldom found in cookbooks.

SHIRLEY CASITY    NEW SPRINGFIELD, OHIO    CANFIELD FAIR

# Chocolate Chip Pecan Pie

Lynda Mackey is an inspired recipe developer who enjoys thinking up new dishes for food-company contests at the Ohio State Fair. She has created prize-winning recipes showcasing ingredients from Spam to sauerkraut. But she also knows how to make a pie with universal appeal. Her Chocolate Chip Pecan Pie was a blue ribbon winner in the open competition at the fair.

She divides the pecans, chopping some of them to mix in the filling and arranging more of them around the filling. Because they are such an important ingredient, she advises using "the plumpest, freshest, handsomest pecans you can find, for flavor and appearance."

*Basic Pie Crust for Single Crusts*
*(page 111) (see Note, below)*
*3 eggs*
*1 cup sugar*
*¾ cup light corn syrup*

*¼ cup butter, melted*
*1 teaspoon vanilla extract*
*½ cup semisweet chocolate chips*
*½ cup coarsely chopped pecans*
*24 pecan halves*

Prepare dough for crust and use to line a 9-inch pie pan. Preheat oven to 350F (175C).

In a medium bowl, beat eggs, sugar and corn syrup until well blended. Beat in butter and vanilla. Fold in chocolate chips and chopped pecans.

Pour into lined pan. Arrange pecan halves on top of filling. Bake 45 to 50 minutes or until top is deep golden brown (filling will not be completely set in the middle of the pie). Cool on a wire rack. Store in refrigerator.

**Makes 1 (9-inch) pie, 8 servings.**

**NOTE**

Lynda uses ¼ cup cold solid vegetable shortening and 2 tablespoons cold butter.

### *Rolling Out a Single Crust*

On a hot day, pie crust will be easier to handle if it is refrigerated until it is firm. Roll it out on a lightly floured surface or between sheets of waxed paper from the center to the edges, keeping the shape as round as possible.

Lift the rolling pin slightly near the edges, so they don't get too thin. Lift the pastry from time to time to make sure it doesn't stick. If it does, loosen it with a spatula and sprinkle a little more flour underneath. Roll the crust to about a ⅛-inch thickness.

With a single-crust pie it's particularly important not to stretch the crust when you put it into the pie plate. To keep it from shrinking during baking, fold the rolled-out crust in quarters or roll half the circle loosely over the rolling pin. Ease the pastry into the pie plate, pressing it down lightly without stretching it. Finish the crust with a high, decorative edge.

LYNDA MACKEY     COLUMBUS, OHIO     OHIO STATE FAIR

# Brandy Chocolate Pie

Julie Dilleshaw-Canada says she does have some low-fat recipes, but she thinks there is nothing like a melt-in-your-mouth, to-die-for dessert. This two-layer pie in a chocolate cookie crust definitely qualifies. Although marshmallows may seem like an unusual ingredient in a gourmet pie, they take the place of gelatin and sugar in the light-textured filling.

The crust must be made ahead and chilled. The recipe makes more than you need for one pie, but you can bake leftovers for the cookie jar.

| | |
|---|---|
| *1 Chocolate Cookie Crust (page 113)* | *1 teaspoon vanilla extract* |
| *30 large or 3 cups miniature marshmallows* | *1 to 2 tablespoons brandy* |
| *½ cup milk* | *1 to 2 tablespoons crème de cacao* |
| *1 cup semisweet chocolate chips* | *2 cups whipping cream, chilled* |

Bake crust in a 9-inch pie pan and cool.

In a heavy saucepan over low heat, combine marshmallows and milk. Cook, stirring constantly, until marshmallows are melted (mixture scorches easily).

Pour half the hot marshmallow mixture into a small bowl. Immediately add chocolate chips and vanilla to remaining marshmallow mixture. Stir to blend in chocolate (if necessary, return mixture to very low heat, stirring constantly, to melt all the chocolate chips). Cool to room temperature.

Stir brandy and crème de cacao into reserved marshmallow mixture. Refrigerate briefly until mixture mounds slightly when dropped from a spoon but is not set.

In a chilled bowl with chilled beaters, whip cream until it thickens and forms soft mounds. Fold half the whipped cream into the cooled chocolate mixture. Spoon into crust. Fold the remaining whipped cream into the thickened brandy mixture; spread over chocolate mixture. Refrigerate 2 hours or until firm. Refrigerate leftovers.

Makes 1 (9-inch) pie, 8 servings.

### Whipping Cream

Cream with 30 to 36 percent fat is called whipping cream or light whipping cream. Heavy whipping cream has between 36 and 40 percent fat. For the best results in whipping, you need cream with at least 35 percent fat. Cream beats up best when it is very cold. Chill the bowl and beaters, too, for best results. Beat the cream only until soft peaks form. If you are using a high-butterfat product, the cream will turn into butter if you beat it too long.

Whipping cream doubles in volume when it is whipped.

JULIE DILLESHAW-CANADA     BAKERSFIELD, CALIFORNIA     KERN COUNTY FAIR

# Orange Cheesecake

Pauline Jenkins has five children who fortunately have a mother who loves to cook. Besides being a talented baker, she has been a sweepstakes winner in preserved food. In 1994 she won the Joe Logan Memorial Trophy at the Kern County Fair for having the highest number of points that year in a combination of baked and preserved foods and needle arts.

Her attractive dessert uses frozen orange juice concentrate and grated orange peel in the cheesecake and is topped with mandarin oranges and a fresh orange glaze.

*1½ cups vanilla wafer crumbs*
*¼ cup butter or margarine, melted*
*3 (8-oz.) packages cream cheese,*
  *softened*
*1 cup sugar*
*3 eggs*
*2 tablespoons all-purpose flour*

*¼ cup frozen orange juice concentrate,*
  *thawed*
*1¼ teaspoons grated orange peel*
*1 (11-oz.) can mandarin orange*
  *segments*
*2 teaspoons cornstarch*
*½ cup orange juice*

Preheat oven to 325F (165C).

In a small bowl, thoroughly combine cookie crumbs and melted butter. Press crumbs firmly into the bottom and 2 inches up the sides of a 9-inch springform pan. Refrigerate the crust while preparing the filling.

In a large bowl, beat softened cream cheese and ¾ cup of the sugar at medium speed until well blended. Beat in eggs, flour, orange juice concentrate and 1 teaspoon of the orange peel until mixture is smooth.

Pour the filling into the crust. Bake about 1 hour or until a wooden pick inserted near the center comes out clean.

While cheesecake is baking, drain mandarin orange segments. Make a glaze by combining remaining ¼ cup sugar, cornstarch, orange juice and remaining ¼ teaspoon orange peel in a small saucepan over medium heat. Cook, stirring constantly, until mixture boils and thickens. Remove from heat and cool slightly.

Cool the cheesecake in the pan on a wire rack for about 15 minutes. Run a metal spatula along side of cheesecake to loosen. Arrange mandarin orange sections to cover top of cheesecake; spoon glaze over the fruit. Cover and refrigerate at least 12 hours.

Before serving, again run a metal spatula along side of the cheesecake; remove side of pan. Refrigerate leftovers, covered.

**Makes 1 cheesecake, serves 16 to 20.**

### Cheesecake
Cheesecake is one of the most popular American desserts. No other country has come up with as many variations on this rich, dense cheese dessert—except possibly ancient Greece and Rome.

Demosthenes, Aristophanes and Socrates all wrote about it. The Roman statesman Cato, who also was known for his cooking skills, created a popular cheesecake that was sweetened with honey and flavored with poppy seeds. Ancient Sicily was renowned for its cheesecake. *Cassata alla Siciliana* is still made today.

PAULINE JENKINS     BAKERSFIELD, CALIFORNIA     KERN COUNTY FAIR

# Coconut Macaroon Pie

Maryn DeBoer's delectable pie not only won a blue ribbon but was given an Award of Excellence as the best of all the single-crust pies at the Ohio State Fair. She baked it in the electric range that she won in an appliance company's contest for the best pumpkin pie. Her husband encourages her to enter cooking contests, possibly because he is such an enthusiastic sampler when she tries new dessert recipes.

*Basic Pie Crust for Single Crusts*
  *(page 111) (see Note, below)*
*2 eggs*
*½ cup water*
*1½ cups sugar*
*5 tablespoons all-purpose flour*

*¼ teaspoon salt*
*1⅓ cups lightly packed moist flaked*
  *coconut*
*½ cup butter, melted and cooled*
*1 teaspoon vanilla extract*
*1 egg white*

Prepare dough for crust and use to line a 9-inch pie pan. Preheat oven to 325F (165C).

In a medium bowl, beat eggs, water, sugar, flour and salt together with an electric hand mixer 2 to 3 minutes, until very well blended. Stir in coconut, butter and vanilla.

Brush unbaked pie shell with unbeaten egg white. Pour filling into the shell. Bake on the bottom oven rack about 45 minutes or until filling is set and very lightly browned. Cool on a wire rack before serving.

Makes 1 (9-inch) pie, 8 servings.

**NOTE**

Maryn uses butter-flavored solid vegetable shortening and adds ¼ teaspoon vanilla extract.

### Baking a Crust at a Low Temperature

Because this pie is baked in a slow oven, to brown the bottom crust you must place the pie on the bottom rack where the temperature is higher. Maryn also seals the crust by brushing it with egg white before pouring in the filling. This prevents the moist filling from soaking into the crust and helps keep it crisp.

MARYN DEBOER      WORTHINGTON, OHIO      OHIO STATE FAIR

# Basic Rich Pie Crust

*2 cups all-purpose flour*
*½ teaspoon salt*

*¾ cup solid vegetable shortening, chilled*
*4 to 5 tablespoons ice water*

In a large bowl, stir together the flour and salt. Using a pastry blender or 2 knives, cut in half the shortening until the mixture resembles coarse crumbs. Cut in the remaining shortening until the mixture is the size of peas. Add the water a little at a time, toss gently and push to the side of the bowl. Repeat until all the flour is moistened. Knead the pastry lightly with finger-tips until the pastry cleans the bowl. Form pastry into 2 flat rounds, wrap tightly in plastic wrap and chill 30 minutes.

Pat out bottom crust on a lightly floured surface or between 2 pieces of waxed paper. Using a lightly floured rolling pin, roll out dough into an 11-inch circle about ⅛ inch thick.

Carefully transfer dough to pie plate without stretching. Trim edge evenly, leaving about a ½ inch overhang.

Roll out top crust into a 10-inch circle. Fold dough in half. Cut small slits along folded edge to allow steam to escape. Lightly brush edge of bottom crust with water after adding filling. Arrange top crust over filling. Trim top crust to a ½-inch overhang. Press top and bottom crust edges together. Fold overhang under itself and flute edge or press tines of a fork around edge.

Bake according to recipe directions.

**Makes 1 (9-inch) double-crust pie shell.**

**NOTE**

For a single crust use a little more than half the dough. Trim edges, leaving a 1-inch overhang. Fold this under itself all around to make a ridge; flute edge. If shell is to be prebaked, using a fork, prick the shell over bottom and sides before baking in a preheated 425F (220C) oven about 15 minutes, until crisp and golden brown. For unbaked shell, follow pie recipe directions.

# Basic Pie Crust for Double Crusts

*3 cups all-purpose flour*                        *1 cup solid vegetable shortening*
*½ teaspoon salt*                                 *7 to 8 tablespoons ice water*

In a large bowl, stir together the flour and salt. Using a pastry blender, 2 knives or fingertips, cut in shortening until flour is well mixed with fat and mixture is crumbly. Sprinkle with water a little at a time, stirring with a fork, until dough holds together. Dryness of flour and humidity will affect amount of water needed.

Divide dough into 2 pieces, using a little more than half for bottom crust. Pat out bottom crust on a lightly floured surface or between 2 pieces of waxed paper. Using a lightly floured rolling pin, roll out dough into an 11-inch circle about ⅛ inch thick.

Carefully transfer dough to pie plate without stretching. Trim edge evenly, leaving about a ½-inch overhang.

Roll out top crust into a 10-inch circle. Fold dough in half. Cut small slits along folded edge to allow steam to escape. Lightly brush edge of bottom crust with water after adding filling. Arrange top crust over filling. Trim top crust to a ½-inch overhang. Press top and bottom crust edges together. Fold overhang under itself and flute edge or press tines of a fork around edge.

Bake according to recipe directions.

**Makes 1 (9-inch) double-crust pie shell.**

**NOTE**

In very hot weather, chilling dough will make it easier to roll. Dough also can be made in advance, wrapped well and refrigerated for several hours or overnight.

---

PIE CRUSTS

Blue ribbon pie bakers often add their own signature touches to pie crust. Most of the recipes are based either on the old standard formula of ⅓ cup shortening to 1 cup of flour (Basic Pie Crust for Single or Double Crusts) or the richer ¾ cup shortening to 2 cups of flour (Basic Rich Pie Crust). The pie recipes indicate which version the winner used, plus any variations.

Two pies call for the popular Never-Fail Pie Crust. This makes a big recipe and freezes well. It is a pliable dough that can be patched and even re-rolled without getting tough.

The recipes also include a Tart Pastry and a Chocolate Cookie Crust.

Standard one-crust pie shell recipes are based on 1½ cups of flour. Our Basic Pie Crust for Single Crusts calls for 2 cups of flour and the basic recipe for double crusts for 3 cups of flour. Prize winners like to have a high, built-up edge. When the crust counts for up to 40 percent of the points in judging pies at a state fair, it doesn't pay to skimp.

The richer version, Basic Rich Pie Crust, calls for the standard 2 cups of flour for a double crust, because this is what the winners indicated they used.

# Basic Pie Crust for Single Crusts

*2 cups all-purpose flour*
*½ teaspoon salt*

*⅔ cup solid vegetable shortening*
*5 to 6 tablespoons ice water*

Preheat oven to 425F (220C). In a large bowl, stir together flour and salt.

Using a pastry blender, 2 knives or fingertips, cut in shortening until flour is well mixed with fat and mixture is crumbly. Sprinkle with water, a little at a time, stirring with a fork, until dough holds together. Dryness of flour and humidity will affect amount of water needed.

Form dough into a ball. Pat out on a lightly floured surface or between 2 pieces of waxed paper. Using a lightly floured rolling pin, roll out dough into an 11-inch circle about ⅛ inch thick.

Carefully transfer dough to pie plate without stretching. Trim edges evenly, leaving about a 1-inch overhang. Fold this under itself all around to make a ridge; flute edge. Using a fork, prick shell over bottom and sides.

Bake about 15 minutes or until crisp and golden brown. For an unbaked shell, follow recipe directions.

Makes 1 (9-inch) single-crust pie shell.

# Never-Fail Pie Crust

*3 cups all-purpose flour*
*1 teaspoon salt*
*1¼ cups solid vegetable shortening*

*1 egg, beaten*
*5 tablespoons cold water*
*1 tablespoon vinegar*

In a large bowl, mix flour and salt. Using a pastry blender, 2 knives or fingertips, cut in shortening until well-blended. In a 1-cup liquid measure, combine egg, water and vinegar. Add all at once to flour mixture, blending with a fork until the flour is moistened.

Divide dough into 2 pieces. Pat out 1 piece on a lightly floured surface or between 2 pieces of waxed paper. Using a lightly floured rolling pin, roll out dough into an 11-inch circle. Carefully transfer to a 9-inch pie plate. Repeat with remaining dough or wrap in plastic wrap and refrigerate up to 2 weeks or freeze. Bake according to recipe directions.

Makes pastry for 1 (9-inch) double-crust pie, 2 (9-inch) single-crust pies or 3 (8-inch) single-crust pies.

**NOTE**

If unbleached flour is used, dough will darken after refrigerating a few days. This will not hurt eating quality of crust. Freezing will prevent darkening.

# Tart Pastry

*1¼ cups all-purpose flour*
*2 tablespoons powdered sugar*
*6 tablespoons butter, chilled*

*1 egg yolk*
*½ teaspoon vanilla extract*
*1 tablespoon water*

Preheat oven to 400F (205C).

In a medium bowl, stir together flour and powdered sugar. Cut in butter until mixture resembles coarse crumbs.

In a small bowl, with a fork, beat egg yolk, vanilla and water together. Add to flour mixture, stirring with a fork, until mixture holds together (add a few more drops of water, if necessary). Form into a ball.

On a lightly floured surface or between 2 pieces of waxed paper, roll out dough into a 13-inch circle. Line a 10-inch tart pan with removable bottom with pastry. Trim edges even with the top of the pan. Prick bottom of pastry with a fork.

Bake about 8 minutes, to partially bake and set crust. Set it on a wire rack to cool while preparing filling. For a fully baked crust, bake about 15 minutes or until lightly browned.

**Makes 1 (10-inch) tart shell.**

# Chocolate Cookie Crust

Julie Dilleshaw-Canada's cookie-dough pastry needs to be made ahead so it can be chilled until firm before slicing. It can be used like tart pastry to line the bottom and sides of the pie pan. Or, if you want a decorative edging, arrange slices around the well-greased edge of the pie pan. (If you don't grease the edge of the pan, the decorative edge will break when you serve the pie.)

Use this cookie crust with chiffon or cream pie fillings or as the base for a fruit tart.

| | |
|---|---|
| *1¼ cups all-purpose flour* | *½ cup butter, softened* |
| *½ cup unsweetened cocoa powder* | *1 cup sugar* |
| *¾ teaspoon baking soda* | *1 large egg* |
| *¼ teaspoon salt* | *1 teaspoon vanilla extract* |

In a small bowl, stir together flour, cocoa, soda and salt. In a medium bowl beat together butter, sugar, egg and vanilla until well blended. Stir in flour mixture just until well blended.

Shape dough into 2 rolls, 1½ inches in diameter. Wrap in plastic wrap and refrigerate for several hours or overnight.

Preheat oven to 375F (190C). Lightly grease a 9-inch pie pan. Cut 1 roll into ⅛-inch-thick slices. Arrange slices, edges just touching, on the bottom and up the sides of prepared pie pan. (Small spaces will fill up as crust bakes.)

Bake 8 to 10 minutes or until cookies are set. Cool on a wire rack before filling.

Makes 2 (8- or 9-inch) crusts or 1 (10-inch) tart crust or 1 (8- or 9-inch) crust with decorative edges plus cookies.

### VARIATIONS

For a decorative edge on the crust, cut ⅛-inch-thick slices from the second roll, cut them in half and arrange them around the well-greased edge of the pie pan.

Freeze remaining dough for up to 6 weeks for later use or slice dough and bake for delicious little chocolate cookies. Bake cookies on greased baking sheets at 375F (190C) 8 to 10 minutes.

# Cookies

Many people think of the holidays as the major cookie-baking time of the year. But for state fair competitors, this is a year-round activity which reaches a heightened state as fair time approaches.

The most striking aspect of this blue ribbon collection is the great variety of cookies that were first-place and sweepstakes winners. Even traditional favorites come with a new twist: white chocolate chip cookies, molasses cookies with a baked-on frosting, Mexican wedding cakes made with a mixture of cornstarch and flour to make a particularly tender, delicate cookie.

Since recipes for cookies came to America from Dutch fur traders who settled on the east coast in the early 1600s, it seems appropriate that the fairs remember this Old World link to our past. A number of major fairs have noted that ethnic cookies were being entered in traditional categories—and often winning. So fairs have been adding new categories for ethnic cookies.

This has given us some exceptionally good winners and an opportunity to get recipes seldom found in any cookbooks. An authentic recipe for Chinese Almond Cookies, Scandinavian Almond Bars, *Bucherie,* an elegant filled vanilla cookie, and an unusual orange coconut bar from Germany are just a sampling.

A category we are calling "hand molded" includes those formed into balls, "ice box" cookies, pinwheels and several molded into bars. Because most of these need to be refrigerated, they are being rediscovered by busy working women. They appreciate the fact that they can mix the dough after work and refrigerate it, then bake the cookies a day or two later.

My children classified cookies at our house as those for "recreational eating," meaning they could eat them freely for snacks, or "not for recreational eating." That meant hands off unless Mom says you can have one.

Every cookie chapter must have some of these family favorites for recreational eating. The categories for these good basic cookies always draw a large number of fair entries and are very competitive, so winning recipes are outstanding.

Recipes for "rock" cookies are found in the earliest American cookbooks. We include an exceptionally good one that has been passed down through several generations. Rolled sugar cookies and a drop sugar cookie give a choice of methods for this all-time favorite. Ranger Cookies and Sun Drops are more contemporary versions of favorite drop cookies to fill the cookie jar.

For times when you need a big batch of cookies in a hurry, nothing beats bars. We have included a range from a kid-pleasing layered cereal bar that is made and baked in the same pan to your choice of rich or even richer frosted brownies.

Winners also offer their blue ribbon tips on equipment they like, special baking techniques, decorating tips and information about ingredients.

Since the first *Blue Ribbon Winners* cookbook was published nearly a decade ago, the cookie-baking problems caused by the proliferation of low-fat spreads has crept up on us. Neither the margarine industry nor others in related food industries did a particularly good job of informing the public how this would affect baking. Since cookies are particularly sensitive, you'll be alerted to recipes where this could be a problem. (See page 118, Low-fat Spreads for Baking.)

Making and receiving cookies promotes a sense of nurturing. Perhaps that's why their popularity has never waned. In this chapter you'll find enough recipes to make a new cookie every day for more than a month. So pick out an old favorite or an interesting new recipe and get ready to turn out some sweet comfort.

# Ruth's Rocks

Rocks are one of the oldest cookie recipes published. Because the rich drop cookies contained dried fruit, they kept well, so some of the old recipes made dozens of cookies.

Ruth Maugeri's mother, Ruth, made these for as long as her daughter can remember, so she named them for her. They are loaded with dates and nuts and have a wonderful spicy flavor. She sometimes makes the dough ahead and freezes it. Freezing some of the baked cookies may be the only way to keep them from being eaten right away.

*3 cups all-purpose flour*
*1 teaspoon baking soda*
*2 teaspoons ground cinnamon*
*1 teaspoon ground cloves*
*½ cup butter, softened*
*½ cup solid vegetable shortening*

*1½ cups packed light brown sugar*
*3 eggs*
*½ to 1 cup chopped nuts*
*2 to 3 cups chopped dates (12 to 16 oz. pitted dates)*

Preheat oven to 350F (175C). Grease baking sheets.

In a medium bowl, sift flour, soda, cinnamon and cloves together. In a large bowl, mix butter and shortening to combine. Add brown sugar and beat until creamy. Beat in eggs until combined. Stir in dry ingredients just enough to blend thoroughly. Stir in nuts and dates.

Drop dough by level measuring tablespoons about 1 inch apart on greased baking sheets. Bake 12 to 15 minutes, until lightly browned. Transfer cookies to wire racks to cool.

**Makes 4½ dozen cookies.**

### Freezing Cookies

Ruth's Rocks and almost all other cookies freeze well. They will keep their oven-fresh quality for several months as long as they are packaged airtight and kept at 0F (−20C). Cool the cookies to room temperature before packaging.

Freezer-weight plastic bags and tightly sealed cookie tins make excellent containers. Label the container with the date and the name of the cookie. (If you keep several kinds of cookies in the freezer, you'll be glad you did.) You also can freeze cookie dough or even unbaked shaped dough for a week or two, as long as they are wrapped to prevent drying out and freezer burn.

RUTH A. MAUGERI   SYRACUSE, NEW YORK   NEW YORK STATE FAIR

# Ranger Cookies

Janet Parkhurst finds baking so relaxing she considers it her mental health time. After she had been sharing her goodies with family and friends for many years, a coworker sent for a state fair book to encourage Janet to compete. She accepted the challenge and has been winning ribbons at the Iowa State Fair ever since.

As with many old cookie recipes, you can find a number of variations for Ranger Cookies, but they all call for several kinds of cereal. Kids will never realize they are eating a healthy snack when they dip into a cookie jar full of these great-tasting Ranger Cookies.

*3½ cups all-purpose flour*
*1 teaspoon salt*
*1 teaspoon baking soda*
*1 teaspoon cream of tartar*
*1 cup margarine*
*1 cup granulated sugar*
*1 cup packed light brown sugar*

*¾ cup vegetable oil*
*2 teaspoons vanilla extract*
*1 egg*
*1 cup flaked coconut*
*1 cup rolled oats*
*2 cups crisp rice cereal*

Preheat oven to 350F (175C).

In a medium bowl, stir together flour, salt, soda and cream of tartar. In a large bowl, beat together margarine and sugars until creamy. Beat in oil, vanilla and egg. Add flour mixture to creamed mixture, stirring until blended. Stir in coconut, oats and cereal.

Drop by measuring tablespoonfuls on ungreased baking sheets. Bake 12 to 14 minutes or until golden. Transfer cookies to wire rack to cool.

**Makes about 7 dozen cookies.**

### 🎀 *Low-fat Spreads for Baking*

Low-fat "spreads" definitely have a place in the diet of anyone who wants to cut down on fat. But don't use them to replace full-fat margarine in a cookie recipe. Besides having a lower amount of fat, these spreads contain more water. Cookies made with them will have a different texture and appearance and won't stay fresh as long.

By law a product labeled "margarine" must contain 80% vegetable oil. If the percentage is not listed on the front label, look at the nutrition label on the back. It will show 1 tablespoon of margarine as having 11 grams of fat.

A 70 percent vegetable oil stick margarine could be your choice for less critical baking. (This will show 10 grams of fat per tablespoon.) But for best results, don't go below that, especially for cookies. Save tub or squeeze margarines for other uses.

JANET PARKHURST     DES MOINES, IOWA     IOWA STATE FAIR

# Sun Crunchies

Kansas is known as the Sunflower State, and Lucille Cline is a strong supporter of its agricultural products. For her rich, crunchy cookies, she uses sunflower kernels in preference to other nuts. She prefers sunflower oil and margarine but says only the sunflower kernels are essential for her cookies.

If you use unsalted sunflower kernels, add ¼ to ½ teaspoon of salt to the recipe. If you prefer, you can chill the soft dough, then shape it into 1½-inch balls. Either way, give the cookies plenty of room on the baking sheet. They spread out to bake as a flat, crisp cookie.

*2 cups all-purpose flour*
*½ teaspoon cream of tartar*
*½ teaspoon baking soda*
*½ cup margarine*
*½ cup granulated sugar*

*½ cup packed light brown sugar*
*½ cup vegetable oil*
*1 egg*
*½ cup roasted, salted sunflower kernels*

Preheat oven to 375F (190C).

In a medium bowl, combine flour, cream of tartar and soda. In another medium bowl, beat together margarine, granulated sugar, brown sugar, egg and oil until well blended. Stir in flour mixture and sunflower kernels.

Drop dough by level tablespoonfuls 2 inches apart onto ungreased baking sheets. Bake 10 to 12 minutes or until cookies are light golden brown. Transfer cookies to wire racks to cool.

**Makes 4 dozen cookies.**

### About Sunflower Kernels

Shelled striped sunflower seeds for baking and snacking usually are marketed as sunflower kernels or nuts. Look for them with other baking nuts or in the produce department of supermarkets or in food co-ops.

They are available raw, unsalted or roasted and salted. They are high in fat and should be refrigerated tightly covered or frozen for longer storage.

LUCILLE CLINE     WICHITA, KANSAS     KANSAS STATE FAIR

# Amish Sugar Cookies

If you'd like a good crunchy sugar cookie that doesn't have to be rolled, you'll treasure this drop cookie recipe. Nancy Gabriel brought it home years ago from a 4-H Club meeting. She seldom made it while she was growing up, because she thought if a cookie didn't include chocolate, it didn't count. Then she rediscovered it among some old family recipes and found she had unearthed a blue ribbon winner.

To dress up the plain cookies, she uses a patterned cookie stamp to flatten the dough.

*4½ cups all-purpose flour*
*1 teaspoon baking soda*
*1 teaspoon cream of tartar*
*1 cup butter*
*1 cup vegetable oil*
*1 cup granulated sugar plus extra for*
   *stamping*

*1 cup powdered sugar*
*2 large eggs*
*1 teaspoon vanilla extract*
*Granulated sugar*

Preheat oven to 375F (190C). Line baking sheets with kitchen parchment paper or grease lightly.

In a medium bowl, mix together flour, soda and cream of tartar. In a large bowl, beat butter, oil and sugars until completely blended and mixture is creamy. Add eggs and vanilla and beat well. Stir in dry ingredients until well blended.

Drop dough, using a cookie scoop or level measuring tablespoonfuls, on prepared baking sheets. Flatten each ball to ⅜-inch thickness using a cookie stamp or bottom of a pretty glass dipped in granulated sugar. Bake 10 to 12 minutes or until cookies are very lightly browned around the edges (do not overbake). Transfer cookies to wire racks to cool.

Makes about 6½ dozen cookies.

### Using a Cookie Scoop
Blue ribbon winners know they must enter a plate of drop cookies that are uniform in size. Many use a cookie scoop, which holds a level measuring tablespoonful of dough. A squeeze of the spring-action handle releases the dough and works equally well for soft or slightly stiff doughs.

NANCY GABRIEL      URBANDALE, IOWA      IOWA STATE FAIR

# White Chocolate Chip Oatmeal Cookies

After years of enjoying the food exhibits at the Iowa State Fair, Joan Randall decided to try her luck with one recipe. Like many others, she was hooked when that recipe won a blue ribbon.

For this blue ribbon winner, she took a favorite oatmeal cookie, added white chocolate chips and topped the cookie with a drizzle of white chocolate for the eye appeal that judges like.

The result is a sweet, reasonably nutritious snack cookie. It's sturdy enough for a lunch box but attractive enough to serve to guests.

| | |
|---|---|
| *1½ cups all-purpose flour* | *½ teaspoon vanilla extract* |
| *½ teaspoon salt* | *2 cups quick-cooking rolled oats* |
| *1 teaspoon baking soda* | *1 cup vanilla-flavor white morsels* |
| *¾ cup butter, softened* | *¾ cup chopped nuts* |
| *1⅔ cups sugar* | *¼ cup vanilla-flavor white morsels* |
| *2 eggs, beaten* | *(optional)* |

Preheat oven to 350F (175C). Lightly grease baking sheets.

In a small bowl, combine flour, salt and soda. In a large bowl, beat together butter and sugar until fluffy. Add eggs and vanilla and beat well. Stir in flour mixture, rolled oats, 1 cup white morsels and nuts. Drop dough, using a cookie scoop or level measuring tablespoonfuls, 2 inches apart on prepared baking sheets.

Bake 12 to 15 minutes or until light golden brown. Let the cookies rest 1 minute on the baking sheets before transferring to wire racks to cool.

If desired, microwave ¼ cup vanilla morsels in a small heavy-duty plastic bag on HIGH 30 to 45 seconds; knead. Microwave for additional 10- to 20-second intervals, kneading until smooth. Cut a tiny corner from the bag and squeeze the melted morsels to drizzle on cooled cookies.

Makes about 5½ dozen cookies.

**VARIATION**

Morsels for drizzling can be melted over hot (not boiling) water. Do not cover. Any moisture will make the morsels "seize" or harden, and they won't melt. When morsels are shiny, stir until smooth and drizzle on cookies from the tip of a teaspoon.

### Storing Cookies

Decorative cookie jars are fun, but unless cookies are all eaten in a day or two, they may not be the best way to preserve fresh-baked flavor and texture.

Airtight storage will keep soft cookies from drying out and crisp cookies crisp. Cookie jars can be used to keep cookies fresh for about a week if they have a gasket lid or screw top. Otherwise, tins, rigid plastic containers and even heavy, well-sealed plastic bags will be better choices.

Always store crisp cookies and soft cookies in separate containers, or the crisp cookies will become soft.

JOAN RANDALL    KELLEY, IOWA    IOWA STATE FAIR

# Buttery Frosted Cashew Cookies

Donna Craig has a home-based wedding cake business and cooks for her church. She enjoys baking more than any other kind of cooking.

Her rich drop cookies have cashews in the batter, more cashews topping the Browned Butter Icing and irresistibly good flavor. They are definitely a drop cookie for a special occasion.

*2 cups all-purpose flour*
*¾ teaspoon baking powder*
*¾ teaspoon baking soda*
*½ teaspoon salt*
*½ cup butter or margarine, softened*
*1 cup packed light brown sugar*
*1 egg*
*½ teaspoon vanilla extract*
*⅓ cup sour cream*

*1¾ cups salted cashew halves plus*
*36 to 40 cashew halves for tops*

*BROWNED BUTTER ICING*
*½ cup butter (no substitute)*
*¼ teaspoon vanilla extract*
*2 cups powdered sugar, sifted*
*2 to 3 tablespoons half-and-half or milk*

Preheat oven to 375F (190C). Line baking sheets with kitchen parchment paper or grease lightly.

In a medium bowl, stir together flour, baking powder, soda and salt. In a large bowl, beat together butter and brown sugar until fluffy. Beat in egg, vanilla and sour cream. Add flour mixture to butter mixture, ½ cup at a time, stirring just enough to blend. Add nuts with the last addition of flour. Drop dough by level measuring tablespoonfuls onto prepared baking sheets.

Bake 8 to 10 minutes or until set and very lightly browned (do not overbake). Transfer to wire racks to cool. Prepare icing and ice when cool. Top each cookie with a cashew half.

**Makes 3½ dozen cookies.**

## BROWNED BUTTER ICING

In a small saucepan over medium heat, lightly brown butter, stirring often to prevent burning. Remove from heat and cool for a few minutes. Add vanilla and gradually add sugar, beating until smooth after each addition. Stir in just enough half-and-half to make an icing that can be spooned over the cookies.

### *About Cashews*

You'll never find cashews in the shell in grocery stores because the shell is toxic. Before they are marketed, the shells are removed, the nuts cleaned and usually roasted.

Cashews have a rich, buttery flavor. Like most nuts, they are high in fat and should be kept in an airtight container in the refrigerator or frozen for storage beyond 1 month.

One pound of whole or half cashews equals 3¼ cups.

DONNA CRAIG     BERLIN CENTER, OHIO     CANFIELD FAIR

# Orange Slices Cookies

The response to these cookies was, "Delicious! But what's in them?" The surprising answer is old-fashioned orange slices candy, very finely chopped.

Helen Kirsch reads and collects cookbooks, then tries new recipes out on her family. She entered state fair competition to prove she could do something well. Many years and ribbons later, she certainly has done that.

Helen says if you make these favorite cookies of hers in a hot kitchen, as she did for her fair entry, the soft dough will be easier to handle if you chill it.

| | |
|---|---|
| 2 cups (about 10 oz.) orange slices candy | 1 cup granulated sugar |
| 2 cups all-purpose flour | 1 cup packed light brown sugar |
| 1 teaspoon baking powder | 2 eggs |
| 1 teaspoon baking soda | 1 teaspoon vanilla extract |
| ½ teaspoon salt | 2 cups quick-cooking rolled oats |
| 1 cup solid vegetable shortening | 1 cup flaked coconut |

Preheat oven to 350F (175C). Lightly grease baking sheets.

Cut orange slices using kitchen scissors dipped in hot water. Cut slices in half lengthwise. Cut each half into 3 strips and snip into small pieces. Toss candy pieces with 2 tablespoons of the flour and set aside.

Stir together remaining flour, baking powder, soda and salt. In a large bowl, beat together shortening and sugars until light and fluffy. Add eggs and vanilla and beat well. Stir flour mixture into the shortening mixture. Stir in rolled oats, coconut and candy pieces. Drop dough by heaping teaspoonfuls 1 inch apart on prepared baking sheets, flattening the tops slightly.

Bake 10 to 12 minutes or until lightly browned. Transfer to wire racks to cool.

**Makes about 6 dozen cookies.**

### Cookie Sheets

Flat baking sheets with just one side allow better heat circulation, so cookies bake more evenly. If you only have a jelly-roll pan, invert it and bake the cookies on the back. Shiny aluminum cookie sheets are best. Avoid dark metal pans. Cookies baked on them will brown unevenly and are more likely to burn on the bottom.

HELEN KIRSCH      ALBUQUERQUE, NEW MEXICO      NEW MEXICO STATE FAIR

# Bird's Nest Cookies

"Cute" isn't an adjective you'd usually associate with a blue ribbon cookie, but it's the best description of these egg-filled little nests.

Vicki Neuharth's young daughter has followed in her mother's footsteps, winning with these no-bake cookies in the junior division at the South Dakota State Fair.

Children love the crunchy little nests filled with pastel M & M candy "eggs," and so do adults. Think of using them as place cards for a spring luncheon or Easter brunch, or for dessert at a meal that includes families.

The mixture of candy coating, cereal and noodles sets up quickly, so make them when you won't have interruptions.

*1 pound vanilla candy coating*
*2 cups chow mein noodles*
*2 cups corn flakes, coarsely crushed*

*⅓ cup M & M's candy, preferably*
  *pastel-colored*

Melt candy coating in the top of a double boiler over simmering water or in the microwave at 50 percent power about 3 minutes, stirring every minute.

In a large bowl, combine chow mein noodles and corn flakes. Pour melted candy coating over noodle mixture, stirring until noodles and cereal are completely coated.

Form nests by mounding heaping tablespoonfuls of the mixture on waxed paper. Make an indentation in the center of each "nest." Place 3 candy "eggs" in each nest. Allow to set at room temperature until firm.

**Makes 18 to 20 cookies.**

**NOTE**
Pastel M & M's candy are available in the spring. Hidden, they will keep all year.

### About Candy Coating

Candy coating, also called confectioner's coating or almond bark, is sold with candy-making supplies and with baking ingredients in grocery stores. It is available in blocks or round disks and comes in chocolate and vanilla flavors.

Vanilla-flavored candy coating sometimes is called white chocolate, but it is an entirely different product. While its primary use is for almond bark and dipping candy, pretzels, fruits and nuts, it also can be used for simple unbaked cookies.

VICKI NEUHARTH    WOLSEY, SOUTH DAKOTA    SOUTH DAKOTA STATE FAIR

# Coconut Macaroons

With the interest in low-fat cooking, egg-white macaroons have gone from being a tea party cookie to a sweet that you can enjoy without guilt. Although Gladys Sykes's light "kisses" include coconut, this adds only a negligible gram of fat per cookie.

As a teenager Gladys helped cook for hired men on the family farm, baking for their coffee breaks and meals. She also has baked for a restaurant. In addition to being a blue ribbon cookie baker, she wins ribbons every year for her canning and preserves.

| | |
|---|---|
| *2 egg whites* | *1 teaspoon vanilla extract* |
| *1 cup sugar* | *1 cup flaked coconut* |
| *1 tablespoon all-purpose flour* | *1 cup corn flakes* |

Preheat oven to 325F (165C). Grease a large baking sheet or line with kitchen parchment paper.

In a medium bowl, beat egg whites until foamy. Beat in sugar, 1 tablespoon at a time. Continue beating until egg whites are stiff but still glossy. Fold in flour, vanilla, coconut and corn flakes. Drop by teaspoonfuls about 1 inch apart on prepared cookie sheet.

Bake about 15 minutes or until tops are set. Cool 10 minutes on baking sheet before removing.

**Makes 3 dozen cookies.**

### Macaroon Tips

Before an electric mixer was standard in almost every kitchen, macaroons used to be considered one of the tests of an expert cook. Now they are easy to make as long as you follow the principles for making meringue:

- Use egg whites at room temperature and clean, grease-free beaters and bowl (not plastic).
- Add sugar gradually, beating at medium speed.
- Make sure all the sugar is dissolved. (Rub a bit of meringue between your immaculately clean fingers. You can feel whether the sugar is totally dissolved.)
- Don't overbeat. Egg whites should be stiff but still glossy.
- Bake at a low temperature just until the macaroons are set.

GLADYS SYKES    BRAINERD, MINNESOTA    MINNESOTA STATE FAIR

# Lemon-Pecan Cookies

Mary Schuman is district director for the Purdue Cooperative Extension Service. Her interest in cooking competitions began when she was a young girl during ten years as a 4-H Club member. Now she enjoys the challenge of state fair competitions.

Her light lemon-flavored cookies won the sweepstakes at the Archway Cookie competition at the Indiana State Fair and then went on to win the regional competition. Archway generously gave us permission to publish the recipe. Toasting extends the flavor of the pecans and makes it seem like there is more than a cupful in the recipe.

*2 cups all-purpose flour*
*½ teaspoon baking soda*
*½ teaspoon cream of tartar*
*¼ teaspoon salt*
*½ cup butter or margarine, softened*
*¼ cup solid vegetable shortening*
*1 cup sugar*

*1 egg*
*2 tablespoons honey*
*1 teaspoon grated lemon peel*
*½ teaspoon lemon extract*
*1 cup pecans, toasted and finely*
*chopped (see below)*

Preheat oven to 375F (190C). Lightly grease baking sheets.

In a small bowl, stir together flour, soda, cream of tartar and salt. In a medium bowl, beat together butter, shortening and sugar until fluffy. Add egg, honey, lemon peel and lemon extract. Beat until smooth. Add flour mixture; stir until a soft dough forms. Stir in toasted pecans. Drop dough by measuring tablespoonfuls 2 inches apart on prepared baking sheets.

Bake 7 to 8 minutes or until a light golden color (do not overbake). Cool cookies on the baking sheets on wire racks 2 minutes before transferring to wire racks to cool.

**Makes about 3 dozen cookies.**

### Toasting Nuts

Because nuts are rich in oil, toasting brings out the flavor and aroma. Toast them in a 350F (175C) oven in a single layer in a shallow pan 5 to 10 minutes, stirring at least once. Smelling the aroma of toasting nuts is a signal that they are ready to use. Once at this stage, they will scorch easily.

MARY E. SCHUMAN     INDIANAPOLIS, INDIANA     INDIANA STATE FAIR

# Spicy Molasses Cutouts

Marjorie Rose graduated from Purdue University with a degree in experimental cooking and restaurant management. Her professional life revolves around institutional food preparation. At fair time she specializes in home-style baking. She has won the prestigious Governor's Cookie Jar Award seven times.

Her cookies have a good spicy flavor and are easy to roll. (Cocoa is added for color, not flavor.) They keep well, or you can bake up part of the dough and refrigerate or freeze the rest.

*3¾ cups sifted all-purpose flour*
*1 teaspoon baking soda*
*½ teaspoon salt*
*2 tablespoons unsweetened cocoa powder*
*2 teaspoons ground ginger*

*1 tablespoon ground cinnamon*
*2 teaspoons ground cloves*
*1 cup butter or margarine, softened*
*1 cup sugar*
*1 egg*
*½ cup molasses*

Sift flour, soda, salt, cocoa, ginger, cinnamon and cloves into a medium bowl.

In a large bowl, beat together butter and sugar until light and fluffy. Add egg and molasses and mix thoroughly. Stir in flour mixture, blending well. Divide dough into 3 portions; wrap in plastic wrap or foil and refrigerate at least 1 hour.

Preheat oven to 350F (175C). On a floured surface, roll out dough 1 portion at a time, keeping remaining dough refrigerated. Roll out to a ⅛-inch thickness. (See Tips for Rolled Cookies, page 124.) Cut out cookies as desired with a floured cookie cutter. Place 1 inch apart on ungreased baking sheets.

Bake about 8 minutes or until cookies are set. Transfer to wire racks to cool.

**Makes about 8 dozen 2-inch round cookies.**

## Bleached Flour for Cookies?

Some baking experts believe that bleached all-purpose flour makes better cookies than unbleached.

The bleaching agents modify the protein in flour, resulting in a more elastic gluten. According to a research official at the American Institute of Baking, this gives a flour with a silkier, finer grain—although even their flour experts don't understand the reason.

We do know that bleached flour has a slightly lower protein content, which improves tenderness.

MARJORIE ROSE     ALBUQUERQUE, NEW MEXICO     NEW MEXICO STATE FAIR

# Pattern Sugar Cookies

Blue ribbon winners at the very competitive Minnesota State Fair usually are women and the occasional man with many years of cooking experience. So when young Lori Beach won a blue ribbon for her first entry a decade ago, everyone knew a serious new contender had arrived.

Lori's mother has been her mentor in the kitchen, and this sugar cookie recipe is from her. Since Lori cuts the rolled dough with variously shaped cookie cutters and then decorates the plain cookies, she named them Pattern Cookies. The dough is easy to roll and vanilla and almond extracts make a lovely flavor combination.

| | |
|---|---|
| *4 cups all-purpose flour* | *1 teaspoon vanilla extract* |
| *2 teaspoons cream of tartar* | *1 teaspoon almond extract* |
| *2 teaspoons baking soda* | *2 eggs* |
| *1 cup butter, softened* | *Colored candies (optional)* |
| *1 cup solid vegetable shortening* | *Colored sugars (optional)* |
| *2 cups powdered sugar* | *Favorite frosting (optional)* |

In a medium bowl, stir together flour, cream of tartar and soda. In a large bowl, beat together butter and shortening until fluffy. Gradually beat in powdered sugar and extracts. Beat in eggs, one at a time. Gradually stir in the flour mixture until well blended. Cover bowl with plastic wrap. Refrigerate at least 4 hours.

Preheat oven to 350F (175C). On a lightly floured surface, roll out a portion of the dough to a ⅛-inch thickness, keeping remaining dough chilled until ready to use. Cut out cookies with a floured cookie cutter. Place cookies 1 inch apart on ungreased or kitchen parchment paper–covered baking sheets.

Sprinkle with colored sugar or candies as desired or leave plain to frost. Bake 8 to 11 minutes or until set but not browned. Transfer to wire racks to cool.

**Makes about 10 dozen 2-inch cookies.**

**NOTE**

Unbaked dough can be refrigerated in a tightly covered container for up to a week. If the dough is too stiff to roll, let it stand at room temperature for a few minutes.

### Tips for Rolled Cookies

Most rolled-cookie recipes call for chilling the dough. The length of time can fit your schedule, but you may have to let the dough warm up a bit if you chill it for several hours.

• Roll a small amount of dough at a time and keep the rest refrigerated, unless you need to let it warm up.

- Some cookie bakers prefer to use a pastry cloth and pastry stocking for the rolling pin. Others like to roll the dough between two sheets of waxed paper.
- Use as little flour as possible to roll the dough. Too much flour will make cookies tough.
- Roll the dough as evenly as possible, from the center to the edge.
- Most doughs are rolled ⅛ inch thick to get a crisp cookie. If you like a softer cookie (e.g. molasses cookies), roll the dough ¼ inch thick.
- Cut the cookies as close as you can with a floured cutter, so you can get as many as possible from your first rolling.
- The scraps of cookie dough will be easier to roll, because of the added flour, but the cookies won't be as tender. If you are baking for the fair, set these aside for your family.
- Most rolled cookies bake very quickly. Don't overbake. Even a few seconds can make a difference.
- Some cookie doughs are easier to roll than others. If you are having problems, it may be the recipe, not your technique.

Lori Beach     Plymouth, Minnesota     Minnesota State Fair

# Molasses Cookies with Baked-on Frosting

Nancy Gabriel's molasses cookies stand out among the competition at the Iowa State Fair. She cuts them with decorative cutters and then adds a baked-on frosting that turns her cookies into snowflakes and leaves.

These semisoft cookies are mildly spiced and have a rich molasses flavor. They are great eating even cut in plain rounds and unfrosted. But for the holidays or parties, anyone who is an artist with food will enjoy following Nancy's blue ribbon tips for decorating cookies using a plastic bag.

*2¾ cups all-purpose flour*
*2 teaspoons ground cinnamon*
*1 teaspoon ground ginger*
*½ teaspoon salt*
*1 teaspoon baking soda*
*⅓ cup packed light brown sugar*
*½ cup butter-flavor solid vegetable*
  *shortening*

*⅔ cup light molasses*
*1 egg*

*DECORATING FROSTING*
*⅓ cup all-purpose flour*
*⅓ cup margarine, softened*
*1½ teaspoons hot water*

Preheat oven to 375F (190C). Lightly grease baking sheets.

In a medium bowl, combine flour, cinnamon, ginger, salt and soda. In a large bowl, beat together brown sugar, shortening, molasses and egg until well blended. Stir in the flour mixture.

Prepare frosting and place in a self-sealing plastic bag or pastry bag.

Roll out dough to a ¼-inch thickness on a floured surface. Cut into desired shapes. Place 1 inch apart on prepared baking sheets.

Make designs on cookies using plastic bag with a tiny corner of the bag snipped off or a pastry bag with small round decorating tube.

Bake 7 to 8 minutes or until edges are firm and no indentation remains when touched. Transfer to wire racks to cool.

Makes about 3½ dozen 3-inch cookies.


**DECORATING FROSTING**

In a small bowl, mix together the flour, margarine and hot water with a fork to make a frosting of piping consistency.


### Nancy Gabriel's Decorating Tips

Nancy Gabriel says she's not a talented decorator, but she has developed a certain comfort level with a self-sealing bag simply because she hates the hassle of washing decorator tips. These are her tips for decorating cookies with a plastic bag.

- Use the heavier storage or freezer-weight bags. Pleated bags don't work very well.
- Use a bag that is generously sized for the amount of frosting you are applying. Be sure you have room to work the frosting into a corner of the bag.
- Begin by cutting only a tiny corner of the bag. You can always make a larger opening.
- Carefully monitor the thickness of your frosting. A too-thick frosting stretches the bag out and makes your hands tired. If your frosting is too thin, you will have too little control for precision decorating.
- The bags are easy to use for a chocolate drizzle. Just put in the chocolate chips, seal the bag shut and microwave 10 to 15 seconds at a time until the chips are melted. By holding the bag close to the cookie, you can decorate with some control. If you hold the bag about 12 inches from the cookie you can make some neat "squiggles."

NANCY GABRIEL   URBANDALE, IOWA   IOWA STATE FAIR

# Apricot-Filled Cookies

Fran Neavoll was one of the four contenders for the million-dollar grand prize at the thirty-seventh Pillsbury Bake-Off Contest with a recipe for Tropical Fruit Scones. But it's her cookies that are the big winners at the Oregon State Fair.

This pretty rolled and filled cookie has a cross cut on the top, so the golden dried apricot filling peeks through. It's a cookie that tastes even more delicious a day or so later, as the flavor of the filling seems to intensify.

Besides being a blue ribbon winner, it was judged the best cookie of all the entries at the 1995 fair.

2¼ cups all-purpose flour
½ teaspoon salt
¾ teaspoon baking powder
½ teaspoon baking soda
¼ cup butter, softened
¼ cup solid vegetable shortening
1 cup sugar
1 egg
½ teaspoon vanilla extract
2 tablespoons milk

APRICOT FILLING
1 cup (6-oz. package) dried apricots, chopped
1 cup water
½ cup sugar
1 tablespoon butter

ICING
1 cup powdered sugar, sifted
2 to 2½ tablespoons orange juice

In a medium bowl, combine flour, salt, baking powder and soda. In a large bowl, beat together butter, shortening and sugar. Add egg and vanilla and beat until fluffy. Add half the flour mixture to the butter mixture, then stir in milk and the remaining flour mixture until dough is well blended. Wrap dough in plastic wrap and refrigerate for several hours or overnight.

Prepare filling. Preheat oven to 400F (205C).

Divide chilled dough into 4 pieces. On a lightly floured surface, roll out 1 piece of the dough to a ⅛-inch thickness (keep remaining dough refrigerated if kitchen is warm). Cut out cookies with a 2-inch round cutter. Place half the rounds on ungreased baking sheets.

Spread 1 heaping teaspoonful of filling in the center of each cookie on baking sheets. Cut a cross in the center of remaining rounds. Place over filled rounds and seal edge. Repeat with remaining dough.

Bake 8 to 10 minutes or until a light golden brown. Transfer cookies to wire racks to cool.

While cookies are baking, prepare icing. Drizzle icing back and forth across slightly cooled cookies.

Makes 2½ to 3 dozen cookies.

**APRICOT FILLING**

In a medium saucepan, combine chopped apricots and water. Bring to a boil over medium heat. Reduce heat and simmer, uncovered, 5 minutes. Put apricots and water, sugar and butter in a blender; puree until smooth. Pour into a bowl and cool to room temperature.

**ICING**

Beat powdered sugar with enough orange juice to make a thin spreading consistency.

### Blue Ribbon or Recipe Contest Winner: What Is the Difference?

Ask someone like Fran Neavoll, who has been both a Bake-Off Contest winner and a frequent blue ribbon winner, what is the biggest difference in the recipes chosen for the major recipe contests.

Taste and appearance are important to both. But the primary difference is originality. In the national food-company contest, submitted recipes may not have been published in cookbooks or magazines or by any food company, or have been winners in any other national contest.

A company like Pillsbury searches its huge computerized recipe collection and hires a team of food experts to further research any recipe being considered as one of the one hundred winners.

Rules say a recipe must contain "significant" changes from a published recipe to be eligible. What does that mean? The "rule of three" applies: Three significant changes are necessary. That could mean differences in ingredients, shaping, preparation methods, etc., not simply twice as much of three kinds of spices.

A few of our blue ribbon recipes *are* original. Some are adaptations of favorite recipes. But the majority are tried and true recipes which probably were published in a magazine or cookbook some time in the past.

Sometimes developing an original contest recipe results in one that seems contrived or overly elaborate. State fair winners can concentrate on quality—and that is the major difference.

FRAN NEAVOLL    SALEM, OREGON    OREGON STATE FAIR

# German Filled Vanilla Cookies (Buckerie)

This old German holiday cookie was handed down to Mary Lou Brousil with the plain vanilla name of Vanilla Cookies. We decided such a special pastry deserved a more descriptive name.

They also are known in her German community as *Buckerie,* which they translate as "bakery." They do look and taste like a cookie that might have a place of honor in a fancy German bakery at holiday time. (*Buckerie* also is similar to the German word for "small baking" or special holiday cookies.)

Mary Lou's profession is nursing, but she says her obsession is baking. She's also a cake decorator, which inspired her to try using a pastry tube to put the nut filling on the ring-shaped cookies, a much quicker method than spreading it with a knife.

Make these very special cookies when you aren't feeling rushed. They admittedly are time-consuming, but the results are worth it.

| | |
|---|---|
| *3 cups sifted all-purpose flour* | *3 egg whites* |
| *¾ cup sugar* | *2 cups walnuts, ground* |
| *1 cup butter, chilled* | *1 cup sugar* |
| *3 egg yolks, beaten* | *1 (12-oz.) can apricot filling* |
| *1 teaspoon vanilla extract* | |

Sift flour and ¾ cup sugar together into a large bowl. With a pastry blender, cut butter into the flour mixture until well blended. Add beaten egg yolks and vanilla. Mix dough together with your hands, using a kneading motion. Divide the dough into 4 parts.

Preheat oven to 325F (165C).

On a floured surface, roll out 1 portion of the dough to about a ⅛-inch thickness. Cut into 2-inch rounds. Cut a small hole in the center of each cookie. (Mary Lou Brousil uses a thimble, "sterilized, of course.") Place cookies on an ungreased baking sheet. Cut remaining dough in the same way. Re-roll and cut leftover dough.

Beat egg whites just enough to mix. Stir in ground nuts and 1 cup sugar. Spread the nut mixture on the unbaked cookies using a knife or a pastry tube with a number 12 opening.

Bake 10 to 12 minutes or until set. Transfer cookies to wire racks to cool.

Spread half the cookies with apricot filling; top with the remaining cookies to make a sandwich.

**Makes about 50 sandwich cookies.**

### 🎗 *German Holiday Baking*

What is known in Germany as "small baking," elaborate little cookies to serve to guests, plays an important part in traditional Christmas holiday food. Years ago German housewives started this baking in July, making and storing away the long-lasting perennials like *Spekulativs* and *Lebkuchen*. Now they are likely to buy these treats closer to the holidays from a neighborhood bakery that still uses family recipes and bakes in small quantities. But elaborate little cookies still are made at home in quantities designed to last through the Feast of the Three Kings, January 6, the last day of Christmas.

One of these cookies, which is similar to this one, is *Mandelplätzchen*, an apricot-filled Bavarian ring cookie that uses almonds instead of walnuts. This recipe could be the original one that came to America with German immigrant friends of Mary Lou Brousil's grandparents. Now adapted for American ingredients and with a plain American name, these filled party cookies have won an all-American state fair blue ribbon.

MARY LOU BROUSIL     STRONGSVILLE, OHIO     OHIO STATE FAIR

# Apple-Walnut Cheese Pillows

Geraldine Sandoval has the reputation of being an innovative and creative cook, as this winning recipe demonstrates. Her attractive pastries are a cross between a filled cookie and a tiny apple dumpling. Like a bite of apple pie with cheese, they combine a flaky cheese pastry with a tasty dried apple puree filling.

Use a good sharp or extra sharp Cheddar for the distinctively rich cheese-flavored dough.

| | |
|---|---|
| *½ cup dried apples* | CHEESE PASTRY |
| *1 cup water* | *½ cup butter-flavor solid vegetable* |
| *½ cup sugar* | *  shortening* |
| *¼ cup finely chopped walnuts* | *1 cup shredded sharp Cheddar cheese* |
| | *1⅓ cups all-purpose flour* |
| | *2 tablespoons water* |

Prepare dough for pastry and chill.

In a medium saucepan, cook apples and water over medium heat, stirring occasionally, until apples are soft. Drain off extra liquid, stir in sugar and return to heat, stirring constantly, just until mixture boils. Cool slightly, then pour into food processor or blender to finely chop apples. Add walnuts and cool to room temperature.

Preheat oven to 375F (190C). On a lightly floured surface roll out 1 portion of dough into a 10-inch square. Cut dough into 2-inch squares. Place a level measuring teaspoonful of filling in the middle of each square. Bring up the corners and seal. Repeat with remaining dough and filling. Place on ungreased baking sheets.

Bake 15 to 18 minutes or until lightly browned. Transfer cookies to wire racks to cool.
**Makes 40 cookies.**

### CHEESE PASTRY

In a mixer bowl, beat together shortening and cheese until well blended. With the mixer on low speed, blend in the flour. Using a fork, mix in the water to form a dough. Divide dough into 2 equal balls. Wrap in plastic wrap and refrigerate 4 hours or overnight.

### NOTE

Chilled dough may need to warm up before rolling.

GERALDINE SANDOVAL      ALBUQUERQUE, NEW MEXICO      NEW MEXICO STATE FAIR

# Scottish Shortbread Cookies

Margaret White's authentic shortbread recipe came from her Scottish grandmother. The addition of rice flour is a clue to its European origins.

One of the simplest cookie recipes, shortbread demands the highest-quality ingredients, especially butter, which provides the main flavoring for the rich, crunchy cookies. Shortbread traditionally is baked in larger circles and cut into wedges, but Margaret's cookie shapes are a more reasonable size to eat and easier to serve.

She is a transplanted Yankee from Massachusetts. At the request of her friends, she has turned her big file of recipes into two volumes of *White House Favorites*.

*3½ cups all-purpose flour*
*1 cup rice flour (see below)*
*1 cup superfine sugar*

*2 cups (1 pound) butter (no substitutes),*
*chilled, cut into pieces*

Preheat oven to 350F (175C).

In a large bowl, stir together flour, rice flour and sugar until very well blended. Rub the butter into the flour mixture until very crumbly and no large particles remain. Divide the dough into 4 parts. Knead each part lightly until it comes together.

Roll out 1 part at a time on a floured board. Roll and pat the dough into about a ⅓- to ½-inch thickness. Cut with a small floured cookie cutter. Place ½ inch apart on an ungreased baking sheet. Repeat with remaining dough. (If kitchen is very warm, chill the dough or chill the cookies before baking. You don't want the butter to become oily.)

Bake 15 to 18 minutes or until the cookies just begin to color, but are not browned. Transfer to wire racks to cool.

Makes about 10 dozen 1½-inch cookies (⅓ inch thick).

**NOTE**

If superfine sugar isn't available, put granulated sugar through the blender.

### About Rice Flour

Rice flour is a fine white flour often used in the past in European countries to extend scarce and expensive wheat flour. It is an excellent flour to use when kneading or rolling out doughs that are sticky or fat-enriched, because it dries the surface of the dough without adhering to it.

Because rice flour has a relatively short shelf life, look for it at food co-ops or health food stores. Not all grocery stores carry it. Buy it in small quantities and store it in the refrigerator or freezer.

Brown rice flour is much coarser than white and should not be substituted to make shortbread.

If you can't find rice flour, Sheila MacNiven Cameron, who has a recipe similar to this in *The Highlander's Cookbook: Recipes from Scotland*, substitutes all-purpose flour, or she has used ¾ cup of cornstarch to replace 1 cup of rice flour.

MARGARET WHITE    CINCINNATI, OHIO    OHIO STATE FAIR

# Strawberry-Nut Hearts

Paula Lonnberg's Strawberry-Nut Hearts won a blue ribbon for the best filled cookie and the Archway Cookie competition at the Kansas State Fair. Then she went on to win the regional Archway competition and finally their top national award in 1996. Archway graciously gave permission to share the recipe for this attractive party cookie.

Paula uses a heart-shaped cookie cutter with a ruffled edge for the bottom cookie and a heart-shaped cookie cutter with a center cutout for the top. Since most of us are not so well equipped, the directions tell how to improvise.

But once you've made the heart-shaped version, you won't want to save the recipe just for Valentine's Day or a bridal shower. Use small round cutters; experiment with other flavors of jam. This is a special cookie, no matter how you cut it.

| | |
|---|---|
| 1 cup butter, softened | 2 cups all-purpose flour |
| ⅔ cup granulated sugar | Powdered sugar |
| ½ teaspoon vanilla extract | About ¼ cup strawberry jam, preferably |
| ½ teaspoon almond extract | home-preserved |
| 1⅓ cups pecans, ground (see below) | |

In a large bowl of an electric mixer, beat butter and granulated sugar until creamy. Beat in vanilla and almond extracts. Gradually add ground pecans and flour and blend until well mixed.

Cover bowl tightly with plastic wrap and refrigerate until dough is easier to handle, about 1 hour. If dough gets too cold, it will be crumbly and hard to roll.

Preheat oven to 375F (190C). Divide dough into 4 pieces for ease in rolling. On a lightly floured surface, roll out each piece of dough to a ⅛-inch thickness. Cut with a floured 2-inch heart-shaped cookie cutter and carefully transfer to ungreased baking sheets, spacing about 1 inch apart. Cut a ½-inch hole in the center of half the cookies using a small bottle cap or tiny cookie cutter.

Bake about 12 minutes or until lightly browned. Carefully transfer to wire racks and cool completely.

Sift a generous layer of powdered sugar over the tops of the cookies with holes. Spread the bottom sides of remaining cookies with jam. Place a sugar-topped cookie on each jam-topped cookie to form a sandwich. Store airtight.

Makes 3 dozen cookies.

### Grinding Nuts

The trick to grinding nuts is to grind them fine without turning them into paste. Try adding a tablespoon of sugar from the recipe to each cup of nuts. Grind small batches, especially if you use a blender. Nuts at the bottom of the container easily become overblended. Quickly start and stop the appliance for better control.

PAULA LONNBERG      JETMORE, KANSAS      KANSAS STATE FAIR

# Mad About Brownies

If you are of the school that thinks it's impossible for brownies to be too rich or too fudgy, then this is your recipe. It also is loaded with walnuts and frosted with a fudge frosting.

Cynthia Clarke doesn't consider herself to be a brownie specialist and admits she was surprised to get a blue ribbon, considering all the competition in that category. But she says cookies in general are her favorite baking category.

*½ cup butter*
*3 (1-oz.) squares unsweetened chocolate*
*1 cup sugar*
*1 teaspoon vanilla extract*
*2 eggs*
*¾ cup all-purpose flour*
*1½ cups chopped walnuts*

*FUDGE FROSTING*
*1 (1-oz.) square unsweetened chocolate*
*2 tablespoons butter*
*¼ cup milk*
*1½ cups sifted powdered sugar*

Preheat oven to 350F (175C). Grease an 8-inch-square baking pan.

In a medium saucepan, melt butter and chocolate over medium-low heat, stirring until blended. Remove from heat. Stir in sugar and vanilla. Beat in eggs, one at a time. Stir in flour and 1 cup walnuts. Mix just until well blended. Spread batter in prepared baking pan.

Bake 25 minutes. Do not overbake; brownies should be fudgy. Remove from the oven and cool in pan on a wire rack.

When brownies are cool, prepare frosting. Spread the warm frosting on the cooled brownies. Sprinkle with remaining ½ cup chopped walnuts. When frosting is set, cut into squares.

Makes 16 brownies.

### FUDGE FROSTING

In a saucepan over low heat, combine chocolate, butter and milk. Heat, stirring constantly, until the chocolate and butter are melted. Beat in powdered sugar, mixing well.

### Origin of Brownies

Some say that brownies originated when a chocolate cake didn't rise in the oven—and everyone loved the result. Actually, the origins are lost in history. We do know brownie recipes began appearing in community cookbooks in the 1920s. Recipes for Fudge Bars and Chocolate Squares in a 1924 church cookbook actually are brownies, so the recipe was being circulated under other names.

The earliest identified recipe is said to be Bangor Brownies, named for the town in Maine, where some believe the recipe originated. That original recipe, as published in a 1954 community cookbook, is similar to Mad About Brownies but it uses only ½ cup sifted flour and 2 squares of chocolate. It also is frosted, supporting the idea it originally was a version of fudge cake.

CYNTHIA CLARKE    LAKEWOOD, CALIFORNIA    LOS ANGELES COUNTY FAIR

# Best Brownies

Fay Peterson's brownies are a more traditional version which received high marks from state fair judges. She likes the convenience of premelted unsweetened chocolate and used that in her winning entry.

Fay started in 4-H Club in Minnesota, entered county fairs in Ohio and graduated to the state fair after she moved back to Minnesota. She says Minnesota has so many great cooks who enter, she enjoys the challenge of seeing if she can win a blue ribbon.

½ cup butter or margarine, melted
2 (1-oz.) envelopes premelted unsweetened
   chocolate product or 2 (1-oz.) squares
   unsweetened chocolate
2 eggs
1 cup sugar
1 teaspoon vanilla extract
⅔ cup all-purpose flour
½ teaspoon salt
1 cup chopped walnuts

CHOCOLATE GLAZE
1½ cups powdered sugar
1 teaspoon vanilla extract
2 tablespoons butter, melted
1 (1-oz.) envelope premelted unsweetened
   chocolate product or 1 (1-oz.) square
   unsweetened chocolate, melted
⅛ teaspoon salt
1½ to 2 tablespoons milk

Preheat oven to 350F (175C). Grease and lightly flour the bottom only of an 11 × 7-inch or 8-inch-square baking pan.

In a medium saucepan, melt butter over low heat, stirring constantly. Add premelted chocolate to the melted butter. Or melt chocolate squares with butter. Remove from heat; cool slightly.

In a large bowl, beat the eggs until thick and creamy; gradually beat in sugar. Stir in chocolate mixture, vanilla, flour, salt and walnuts. Spread in the prepared pan.

Bake 20 to 25 minutes or until set in the center and a crust forms on top. Cool in pan on a wire rack.

Prepare glaze and spread over cool brownies. Cut into bars.

**Makes 16 brownies.**

### CHOCOLATE GLAZE

In a small bowl, beat together all ingredients, adding enough milk to make a smooth and creamy glaze.

### *Premelted Unsweetened Chocolate*

To make the semiliquid premelted chocolate, cocoa powder is combined with vegetable oil. Pure unsweetened baking chocolate bars contain about 50 percent cocoa butter. Because legal standards of identity define what can be called "chocolate," premelted unsweetened chocolate is known as a "chocolate product," although it is used in the same way as unsweetened baking chocolate.

A 1-ounce envelope of premelted chocolate can replace a 1-ounce square of unsweetened baking chocolate in a recipe. To replace ¼ cup unsweetened cocoa powder, use 1 envelope of premelted chocolate and reduce fat in the recipe by 1 tablespoon.

FAY PETERSON    APPLE VALLEY, MINNESOTA    MINNESOTA STATE FAIR

# Walnut Pie Bars

Registered nurse Leisa Lower finds entering fair competitions a challenge and baking a release from her fast-paced work day. As a child she was encouraged to help her mother and grandmother cook and was allowed to experiment on her own. She especially enjoys using recipes handed down through her family.

These luscious two-layer bars also won a special award from Hammon's, the world's largest processor of black walnuts. Using toffee bits makes an interesting change from the more usual chocolate chips, and black walnuts add a rich flavor.

| | |
|---|---|
| 2 cups all-purpose flour | 1 teaspoon vanilla extract |
| ½ cup powdered sugar | ¼ teaspoon salt |
| 1 cup margarine, cut into chunks | 1 cup (6-oz. package) toffee-flavored |
| 1 (14-oz.) can sweetened condensed milk | baking chips |
| 1 egg | 1 cup chopped black or California walnuts |

Preheat oven to 350F (175C). Grease a 13 × 9-inch baking pan.

In a medium bowl, stir together flour and powdered sugar. Cut in margarine until mixture resembles coarse meal. Press firmly into prepared baking pan. Bake 15 minutes.

Meanwhile, beat together condensed milk, egg, vanilla and salt. Stir in baking chips and walnuts. Spread evenly over baked crust.

Bake 20 to 25 minutes or until topping is set and very lightly browned. Cool in pan on a wire rack, then refrigerate. When chilled, cut into bars. Store refrigerated.

**Makes 48 bars.**

### Freeing Up the Baking Pan

It's convenient to store bars right in the pan. But if you don't want to tie up a baking pan, line it with foil, extending the foil over the edges of the pan. Grease the foil and spread the batter evenly in the pan. After the bars are baked and cooled, you can lift them out by the edges of the foil. Cut the bars and overwrap them with foil or store them in an airtight container.

LEISA LOWER    SPRINGFIELD, MISSOURI    OZARK EMPIRE FAIR

# German Orange Coconut Bars

## *(Orangenkekse mit Kokosnuss)*

Cheryl Ashwill has a special interest in ethnic baking, a category that is gaining popularity at fairs across the country. She is a registered pharmacist with two children. Since baking time is at a premium, she concentrates on cookies, because of their versatility. In a two-day baking marathon to get ready for the fair last year, she baked more than thirty different cookies and received ten blue ribbons.

These cakelike bars have a refreshing orange flavor. One way she achieves this is to whiz the orange peel and sugar together in the blender, which releases the essential oils in the peel and adds distinctive flavor to the bars. Her recipe is from *The German Village Cookbook,* collected and edited by the German Village Society of Columbus, Ohio.

| | |
|---|---|
| *2 cups all-purpose flour* | *1 egg* |
| *2 teaspoons baking powder* | *½ cup milk* |
| *¼ teaspoon salt* | |
| *3 tablespoons shredded orange peel* | *TOPPING* |
| *(from 3 large oranges)* | *1 egg* |
| *1 cup sugar* | *¼ cup sugar* |
| *½ cup butter, softened* | *1¼ cups shredded coconut* |

Preheat oven to 350F (175C). Grease a 15 × 10-inch jelly-roll pan.

In a medium bowl, stir together flour, baking powder and salt. In a blender or food processor, pulse orange peel and sugar together. In a medium bowl, beat together butter and orange-sugar mixture until light and fluffy. Beat in egg. Add flour mixture, alternately with milk, mixing well after each addition. Press dough evenly into prepared pan.

Prepare topping. Spread evenly over dough. Sprinkle with reserved coconut.

Bake 14 to 17 minutes or until top is lightly browned. Cool in pan on a wire rack. Cut into bars when cool.

**Makes 30 to 40 bars.**

**TOPPING**

In a small bowl, beat egg lightly. Stir in sugar and 1 cup coconut, reserving ¼ cup for sprinkling.

### *Fund-Raiser Cookbooks*

The soft-cover, spiral-bound fund-raising cookbooks, which are generally classified as charitable cookbooks, can be a source of unusual regional and ethnic recipes, as well as fascinating reading. Cheryl Ashwill discovered her prize-winning bar cookie in one of these books.

The idea of publishing recipes to raise money for charity dates back to the Civil War, when

Ladies Aid Societies sold recipe booklets to raise money to help support military casualties and their families. The idea caught on, and after the war women's organizations and church groups collected and sold recipes in formats ranging from pamphlets to hard-cover books.

Cookbook collectors look at flea markets and estate sales for older volumes, which are more likely to have the most authentic regional and ethnic recipes. These may also assume the reader knows how to cook and bake, so detailed instructions may be left out. One caveat: The recipes in most old and many newer charitable cookbooks have been published without being tested.

CHERYL ASHWILL      DES MOINES, IOWA      IOWA STATE FAIR

# Pumpkin Bars with Cream Cheese Frosting

When you need to bring a big pan of bars to some event, spicy pumpkin bars thickly frosted with cream cheese frosting will be a hit. Lori Beach uses a recipe a friend gave her years ago. Since it calls for vegetable oil rather than solid shortening, it is quick to mix and is moist. The bars keep well but must be stored in the refrigerator because of the cream cheese frosting.

*2 cups all-purpose flour*
*2 teaspoons baking powder*
*1 teaspoon baking soda*
*½ teaspoon salt*
*2 teaspoons ground cinnamon*
*½ teaspoon ground ginger*
*½ teaspoon ground cloves*
*½ teaspoon ground nutmeg*
*4 eggs*
*1 cup vegetable oil*

*2 cups sugar*
*1 (15-oz.) can pumpkin*

*CREAM CHEESE FROSTING*
*2 (3-oz.) packages cream cheese, softened*
*6 tablespoons butter, softened*
*1 tablespoon half-and-half or milk*
*1 teaspoon vanilla extract*
*4 cups powdered sugar, sifted*

Preheat oven to 350F (175C). Grease and flour a 15 × 10-inch jelly-roll pan.

In a medium bowl, stir together flour, baking powder, soda, salt, cinnamon, ginger, cloves and nutmeg. In a large bowl, beat eggs until foamy. Add oil, sugar and pumpkin and beat until thoroughly blended. Stir in dry ingredients, beating just enough to combine thoroughly. Pour into prepared pan.

Bake 25 to 30 minutes or until a wooden pick inserted in the center comes out clean. Cool in pan on a wire rack.

Prepare frosting and spread over cooled bars. When frosting has set, cut into bars. Refrigerate leftover frosted bars.

**Makes 48 dessert bars.**

### CREAM CHEESE FROSTING

In a medium bowl, beat cream cheese, butter, half-and-half and vanilla until fluffy. Gradually beat in powdered sugar; blend until smooth.

### Storing Spices

A decorative spice rack may dress up a kitchen counter, but it is not a good way to store spices. They will keep their flavor longer if they are stored tightly covered in a cool, dry cupboard.

Many blue ribbon winners say they replace spices before they do their fair baking. Ground spices begin to lose their flavor after 6 months and should be replaced at least once a year. You can tell by the strong aroma and rich color if spices are fresh. You can save money by buying spices you don't use often in small containers.

LORI BEACH      PLYMOUTH, MINNESOTA      MINNESOTA STATE FAIR

# Crunch Bars

Busy working moms will love these bars. They go together in just minutes and are assembled right in the baking pan, so there's practically no cleanup.

Jean Meiers collects cookbooks and likes to try new recipes from them. This is one she discovered and liked so well, she entered it at the fair. The rich, moist bars keep well—in fact, the flavor is even better the second day.

*½ cup butter or margarine*
*5 cups bite-sized rice squares cereal,*
*   coarsely crushed*
*1 cup butterscotch-flavored chips*

*1 (3½-oz.) can (1⅓ cups) flaked coconut*
*1 (14-oz.) can sweetened condensed milk*
*1 cup chopped pecans*

Preheat oven to 350F (175C).

Melt butter in a 13 × 9-inch baking pan in the oven. Spread 1½ cups of crushed cereal over the melted butter; sprinkle evenly with layers of chips, coconut, condensed milk, pecans and the remaining cereal. Press down firmly.

Bake 25 to 30 minutes or until bars are set and very lightly browned. Cool on a wire rack. Cut into bars. Store, loosely covered, at room temperature.

**Makes 36 bars.**

**VARIATION**

Jean also makes these with wheat squares cereal and peanut butter chips. When she uses a glass baking pan, she bakes the bars at 325F (165C).

### About Sweetened Condensed Milk

During the Civil War, soldiers were given a new product, canned sweetened condensed milk. Even though all the principles of sterilization were not known at the time, Gail Borden had discovered that adding a quantity of sugar to condensed milk inhibited bacterial growth.

Because fresh milk could not be transported great distances and the sanitation in many dairies was suspect, after the war soldiers continued to buy the condensed milk and civilians discovered its convenience.

Today condensed milk is used primarily in desserts. It can be stored, unopened, 6 months. Once opened, any leftover condensed milk should be poured into a tightly sealed glass container and refrigerated 2 to 3 days or frozen. (However, most dessert recipes call for 1 can of condensed milk.)

Evaporated milk has had about the same amount of water removed, but sugar hasn't been added. The two products cannot be substituted for each other.

JEAN MEIERS     ARMOUR, SOUTH DAKOTA     SOUTH DAKOTA STATE FAIR

# Frosted Applesauce Raisin Bars

Joyce Dubois's Applesauce Raisin Bars is one of those unbeatable entries at the South Dakota State Fair. At last count, they had won the top award in the category for nine years. While this may be frustrating for other fair competitors, it's a sure sign of a great recipe.

Joyce has furnished her kitchen with appliances won for the top homemaker's award, the prize given to the person receiving the most premium money in women's activities that year.

Her lightly spiced cakelike bars have a generous amount of raisins and nuts and a particularly good caramel frosting.

*2 cups all-purpose flour*
*2 teaspoons baking soda*
*½ teaspoon ground cinnamon*
*½ teaspoon salt*
*¾ cup solid vegetable shortening*
*1 cup sugar*
*2 eggs*
*2 cups sweetened applesauce*
*1 teaspoon vanilla extract*

*1 cup raisins*
*1 cup chopped walnuts*

*CARAMEL FROSTING*
*1 cup packed light brown sugar*
*½ cup margarine*
*¼ teaspoon salt*
*¼ cup milk*
*2 cups sifted powdered sugar*

Preheat oven to 350F (175C). Grease and flour a 15 × 10-inch jelly-roll pan.

In a small bowl, mix flour, soda, cinnamon and salt. In a medium bowl, beat together shortening and sugar until well blended. Beat in eggs, one at a time. Stir in applesauce and vanilla. Add flour mixture to egg mixture, stirring until well blended. Stir in raisins and walnuts. Pour into prepared pan.

Bake about 25 to 30 minutes or until dark golden brown and a wooden pick inserted in the center comes out clean.

Cool in pan on a wire rack while making frosting. Quickly spread warm frosting on cooled bars. After frosting has set, cut into bars.

**Makes 48 bars.**

### CARAMEL FROSTING

In a medium saucepan, combine brown sugar, margarine and salt. Bring to a boil over medium heat; cook 2 minutes, stirring constantly. Add milk and bring to a boil. Remove from heat.

Using an electric mixer, gradually beat in powdered sugar until frosting is smooth and creamy. Spread warm frosting on cooled bars.

### ⬗ *Pan Sizes*

No jelly-roll pan? Rather than baking a recipe that calls for a 15 × 10-inch pan in a 13 × 9-inch pan, use two 9-inch-square pans for blue ribbon results. The bars will bake in a little less time in the smaller pans, so check them at least 5 minutes before the minimum baking time.

JOYCE DUBOIS     WOLSEY, SOUTH DAKOTA     SOUTH DAKOTA STATE FAIR

# Ginger Crinkles

Using vegetable oil instead of solid shortening in Vicki Neuharth's gingersnaps makes a dough that's very easy to handle and doesn't need to be refrigerated before molding. They are mildly spiced and have an attractive crinkled top. Vicki warns that these cookies shouldn't be overbaked or they'll get hard.

Ginger Crinkles will be a favorite for the cookie jar, but expect it to empty quickly.

*2 cups all-purpose flour*
*2 teaspoons baking soda*
*¼ teaspoon salt*
*1 teaspoon ground cinnamon*
*1 teaspoon ground ginger*

*⅔ cup vegetable oil*
*1 cup plus 3 tablespoons sugar*
*1 egg*
*¼ cup molasses*

Preheat oven to 350F (175C).

In a small bowl, combine flour, soda, salt, cinnamon and ginger.

In a large bowl, beat together oil and the 1 cup sugar until well mixed. Beat in egg and molasses. Stir in flour mixture just until well blended. Drop dough by level measuring tablespoonfuls into remaining 3 tablespoons sugar, in a small bowl. Form into balls. Place about 2 inches apart on ungreased baking sheets.

Bake 8 to 10 minutes or until tops are crinkly and some of the cracks are still slightly moist. Cool on wire racks.

Makes about 3 dozen cookies.

### Greased vs. Ungreased Pans

Molded cookies usually are high in fat, so they are baked on ungreased baking sheets. If pans are greased they can cause these cookies to spread too much.

VICKI NEUHARTH       WOLSEY, SOUTH DAKOTA       SOUTH DAKOTA STATE FAIR

# Dutch St. Nicholas Cookies

## (Sint Nikolaas Koekjes)

Cookies are a Dutch specialty. Our word for cookie is a phonetic approximation of *koek-jes,* which translates as "little cakes." Cheryl Ashwill's recipe is similar to *Spekulaas,* the spicy holiday cookie, which traditionally is shaped by pressing the dough into a mold. Cheryl forms this dough into balls and then presses them flat with a patterned cookie stamp.

This is a nice cookie to serve with ice cream or a cup of tea or coffee. You won't want to reserve it just for Christmas!

| | |
|---|---|
| *2 cups all-purpose flour* | *1 cup sugar* |
| *1½ teaspoons ground cinnamon* | *¼ cup sour cream* |
| *½ teaspoon ground allspice* | *½ cup finely chopped nuts (pecans,* |
| *½ teaspoon ground nutmeg* | *cashews, almonds or a mixture)* |
| *¼ teaspoon ground cloves* | *1 egg white beaten with 2 teaspoons* |
| *¼ teaspoon salt* | *water* |
| *½ teaspoon baking soda* | *Coarse decorating sugar* |
| *1 cup butter, softened* | |

In a medium bowl, combine flour, spices, salt and soda. In a large bowl, beat together butter and sugar until light and fluffy. Beat in sour cream. Stir in the flour mixture ½ cup at a time, blending well after each addition. Add nuts with final addition of flour.

Form dough into a ball; wrap well in plastic wrap or foil and refrigerate for several hours or overnight.

Preheat oven to 350F (175C). Line baking sheets with kitchen parchment paper or grease lightly.

Roll rounded tablespoons of dough into 1¼-inch balls. Arrange 1½ inches apart on prepared baking sheets. Press with the bottom of a glass or a cookie stamp dipped in sugar. Brush with egg white and water glaze and sprinkle with coarse sugar.

Bake 9 to 12 minutes or until cookies are set and light golden brown on the top. Cool on wire racks.

Makes 4 dozen cookies.

### Kitchen Parchment Paper
More blue ribbon bakers are discovering the convenience of using kitchen parchment paper to line baking sheets. Cookies bake evenly on it, and most can be baked without greasing the paper.

You'll find kitchen parchment paper in tear-off rolls in supermarkets, usually in the section where kitchen baking equipment is sold.

CHERYL ASHWILL     DES MOINES, IOWA     IOWA STATE FAIR

# Pecan Shortbread Cookies

Susan Moser's cookies are a very good variation of classic shortbread. Vanilla and chopped pecans add a pleasing flavor and rolling the baked cookies in powdered sugar is a sweet touch. The recipe is one she's had since a high school home economics class, where the cookies were baked in a finger shape.

*1 cup butter, softened*
*½ cup powdered sugar plus extra for rolling*
*2 teaspoons vanilla extract*

*1 tablespoon water*
*2 cups all-purpose flour*
*1 cup chopped pecans*

In a large bowl, beat together butter and sugar until light and fluffy. Stir in vanilla, water, flour and pecans, mixing until well blended, using a large wooden spoon or hands. Refrigerate dough for several hours or overnight.

Preheat oven to 325F (165C). Using measuring tablespoonfuls of dough, firmly press into 1-inch balls. Place 1 inch apart on ungreased baking sheets. Press to flatten.

Bake 15 to 20 minutes or until cookies are set, but not brown. While cookies are still warm, gently roll in powdered sugar. Cool on wire racks.

**Makes 4 dozen cookies.**

### About Vanilla
Pure vanilla is made from the seed of an orchid. The slender pod, called a vanilla bean, is dried and cured, then finely chopped. Vanilla extract is made by circulating diluted alcohol through the chopped bean until the full flavor has been extracted.

Imitation vanilla is made from synthetic flavors and food coloring. Different brands vary in composition. Some may contain some pure vanilla extract. Pure vanilla extract adds a richer flavor but is more expensive.

Vanilla should be stored tightly closed in a cool, dark place.

SUSAN C. MOSER     KING, NORTH CAROLINA     NORTH CAROLINA STATE FAIR

# Walnut Frosties

In her upscale version of thumbprint cookies, Leisa Lower fills the depression in her crunchy brown sugar cookies with a baked-in topping of walnuts, brown sugar and sour cream. This treasured recipe from her grandmother has been a family favorite for many years.

Leisa lives in southwest Missouri in the heart of black walnut country, so that's her preference when she bakes. Hammon's Products, the world's largest processor of black walnuts, gave her a special award for Walnut Frosties, in addition to her blue ribbon.

*1 cup black or California walnuts, chopped*　　*¼ teaspoon salt*
*1½ cups packed light brown sugar*　　　　　*½ cup margarine, softened*
*¼ cup sour cream*　　　　　　　　　　　　*1 egg*
*2 cups all-purpose flour*　　　　　　　　　　*1 teaspoon vanilla extract*
*½ teaspoon baking soda*

Make topping by combining chopped walnuts, ½ cup brown sugar and sour cream. Set aside.

Preheat oven to 350F (175C). In a medium bowl, sift together flour, soda and salt. In a large bowl, beat together margarine, remaining 1 cup brown sugar, egg and vanilla until light and fluffy. Gradually stir in flour mixture, mixing thoroughly.

Shape level measuring tablespoonfuls of dough into 1-inch balls. Place on ungreased baking sheets. Make a depression in the center of each cookie. Fill with a heaping teaspoonful of topping. Bake about 10 minutes or until cookies are set. Cool on wire racks.

**Makes 3½ dozen cookies.**

### About Black Walnuts

Black walnuts are native to America. They grow over a much wider geographic area than the English (California) walnut. The meat of the black walnut is richer and has a much more intense flavor.

Black walnut trees have been raised more for their beautiful wood than the nut. One reason may be that the nuts are notoriously difficult to hull and shell, although some thinner-shelled nuts have been propagated. They are not as widely available in grocery stores as California walnuts.

Store the shelled nuts in airtight containers in the refrigerator for a few months or freeze them for longer storage.

LEISA J. LOWER　　　SPRINGFIELD, MISSOURI　　　OZARK EMPIRE FAIR

# Chinese Almond Cookies

While we think of fortune cookies as the quintessential Chinese cookie, Cheryl Ashwill's Chinese Almond Cookies are more authentic. Lard gives these little cookies their characteristic crunchy texture. The flavor is a delicate almond.

If you'd prefer not to use lard, substitute solid vegetable shortening, not butter or margarine, to get similar results. This recipe won a sweepstakes award as well as a blue ribbon.

*3 cups sifted all-purpose flour*
*1 teaspoon baking soda*
*¼ teaspoon salt*
*1 cup lard, at room temperature*
*1 cup sugar*

*1 egg*
*1 teaspoon almond extract*
*About 30 whole blanched almonds,*
 *split in half*

Preheat oven to 375F (190C). Line baking sheets with kitchen parchment paper.

In a medium bowl, sift together flour, soda and salt. In a large bowl, beat together lard and sugar until light. Add egg and almond extract and mix well. Stir in flour mixture.

Shape into 1-inch balls and place 2 inches apart on lined or ungreased baking sheets. Flatten slightly by pressing center of cookie with your thumb. Press an almond half in the center of each cookie. Bake 10 to 12 minutes or until set. Transfer cookies to wire racks to cool.

**Makes about 4½ dozen cookies.**

**VARIATION**

If you prefer, use whole blanched almonds.

### Using Lard

Lard is a white fat processed from pork. Until we became concerned about saturated fat and cholesterol, it often was used in pie crusts and for deep-fat frying. Some good home bakers still swear by it.

Lard is comparable to solid vegetable shortening and higher than butter or margarine in total fat, one of the main reasons it makes tender, flaky pastry. Chinese Almond Cookies are unusual in that the special texture of this traditional old cookie depends on using lard.

Lard is available in 1-pound packages and usually is found in the meat case at the supermarket. It must be refrigerated and can be frozen for longer storage.

CHERYL ASHWILL    DES MOINES, IOWA    IOWA STATE FAIR

# Karen's Pinwheels

Biologist Karen Cope works in the food industry in quality assurance, but outside of work her interest is in gourmet cooking. She has taken cooking classes at the famed Le Cordon Bleu in Paris and in her spare time she assists at a cooking school in St. Paul.

Although the pastry she most enjoys making is puff pastry, she wins her blue ribbons with cookies. To get ready for fair baking, she tosses out all the old ingredients like leavening, buys a new supply and then bakes from early morning to midnight, so all her entries are fresh for the competition.

| | |
|---|---|
| *3 cups all-purpose flour* | *1½ cups powdered sugar* |
| *¼ teaspoon salt* | *1 egg* |
| *1¼ cups butter, softened* | *¼ cup unsweetened cocoa powder* |

In a medium bowl, stir together flour and salt. In another medium bowl, beat together butter, powdered sugar and egg until light and fluffy. Stir in the flour mixture. Divide the dough into 2 equal portions. Mix cocoa into 1 portion.

Wrap doughs in plastic wrap and refrigerate at least 1 hour. Roll out chocolate dough into a 16 × 9-inch rectangle on waxed paper or a lightly floured board. Roll out the white dough into a 16 × 9-inch rectangle and place on the chocolate rectangle. Roll tightly, jelly-roll fashion, beginning at a long side. Wrap roll in plastic wrap or waxed paper. Refrigerate at least 8 hours.

Preheat oven to 400F (205C). Cut rolls into ⅛-inch-thick slices. (If dough crumbles, let it warm up slightly.) Place cookies about 1 inch apart on ungreased baking sheets.

Bake about 8 minutes or until cookies are set. Immediately remove from baking sheets and cool on wire racks.

**Makes about 8 dozen cookies.**

### ✿ *Tips for Perfect Pinwheels*

Since appearance can add or subtract important points when baked goods are judged, fair contestants want to submit well-shaped cookies with a distinct pinwheel pattern.

Karen Cope, who honed her pastry-baking skills at Le Cordon Bleu, shares these tips:

- Using a Magic Marker™, she draws a rectangle of the specified size on one side of a sheet of waxed paper. Then she rolls the dough to that size, being careful to keep it an even thickness. She prefers waxed paper to a floured board, because it's easier to move the dough on it.
- Her original recipe called for putting the light dough on the outside. She prefers having the darker dough on the outside. This hides any browning along the outside edge and gives a more distinct contrast between light and dark doughs.
- She rolls the dough as tightly as possible. If there is a filling, spread it just to within ½ inch of the edges, so it won't run out as the cookies bake.

● Read the recipe in advance. Some doughs need to be refrigerated before they are rolled, and all rolls need to be refrigerated before they are sliced. Refrigerated dough may need to rest at room temperature for a few minutes if it is difficult to roll or is crumbly when cut.

KAREN COPE    MINNEAPOLIS, MINNESOTA    MINNESOTA STATE FAIR

# Mexican Wedding Cakes

Whether you call them Russian tea cakes, Mexican wedding cakes or one of several other names, these buttery, rich snowball cookies are a favorite holiday treat in many countries.

Becky Daugherty and her two sisters all got their start competing in food events in 4-H Club. Now they all participate in the state fair, where competition remains friendly. Becky enjoys browsing through cookbooks, looking for new and unusual recipes to try.

*1 cup all-purpose flour*
*¾ cup cornstarch*
*½ cup butter*
*½ cup margarine*

*⅓ cup powdered sugar plus extra*
*    for coating*
*1 teaspoon vanilla extract*
*1 cup chopped pecans*

In a small bowl, thoroughly combine the flour and cornstarch. In a medium bowl, beat together butter and margarine until softened. Beat in ⅓ cup powdered sugar and vanilla. Blend in flour mixture and pecans. If dough is too soft to handle, wrap in waxed paper and refrigerate about 1 hour.

Preheat oven to 350F (175C). Roll teaspoonfuls of dough into balls. Arrange on ungreased baking sheets. Bake 12 to 14 minutes or until cookies are set, but not browned, and very lightly browned on the bottom. While still warm, roll cookies in sifted powdered sugar. Cool on wire racks.

**Makes 3½ to 4 dozen cookies.**

BECKY DAUGHERTY    SELMA, INDIANA    INDIANA STATE FAIR

# Aunt Molly's Almond Cookies

Berta Shapiro has had two remarkable cooking mentors—her own Aunt Sadie and her husband's Aunt Molly. Berta put together a family cookbook, *Aunt Sadie's Strudel,* to honor her own aunt's memory. Aunt Molly, a contestant in an early Pillsbury Bake-Off Contest, went on to win a number of recipe contests, so it seemed appropriate that her cookie recipe should bring a blue ribbon to Berta. These look like Chinese Almond Cookies but have more of a buttery, melt-in-the-mouth texture.

*1 cup butter, softened*
*1 cup powdered sugar*
*1¼ cups ground blanched almonds*
*2 teaspoons almond extract*

*1 teaspoon vanilla extract*
*2 cups all-purpose flour*
*¼ teaspoon salt*
*40 whole blanched almonds*

Preheat oven to 350F (175C).

In a large bowl, beat together butter and powdered sugar until light and fluffy. Beat in ground almonds, almond extract and vanilla. Blend in flour and salt. If dough is too soft to mold easily, wrap in waxed paper and refrigerate up to 1 hour. Using level tablespoonfuls of dough, shape dough into balls and place 2 inches apart on ungreased baking sheets. Flatten balls with a glass dipped in sugar. Press an almond in the center of each cookie.

Bake 8 to 10 minutes or until tops of cookies are set. (Cookies do not brown.) Remove to wire racks to cool.

**Makes 40 cookies.**

### Learning About Flour

When we bake molded cookies, we tend to think of the butter, nuts, spices and flavorings as the important ingredients. Flour is just flour. I learned differently when I started testing some of these molded cookie recipes during the coldest winter in recorded history in Minnesota.

Flour can absorb or lose small amounts of moisture. During the very cold weather, it becomes drier and takes up more liquid in a recipe. Molded cookies have very little liquid—in the case of Aunt Molly's Almond Cookies, only 3 teaspoons of flavoring.

You may find you need to make slight adjustments in these recipes for molded cookies. You might need to use a little less flour or add a tiny amount of water. You might need to let chilled dough warm up a little before shaping it, or in hot weather you might need to chill it longer than the recipe specifies.

By the nature of their ingredients, molded cookies are deliciously rich and have a good crunchy texture. But the recipes also are a little less forgiving than most other kinds of cookies. However, they will be worth your extra attention.

BERTA SHAPIRO    MINNETONKA, MINNESOTA    MINNESOTA STATE FAIR

# Butter-Pecan Ice Box Cookies

If you are a fan of butter pecan ice cream, you will love these delicious refrigerator cookies. Peggy Russell thinks one of the secrets of her success is that she used her pet chicken's fresh egg to make her fair entry. Experience also may have entered in. She gets up early and bakes every morning before she goes out to her work of caring for injured and abandoned wildlife. At Christmas she bakes about three thousand cookies to give as gifts. Her dream is to own a small-town bakery, so she could give free cookies to all the children who come in.

| | |
|---|---|
| 2¼ cups all-purpose flour | 1 cup packed light brown sugar |
| ¼ teaspoon salt | 1 egg |
| 1 teaspoon cream of tartar | 1 teaspoon vanilla extract |
| 1 cup butter, preferably salted, softened | 1 cup coarsely chopped pecans |

In a medium bowl, stir together flour, salt and cream of tartar. In a large bowl, beat together butter and brown sugar until light and fluffy. Beat in egg and vanilla. Blend in flour mixture and pecans.

Form into 2 rolls, 8 to 10 inches long. Wrap in plastic wrap and refrigerate until firm enough to slice.

Preheat oven to 350F (175C). Lightly grease baking sheets. Slice dough into ¼-inch-thick rounds. Arrange on ungreased baking sheets about 1 inch apart. Bake 8 to 10 minutes or until light golden brown. Cool slightly on baking sheets before removing to wire racks.

Makes 4½ to 5 dozen cookies.

### About Refrigerator Cookies

Most refrigerator cookies contain a high proportion of fat and are crisp rather than chewy. For blue ribbon results, use butter.

For the best shaped cookies, keep the dough refrigerated until you start slicing it. Use your sharpest knife. A dull knife will push the dough out of shape.

Rotating the roll a quarter turn each time you cut it also will give you a better shape. If your hands are warm, slip a plastic bag over the one that holds the roll to insulate it. Heat from your hand can soften the dough.

PEGGY RUSSELL     ALTADENA, CALIFORNIA     LOS ANGELES COUNTY FAIR

# Rainbow Slices

Marjorie Rose's pretty triple-layer cookies look complicated to make, but the recipe is easy to follow, one step at a time. The pink, white and green cookies make an attractive addition to a cookie tray. They have won a blue ribbon in their category five times at the New Mexico State Fair.

One caveat: add the food coloring slowly, one drop at a time. It's much easier to put it in than to take it out!

*2½ cups all-purpose flour*
*1 teaspoon baking powder*
*¼ teaspoon salt*
*1 cup butter, softened*
*¾ cup sugar*
*1 egg*
*1 teaspoon vanilla extract*
*4 drops red food coloring*

*¼ cup finely chopped, well-drained*
*   maraschino cherries or*
*   candied cherries*
*¼ cup flaked coconut*
*4 drops green food coloring*
*½ teaspoon almond extract*
*¼ cup chopped pistachio nuts*

Line the bottom and sides of a straight-sided 8 × 4-inch loaf pan with waxed paper or foil.

In a medium bowl, stir together the flour, baking powder and salt. In a large bowl, beat together butter and sugar until light and fluffy. Beat in egg and vanilla. Stir in flour mixture until well blended. Divide dough evenly into 3 parts. Cover with plastic wrap and refrigerate about 15 minutes.

To make pink layer, remove 1 portion of dough from the refrigerator. Adding 1 drop at a time, add red food coloring to make a pink dough. Stir in cherries. Press dough firmly and evenly in the bottom of the prepared pan. Refrigerate dough.

For the white layer, stir coconut into a second portion of dough. Press it firmly and evenly over the pink layer. Refrigerate dough.

For the green layer, add green food coloring, a drop at a time, to remaining portion of dough. Add almond extract and pistachio nuts and mix well. Press firmly and evenly over the white layer. Cover with plastic wrap. Refrigerate for several hours or overnight.

Preheat oven to 350F (175C). Invert pan of cookie dough onto a cutting board. Remove waxed paper or foil. Cut crosswise into ¼-inch-thick slices. Then cut each slice vertically into 3 equal pieces. Place 1 inch apart on ungreased baking sheets.

Bake 8 to 10 minutes or until edges are lightly browned. Remove to a wire rack to cool.

**Makes 6 dozen cookies.**

### Using Food Coloring in Cookies

Decorating colors are available in paste and liquid forms. Professional cake decorators like the little jars of pastel colors, but they are more difficult for amateurs to use when only a few drops of color are called for.

Stores that sell cake decorating equipment carry liquid colors in containers that release one drop at a time. It's very difficult to get just 1 drop from the 1-ounce bottles of liquid food coloring, unless you use an eye dropper.

MARJORIE ROSE     ALBUQUERQUE, NEW MEXICO     NEW MEXICO STATE FAIR

# Date Pinwheels

Date Pinwheel Cookies were Ellen Ebner's very first entry and her first blue ribbon at the historic Bloomsburg Fair more than a quarter century ago—and it's still a winner. She has expanded her repertoire considerably since then. Now she excels in pies, other baked goods and jams and jellies.

Her Date Pinwheel Cookies bring back wonderful memories, because they were always one of the many special cookies my mother made for Christmas. They don't need to be saved for holiday baking, though. They fit into any busy schedule, because you can make the filled cookie rolls one day and bake them the next.

For best results, see Tips for Perfect Pinwheels (page 152).

*2½ cups chopped pitted dates*
*1 cup granulated sugar*
*1 cup water*
*1 cup finely chopped nuts*
*4 cups all-purpose flour*

*½ teaspoon salt*
*½ teaspoon baking soda*
*1 cup butter, softened*
*2 cups packed light brown sugar*
*3 eggs*

Prepare date filling by combining dates, granulated sugar and water in a medium pan. Bring to a boil over high heat. Reduce the heat and simmer, stirring constantly and mashing with a spoon, until the mixture is thick and smooth, about 8 minutes. Remove from heat and let cool. Add nuts to the cooled date mixture.

In a medium bowl, stir together the flour, salt and soda. In a large bowl, beat together butter and sugar until creamy; beat in eggs. Gradually add flour mixture, blending to make a stiff dough. Divide dough into 3 parts, cover with plastic wrap and refrigerate at least 30 minutes.

On a floured board or between sheets of waxed paper, roll out 1 portion of dough at a time into a 10 × 8-inch rectangle. Spread ⅓ of the date filling to within ½ inch of the edges. Roll up, jelly-roll fashion, starting with a long edge. Wrap rolls in plastic wrap or waxed paper and refrigerate at least 12 hours or up to 3 days.

Preheat oven to 350F (175C). Using a sharp knife, cut rolls into ¼-inch-thick slices. Place ½ inch apart on ungreased baking sheets and bake 8 to 10 minutes or until lightly browned. Transfer cookies to wire racks to cool.

**Makes about 11 dozen cookies.**

ELLEN EBNER      BLOOMSBURG, PENNSYLVANIA      BLOOMSBURG FAIR

# Scandinavian Almond Bars

For many Minnesotans, even non-Scandinavians, Paula Downing's rich, crunchy almond bars are a favorite addition to a holiday cookie tray. More flavorful than many of the Scandinavian pastries, the diagonally cut strips with a drizzle of frosting also have an interesting shape.

The problem with these delicious cookies is that the recipe seldom appears in cookbooks. It is handed down in the family or passed on to a friend. We can rejoice that Paula won a blue ribbon and is sharing her recipe.

When you see these attractive cookies, they look like they are difficult and time-consuming to make. But Paula, a mother of two who works full time, says she likes recipes that are quick and easy—and this one fills the bill.

*1¾ cups all-purpose flour*
*2 teaspoons baking powder*
*¼ teaspoon salt*
*½ cup butter, softened*
*1 cup sugar*
*1 egg*
*½ teaspoon almond extract*
*2 tablespoons milk*

*½ cup (2-oz. package) slivered almonds, coarsely chopped*

*ALMOND ICING*
*1 cup powdered sugar, sifted*
*¼ teaspoon almond extract*
*3 to 4 teaspoons milk*

Preheat oven to 325F (165C).

In a medium bowl, combine flour, baking powder and salt. In a large bowl, beat together butter and sugar until fluffy. Beat in egg and almond extract. Stir in flour mixture until well mixed.

Divide dough into 4 pieces. Form each piece into a 12-inch-long roll. Place 2 rolls 5 inches apart on kitchen parchment paper–covered or ungreased baking sheets. Flatten until rolls are 3 inches wide. Repeat with remaining 2 rolls. Brush rolls with milk and sprinkle with almonds.

Bake 12 to 14 minutes or until cookies are firm and edges are lightly brown. While cookies are still warm and on the baking sheet, cut crosswise on a diagonal into 1-inch strips. Transfer to wire racks to cool.

Make icing and drizzle over cooled cookies.

**Makes 48 bars.**

### ALMOND ICING

In a small bowl, stir together powdered sugar, almond extract and enough milk to make an icing of drizzling consistency.

PAULA DOWNING     YOUNGSTOWN, OHIO     CANFIELD FAIR

# Cakes & Frostings

*Delicious endings depend on exact beginnings.*
Anonymous

Several years ago, shortly before state fair time, the Portland *Oregonian's* food staff decided to test the theory that if you gave the same cake recipe to a group of people to bake, they'd bring back entirely different products.

The recipe they chose was Chocolate Sauerkraut Cake with Seafoam Frosting. It had just been published in the state fair premium book, because it was being promoted as the cake state fair contestants had to bake to enter a special contest sponsored by the Oregon Wheat Growers.

As part of its pre-fair publicity, the paper held its own mini-contest, with five contestants ranging from professional bakers (both female) to a male bank executive who was interested in cooking. After the judging by food professionals, the paper published photos of the cakes, along with comments.

Anyone who has been involved in an event like a church supper where several people are asked to prepare the same recipe will not be surprised at the results. The judges reported that none of the cakes tasted the same, although all but one were the same color. The winning cake was half again as high as the one with the least volume. Texture varied from tender to tough. A baker's cake had the best texture, but many children would have done a better job with the frosting. The winning cake, baked in a 1928 gas range by an exercise specialist, looked like a blue ribbon winner, with both cake and frosting scoring high on appearance, taste and texture.

Compared with yeast baking, cake baking is a more exact process. Perhaps that is why many of today's most popular cakes still are heritage recipes that have stood the test of time. Different flavorings, added ingredients, frostings and fillings offer creative ways to change these basic cakes.

In addition to a reliable recipe, technique is important, especially for the more delicate butter layer cakes or angel food cakes. There's a technique to creaming the butter and sugar so the delicate air cells don't break down. Having ingredients at the optimum temperature is important. Being able to beat egg whites to just the right stage and then gently fold them in is a learned technique. Since few of us have degrees in food chemistry, like our blue ribbon winners we learn these things by trial and error and by practice. Having recipes like those in this chapter that give detailed instructions make this learning process much quicker.

These recipes cover a range of complexity. Texas Sheet Cake, a regional specialty that is a cross between a bar cookie and a cake, is both quick and easy to make. Spicy Prune Bundt Cake and Honey Apple Nut Cake are sturdy family-oriented cakes with very simple or no frosting.

Thanks to a veteran blue ribbon baker we've included the most detailed instructions for making the most perfect angel food cake you may ever find. Following her recipe and tips, you'll discover this delicate foam cake is not difficult to make from scratch.

However, most of the recipes are the beauty queens of the culinary exhibit at the fairs—the frosted layer cakes. Chocolate cakes predominate. The four recipes may sound similar, but with their special fillings and frostings, the recipes produce four very different desserts.

While none of these cakes should be difficult for anyone who even occasionally makes cakes from scratch, be sure to read the recipe through before starting. For example, some recipes require advance preparation of ingredients. A few need three 9-inch cake pans, so you will want to be sure you have the necessary equipment. In return, you will find a group of truly outstanding cakes that you will treasure.

The careful observer will discover some discrepancies in methods. For example, several call for lining cake pans with waxed paper. Not all the recipes say to grease the waxed paper. Because this is the way these recipes won blue ribbons, they were tested as written. The method works.

The one change is that all the recipes have been rewritten so the ingredients and the steps are given in the order used. In a number of cases we went back to the winners for more detailed instruction or clarification. This additional information is, of course, included in the recipes. Enjoy them!

# Angel Food Cake

Since all angel food cake recipes are similar, technique makes the blue ribbon difference. For that reason, consistent winners are reluctant to reveal their tips. But Marjorie Johnson has been such a big winner for many years in every baking category at the highly competitive Minnesota State Fair that she agreed to share her detailed recipe plus additional tips.

*1 cup sifted cake flour*
*1½ cups sifted powdered sugar*
*1⅔ cups egg whites, at room temperature*
   *(about 13 eggs)*
*½ teaspoon salt*

*1½ teaspoons cream of tartar*
*1 teaspoon almond extract*
*1 teaspoon vanilla extract*
*1 cup granulated sugar*

Preheat oven to 350F (175C). Have an ungreased 10 × 4-inch tube pan ready. Sift sifted flour and sifted powdered sugar together 4 times into a medium bowl.

In a large bowl, beat together egg whites, salt, cream of tartar and almond and vanilla extracts with an electric mixer at medium speed 30 seconds, then on medium-high speed until frothy. Continue beating on medium-high speed while adding granulated sugar, 2 tablespoons at a time, beating 10 seconds after each addition. Continue beating on high speed until the mixture is stiff and glossy. Do not underbeat.

Sift the flour mixture over the egg whites about ¼ cup at a time. With a rubber spatula, gently fold in the flour mixture. Gently push the batter into the ungreased tube pan. Cut through the batter a few times with a metal spatula to remove large air bubbles.

Bake 35 to 40 minutes or until the top springs back when touched lightly and the cracks feel dry. Invert the pan on an empty soda bottle or funnel 1 hour or until completely cool before removing from the pan.

Makes a 10-inch tube cake, 12 to 16 servings.

### Secrets for a Blue Ribbon Angel Food Cake
Marjorie Johnson uses her Kitchen Aid mixer with the wire whisk attachment to beat the egg whites (and uses 1 more egg white than most recipes call for). Then she very carefully transfers the stiffly beaten whites to a 6-quart bowl. She feels it is easier to fold the flour mixture in without overmixing in this wider-bottomed bowl.

She bakes the cake on the lowest rack, using an angel food cake pan with a removable bottom. To remove the cake from the pan, she runs a thin-bladed spatula carefully around the edge of the pan and the tube. When she tips the cake over, the bottom stays attached. She runs the spatula between the cake and the bottom section and comes out with a perfect bottom on her cake.

To accumulate egg whites for her angel food cakes, she drops any extra egg whites into a pint jar which she keeps in the freezer. She marks the jar with the number of whites and the date and stores them in the freezer for up to 6 months. She uses 2 egg yolks instead of 1 egg in products like yeast rolls, when she needs to accumulate egg whites.

MARJORIE JOHNSON    ROBBINSDALE, MINNESOTA    MINNESOTA STATE FAIR

# Honey Apple Walnut Cake

Thelma Atkinson's daughter is test kitchen director for a major publishing company. Like her mother, she started baking when she was barely into grade school. Since the Atkinsons raise bees, Thelma likes to find ways to use honey in cooking. Living in the heart of Missouri's black walnut country, she also favors their walnuts' rich, distinctive flavor. Her unfrosted cake combines these two favorites, with the honey contributing to its moist texture and good keeping qualities. Fresh from the oven, served with a dollop of whipped cream, it makes a dessert you could serve to special guests.

| | |
|---|---|
| ¼ cup solid vegetable shortening | ½ teaspoon baking powder |
| ½ cup sugar | ½ teaspoon salt |
| ½ cup honey | ¾ teaspoon ground cinnamon |
| 1 teaspoon vanilla extract | 1½ cups chopped, peeled apples |
| 1 egg, well beaten | ¾ cup black or California walnuts, |
| 1 cup all-purpose flour | chopped |
| 1 teaspoon baking soda | |

Heat oven to 350F (175C). Grease and flour a 9-inch-square baking pan.

In a large bowl, beat together shortening, sugar, honey, vanilla and beaten egg until mixture is creamy. Sift in flour, soda, baking powder, salt and cinnamon. Stir until well blended. Fold in apples and nuts.

Spoon batter into prepared pan. Bake 40 to 45 minutes or until the cake starts to pull away from sides of the pan and a wooden pick inserted in the center comes out clean. If cake seems to be browning too fast, cover loosely with foil after 30 minutes.

Makes a 9-inch-square cake, 9 servings.

### Using Honey in Baking

It's best to use recipes formulated for honey, but if you want to experiment, substitute honey for no more than half the sugar in a recipe. Reduce the liquid by 2 tablespoons for each ½ cup of honey.

Usually, the lighter the color of the honey, the milder the flavor. A 12-ounce jar of honey is 1 cup.

Food made with honey browns quicker, so you can reduce the oven temperature 25 degrees Fahrenheit (10 degrees Celsius) or cover the product with foil toward the end of baking.

THELMA ATKINSON        SPRINGFIELD, MISSOURI        OZARK EMPIRE FAIR

# Almond Torte

Whole-wheat flour intensifies the crunchiness of the ground almonds in this melt-in-your-mouth torte, which won both a blue ribbon and the sweepstakes award for Linda Pauls. The cake is very rich and moist because nuts replace some of the flour. Even with a filling of seedless raspberry jam and powdered sugar sprinkled on top, it is not overly sweet. A small piece makes a very satisfying dessert.

*1½ cups sliced almonds (1⅓ cups after*
   *finely grinding)*
*¾ cup butter, softened*
*¾ cup sugar*
*4 eggs, separated*
*2 teaspoons vanilla extract*

*⅛ teaspoon salt*
*¼ cup all-purpose flour*
*¼ cup whole-wheat flour*
*½ cup seedless raspberry jam*
*Powdered sugar*

Preheat oven to 350F (175C). Grease bottom of a 9-inch round cake pan or springform pan and line it with waxed paper. Finely grind almonds in a food processor or blender.

In a large bowl, beat together butter and 6 tablespoons of the sugar until creamy. Beat in yolks, one at a time. Stir in vanilla and almonds. In a medium bowl, with clean beaters, beat egg whites and salt until soft peaks form. Gradually add the remaining sugar, beating until soft, glossy peaks form.

Sift flours over the batter; gently fold in. Fold in beaten egg whites. Pour into the prepared pan. Bake about 30 minutes or until a wooden pick inserted in the center of the cake comes out clean. Cool in the pan on a wire rack 10 minutes. Remove from pan and finish cooling on a waxed paper–covered rack.

When cool, slice horizontally into 2 layers. Place bottom layer, cut side up, on a serving plate. Spread with jam. Top with remaining layer, cut side down. Place a paper doily on top; sprinkle with powdered sugar. Carefully remove doily.

Makes a 9-inch layer cake, 10 servings.

### Splitting a Cake Evenly into Two Layers
Measure the height of the cake layer with a ruler. Then insert 4 to 6 wooden picks in the side of the cake at the center. Using a sharp, thin-bladed knife, cut across just above the picks. Or, instead of using a knife, you can place dental floss around the cake, resting on the wooden picks. Cross the two ends in front, then pull the ends in opposite directions, drawing the floss through the cake.

LINDA PAULS    BUHLER, KANSAS    KANSAS STATE FAIR

# Martha's Orange Pecan Torte

Martha York likes to enter the "favorite cake" category, because it gives her the best opportunity to express her creativity. She won her fourth blue ribbon in recent years for a favorite cake with this European-style nut torte. It combines a light, tender-textured four-layer cake with a rich cream cheese filling and whipped cream frosting.

In the summer she likes to decorate her lovely party cake with fresh flowers and calls it her "Summer Bouquet Cake." She cautions that the pecans must be ground fine but should not be ground to a paste.

*2½ cups pecan pieces*
*3 tablespoons all-purpose flour*
*4 teaspoons baking powder*
*6 eggs*
*1 cup sugar*
*Pecan halves (optional), for decoration*

*ORANGE SYRUP*
*¼ cup sugar*
*¼ cup water*
*2 tablespoons Grand Marnier liqueur or*
*½ teaspoon pure orange extract*

*CREAM CHEESE FILLING*
*1 (8-oz.) package cream cheese, softened*
*¼ cup butter, softened*
*½ cup packed light brown sugar*
*1 teaspoon grated orange peel*
*1 teaspoon pure orange extract*

*CHANTILLY CREAM*
*1½ cups whipping cream, well chilled*
*3 tablespoons light brown sugar*
*1½ teaspoons grated orange peel*
*2 teaspoons Grand Marnier liqueur or*
*½ teaspoon pure orange extract*

Preheat oven to 350F (175C). Grease and flour 2 (8-inch-round) cake pans. Toast pecans 12 to 15 minutes, stirring several times as they toast. Cool.

In a blender, grind the pecans, in 2 batches, until fine. In a small bowl, combine the pecans, flour and baking powder. In the blender, process eggs and sugar until smooth. Add the nut mixture and blend, scraping the sides as needed.

Spread the batter in prepared pans. Bake 20 to 25 minutes or until a wooden pick inserted in the center comes out clean. Cool in the pans on a wire rack for 10 minutes; remove layers and cool.

Make syrup and filling while cake is cooling. Cut the cake layers in half horizontally to make 4 layers. Sprinkle the cut surfaces with syrup. Stack the layers on a serving plate, spreading ⅓ of the filling mixture between the layers.

Make Chantilly Cream and spread on the top and sides of the cake. Decorate with pecan halves, if desired. Refrigerate covered.

**Makes an 8-inch, 4-layer cake, 10 to 12 servings.**

**ORANGE SYRUP**

In a small pan, combine sugar and water and boil 5 minutes. Remove from heat. Add liqueur.

## CREAM CHEESE FILLING

In a small bowl, beat cream cheese and butter until fluffy. Gradually beat in brown sugar until mixture is smooth. Stir in orange peel and extract.

**Makes enough filling to cover 3 (8-inch) layers.**

## CHANTILLY CREAM

In a medium bowl, combine cream, sugar, orange peel and orange liqueur or extract. Beat until soft peaks form. Immediately spread on the top and sides of the cake.

**Makes about 3 cups of frosting.**

### *Grating Orange Peel*

Oranges should be washed well and thoroughly dried before grating. Use only the outside orange part of the peel; the white membrane is bitter.

Measure grated peel lightly in the spoon; do not pack down. A large orange will yield about 4 teaspoons of grated peel.

An easy way to have grated peel on hand is to first grate the peel whenever you are using whole oranges. Freeze it in a small glass jar or plastic snack bag.

MARTHA YORK     LOUISVILLE, KENTUCKY     KENTUCKY STATE FAIR

# Marge's Perfect Chocolate Cake

One of the highlights of the Oregon State Fair is the Gerry Frank Chocolate Layer Cake Contest. Chocolate aficionado Frank judges it, tasting his way through the dozens of entries. It takes an outstanding cake, like Marge Cuff's Perfect Chocolate Cake, to win.

Her three-layer beauty combines a moist, light-textured chocolate cake with a whipped cream filling and an outstanding fudge frosting. The light whipped cream filling contributes a pleasing contrast to the rich chocolate cake and frosting.

Because of the whipped cream, the cake should be stored covered in the refrigerator. For best flavor, bring it to room temperature before serving.

*1 cup unsweetened cocoa powder*
*2 cups boiling water*
*2¾ cups all-purpose flour*
*2 teaspoons baking soda*
*½ teaspoon baking powder*
*½ teaspoon salt*
*1 cup butter, softened*
*2½ cups sugar*
*4 eggs*
*1 teaspoon vanilla extract*
*1 teaspoon chocolate extract*

*CHANTILLY CREAM FILLING*
*1 cup heavy cream, chilled*
*¼ cup powdered sugar*
*1 teaspoon vanilla extract*

*CREAMY FUDGE FROSTING*
*1 cup (6-oz. package) semisweet*
   *chocolate chips*
*½ cup half-and-half*
*1 cup butter*
*Ice cubes*
*2½ cups powdered sugar, sifted*

Preheat oven to 350F (175C). Grease and flour 3 (9-inch-round) cake pans.

In a medium bowl, combine cocoa and boiling water until smooth. Cool. Sift together flour, soda, baking powder and salt.

In a mixer bowl, beat butter, sugar, eggs, vanilla and chocolate extract with an electric mixer at low speed about 5 minutes. Scrape sides of the bowl occasionally. At low speed, alternately blend in ¼ of flour mixture and ⅓ of cocoa mixture, beginning and ending with flour. Do not overbeat.

Divide batter evenly among the prepared pans. Bake 25 to 30 minutes or until a wooden pick inserted in the center of a cake comes out clean. Cool in pans on a wire rack 10 minutes, then turn out and cool completely.

Prepare filling and frosting. Assemble cake with filling between layers and frosting on top and sides of cake. Refrigerate covered. Serve at room temperature.

Makes a 9-inch, 3-layer cake, 12 servings.

### CHANTILLY CREAM FILLING

In a medium bowl, whip cream with sugar and vanilla until it forms soft peaks.

**CREAMY FUDGE FROSTING**

In a medium saucepan over low heat, stir chocolate chips, half-and-half and butter until mixture is smooth. Pour into a medium bowl over a bowl of ice. With an electric mixer, beat in powdered sugar until mixture is creamy and spreadable. When mixture begins to change from dark brown to a milk chocolate color, it is nearly ready to spread. If it should get too thick, remove it from the ice and let it warm a bit.

## Storing Cake

When making a filled and frosted butter cake for a special occasion, it may be more convenient to bake the layers one day and fill and frost the cake the next. The unfrosted layers, tightly wrapped in foil or stored in self-sealing plastic bags, keep well for a day or two at room temperature. Or, they can be made well ahead of time and frozen for several months.

Once filled and frosted with a butter cream frosting, the cake will keep best covered in the refrigerator if it will not be served in a few hours. Most butter cream frosting will begin to soften at room temperature. Cakes with a whipped cream or cream filling must be refrigerated.

Cakes with fluffy frosting are best eaten the same day, as this kind of frosting breaks down during storage. (This is the reason you most often find butter cream frostings used on cakes to be judged at a fair.)

MARGE CUFF     SALEM, OREGON     OREGON STATE FAIR

# Old-Fashioned Devil's Food Layer Cake

Besides being an experienced baker, Denise Turnbull has steady nerves. She was declared Grand Champion winner in cakes after preparing her Devil's Food Cake before an audience of fair goers and judges at the Illinois State Fair.

This great-tasting cake has a fine, delicate structure and needs to be handled carefully. Let the cake layers cool in the pans 15 minutes, so they will be easier to remove. Cover the wire rack with waxed paper, so the wires won't mark the top of the cake. Sprinkling a little sugar on the paper also helps keep the tops from sticking. The batter generously fills 2 (9-inch) pans. If you must use 8-inch pans, make a few cupcakes with the extra batter.

2¼ cups sifted cake flour
½ cup unsweetened cocoa powder
1½ teaspoons baking soda
1 teaspoon salt
½ cup solid vegetable shortening
1¾ cups sugar, divided
1 teaspoon vanilla extract
3 large eggs, separated
1⅓ cups cold water

DARK CHOCOLATE FROSTING
2⅔ cups powdered sugar, sifted
¾ cup unsweetened cocoa powder
6 tablespoons butter, softened
4 to 5 tablespoons milk
1 teaspoon vanilla extract
1 tablespoon light corn syrup

Preheat oven to 350F (175C). Heavily grease and flour 2 (9-inch-round) cake pans. In a medium bowl, sift together flour, cocoa, soda and salt.

In a large mixer bowl, beat shortening until fluffy. Add 1 cup of the sugar and vanilla; beat until light and fluffy. Add egg yolks, one at a time, beating well after each addition. Add dry ingredients alternately with water, mixing until just combined.

In a medium bowl, beat egg whites until soft peaks form. Gradually beat in the remaining ¾ cup sugar, beating until stiff peaks form. Gently fold egg whites into the batter just until completely mixed.

Pour batter evenly into prepared pans. Bake 30 to 35 minutes or until a wooden pick inserted in the center of a cake comes out clean. Cool layers in pans on cooling rack 15 minutes, then carefully turn out on waxed paper–covered cooling rack and cool right side up. Cool completely before frosting.

Make frosting. Spread about ½ cup of the frosting on 1 layer. Place second layer on top. Spread a thin layer of frosting on the sides and swirl the rest on top.

**Makes a 9-inch, 2-layer cake, 12 servings.**

**DARK CHOCOLATE FROSTING**

In a small bowl, blend together powdered sugar and cocoa powder. In a medium bowl, cream butter and ½ cup cocoa mixture. Add remaining cocoa mixture, 3 tablespoons milk, vanilla and corn syrup. Beat to spreading consistency, adding more milk as needed.

Makes enough frosting to fill and frost 2 (8- or 9-inch) layers.

## Beating Egg Whites

Egg whites beat to their highest volume at room temperature, but separate easier while the eggs are still cold. Let the whites stand about 30 minutes at room temperature before beating.

Be sure the beater blades and bowl are very clean. Even the most minute amount of fat on them will keep the whites from beating properly. That's why it's best to use a glass or stainless steel bowl; a plastic bowl can absorb fat.

Start beating at low speed until the eggs are foamy. Add sugar gradually, beating at medium-high speed (high speed with a hand-held beater). The stiffly beaten egg whites should stand in straight peaks and should look moist and glossy. If they begin to look curdled, start again with new egg whites, because the whites are overbeaten. Overbeaten egg whites will make a dry cake.

Any bit of egg yolk in the whites will keep them from beating properly. You often can scoop out a small amount of yolk with the broken shell. If not, start with a new egg.

DENISE TURNBULL      MONMOUTH, ILLINOIS      ILLINOIS STATE FAIR

# Chocolate Mocha Hazelnut Cake

Florence Neavoll and her sister Fran are frequent winners at the Oregon State Fair, and both were chosen as finalists in the thirty-seventh Pillsbury Bake-Off Contest.

Florence's notepaper reads: "I never met a dessert I didn't like." Her show-stopper of a party cake is proof she also knows how to create memorable desserts, this one a winning combination of Oregon hazelnuts and chocolate.

Read the recipe through before starting it and allow yourself plenty of time. If more convenient, you can bake and glaze the layers one day and fill and frost the cake the next day (see page 169, "Storing Cake").

⅔ cup unsweetened cocoa powder
¾ cup boiling water
1¾ cups sifted cake flour
1¾ cups sugar
4 teaspoons baking powder
½ teaspoon salt
½ cup vegetable oil
8 eggs, separated
3 teaspoons vanilla extract
¼ teaspoon red food coloring
½ teaspoon cream of tartar

*HAZELNUT MOCHA CREAM FILLING*
½ cup sugar
¼ cup cornstarch
2 tablespoons instant coffee
1¼ cups milk
1 cup butter, softened
¼ cup powdered sugar
1 cup finely ground roasted hazelnuts

*CHOCOLATE HAZELNUT GLAZE*
2 squares (2 oz.) unsweetened chocolate
2 tablespoons softened butter
½ teaspoon vanilla extract
2½ cups sifted powdered sugar
2 teaspoons hazelnut liqueur
6 to 8 tablespoons milk

*COCOA HAZELNUT ICING*
6 tablespoons butter, softened
2 cups sifted powdered sugar
½ cup unsweetened cocoa
⅛ teaspoon salt
1 teaspoon vanilla
1 teaspoon hazelnut liqueur
3 tablespoons half-and-half
⅓ cup marshmallow creme

*FOR DECORATION*
1 cup chopped toasted hazelnuts
8 chocolate-covered whole hazelnuts
   (optional)

Preheat oven to 350F (175C). In a small bowl, combine cocoa and boiling water. Set aside to cool. Grease 3 (9-inch-round) cake pans and line with waxed paper. Do not grease waxed paper.

Into a large mixer bowl, sift flour, sugar, baking powder and salt; make a well in the flour mixture. Add oil, egg yolks, cocoa mixture, vanilla and food coloring. Beat at medium speed about 1 minute or until mixture is smooth.

In a separate bowl, with clean beater blades, beat egg whites with cream of tartar until whites are stiff but still moist. With a rubber spatula, gently fold the egg whites into the cake batter.

Carefully pour batter into prepared pans. Bake about 25 minutes or until a wooden pick inserted in the center of a cake comes out clean. Cool cake in pans on a wire rack about 15 minutes. Carefully remove from the pans and finish cooling.

While cake is cooling, prepare filling and cool. Prepare glaze. Spread the glaze on the tops of the cooled layers and set aside for glaze to harden. While filling is cooling and glaze is hardening, prepare icing.

Spread cooled filling on top of hardened chocolate glaze on all 3 layers. Stack the cakes, filling side up. Frost sides of cake with icing. Press chopped hazelnuts gently into the icing. If desired, place chocolate-covered hazelnuts on the top to decorate.

**Makes a 9-inch, 3-layer cake, 12 servings.**

### Hazelnut Mocha Cream Filling

In a medium saucepan, combine sugar, cornstarch, instant coffee and milk. Cook over medium heat, stirring constantly, until mixture boils and thickens. Remove from heat. Cover surface with plastic wrap and refrigerate 30 minutes or until cool. In a large bowl, beat butter and powdered sugar until well blended. Gradually add cooled coffee mixture and beat until light and fluffy. Fold in hazelnuts.

### Chocolate Hazelnut Glaze

In a medium saucepan, melt chocolate and butter over medium heat. Add vanilla, powdered sugar, hazelnut liqueur and milk and blend well.

### Cocoa Hazelnut Icing

In a medium bowl, beat butter, powdered sugar, cocoa, salt, vanilla, hazelnut liqueur and half-and-half until smooth and creamy. Blend in marshmallow creme. Use to frost the sides of the cake.

### Note

Look for hazelnut liqueur in small bottles with other liqueurs in liquor stores. The Italian import is called Frangelico. It is used to enhance the hazelnut flavor, so there is no good substitute.

### All About Hazelnuts

Hazelnuts (also called filberts) often are roasted when they will be used in baking to develop their mild, sweet flavor. Because of their brown skin, it's easy to overroast them. Roast them at 325F (160C) about 8 to 10 minutes or until you just begin to smell them. The skinless nuts should only be lightly colored, not golden brown.

Many recipes suggest skinning the roasted hazelnuts by rubbing them vigorously in a clean terrycloth towel. The problem with that is that the ones most available in this country come from Oregon or Turkey. Both places raise varieties of hazelnuts with remarkably tenacious skins. Unless you need perfectly skinned hazelnuts for decoration, just rub off as much as you can. If you freeze the nuts right from the oven, the skins will come off more easily.

Because of their high fat content, they can develop a rancid flavor, so it's best to store them in the freezer. Fresh hazelnuts will keep for at least a year in a freezer, if they are stored in a tightly covered container.

FLORENCE NEAVOLL      SALEM, OREGON      OREGON STATE FAIR

# Fudgy Chocolate Layer Cake

Jean Meiers's chocolate cake will especially please anyone who prefers bittersweet chocolate to milk chocolate. A high level of cocoa plus brown sugar give it a deep color and a rich but not-too-sweet flavor. To double the chocolate flavor, use Dark Chocolate Frosting (page 170) for filling and for frosting. Or, for a lighter dessert, use a whipped cream filling and a thin chocolate glaze on top.

*1¾ cups all-purpose flour*
*¾ cup plus 3 tablespoons unsweetened cocoa powder*
*1¼ teaspoons baking soda*
*⅛ teaspoon salt*
*¾ cup butter, softened*

*⅔ cup granulated sugar*
*⅔ cup firmly packed brown sugar*
*2 eggs*
*2 teaspoons vanilla extract*
*1½ cups buttermilk*

Preheat oven to 350F (175C). Line the bottoms of 2 (9-inch-round) cake pans with waxed paper. Grease paper and sides of pans and dust with flour.

In a medium bowl, sift together flour, cocoa, baking soda and salt. In a large bowl, beat together butter and sugars until light and fluffy. Add eggs, one at a time, beating after each addition. Add vanilla. At low speed alternately add flour mixture and buttermilk, beating just until blended.

Divide batter evenly between prepared pans. Bake about 25 minutes or until a wooden pick inserted in a cake center comes out clean. Cool in pans on a wire rack 10 minutes.

Turn out onto racks; remove waxed paper. Turn layers top side up and cool completely before frosting with Dark Chocolate Frosting (page 170).

**Makes a 9-inch, 2-layer cake, 12 servings.**

## *Which Cocoa to Use?*

Chocolate cake recipes are developed for unsweetened cocoa powder that has no added ingredients. It is made by pressing most of the cocoa butter from pure chocolate. Presweetened cocoa mix for making hot cocoa has sugar and flavoring added; it cannot be substituted for cocoa powder.

Dutch-process cocoa is pure cocoa powder treated with alkali to partially neutralize the acids in the cocoa bean. This darker cocoa has a more mellow flavor.

Some baking experts feel you should use baking powder rather than baking soda if you use "Dutched" cocoa. The process that produces Dutch-process cocoa takes the place of soda, while baking powder is needed as the leavening. Too much soda results in a coarser texture and "soapy" flavor.

The prudent solution for a cake like Fudgy Chocolate Layer Cake is to use a regular domestic cocoa, but use Dutch-process cocoa in recipes that specify it.

JEAN MEIERS       ARMOUR, SOUTH DAKOTA       SOUTH DAKOTA STATE FAIR

# Coconut Supreme Cake

Linda Cranmer baked her first cake from scratch when she was eight years old. Many years later she still reads cookbooks as if they were novels and confidently alters the recipes to make them her own. Her fine-textured, three-layer white cake with coconut frosting won Best of Show at the South Plains Fair. Her recipe is based on the classic 1-2-3-4 cake, said to be one of the most popular American cakes because it was easy to remember the recipe.

| | |
|---|---|
| *3 cups sifted cake flour* | *COCONUT FROSTING* |
| *1 tablespoon baking powder* | *⅔ cup butter, softened* |
| *½ teaspoon salt* | *⅛ teaspoon salt* |
| *½ cup butter, softened* | *5½ to 6 cups powdered sugar* |
| *½ cup solid vegetable shortening* | *½ cup milk* |
| *2 cups sugar* | *1 tablespoon vanilla extract* |
| *4 eggs* | *1 teaspoon coconut flavoring* |
| *1 teaspoon vanilla extract* | *3 cups flaked coconut* |
| *½ teaspoon almond extract* | |
| *½ teaspoon coconut flavoring* | |
| *1 cup milk* | |

Preheat oven to 325F (165C). Grease and flour 3 (9-inch-round) cake pans. In a medium bowl, sift sifted cake flour with baking powder and salt.

In a mixer bowl, beat together butter and shortening until blended. Gradually beat in sugar with mixer at medium-low speed. Increase speed to medium and beat a total of 10 minutes. Add eggs, one at a time, beating well after each addition. Add vanilla and almond extracts and coconut flavoring. Add flour mixture alternately with milk, beginning and ending with flour.

Divide batter evenly among the prepared pans. Bake 25 to 35 minutes or until a wooden pick inserted in the center of a cake comes out clean. Cool in pans on wire rack 10 minutes. Then turn out on wire rack and cool completely before frosting.

Spread frosting on tops of 2 layers and stack layers, frosting side up, with unfrosted layer on top. Frost top and sides of cake, pressing coconut lightly into the frosting.

**Makes a 9-inch, 3-layer cake, 12 servings.**

#### COCONUT FROSTING

In a medium bowl, beat together butter, salt and 2 cups powdered sugar until light and fluffy. Add milk, flavorings and enough powdered sugar to make a spreading consistency. Beat until smooth and fluffy.

## 🏅 *Baking a Three-Layer Cake*

If you have one oven and a three-layer cake to bake, divide the oven into thirds with the two racks. Bake two layers on the bottom and one on top, staggering them so one is not above another.

Since layers bake relatively quickly, if your oven is small, you could refrigerate one layer while you bake the other two. This works best when you make a cake leavened with double-acting baking powder, the kind most commonly used for home baking. A cake leavened with baking soda must be baked right away, or it will lose volume.

If three layers are more than you can manage, half the recipe for a three-layer cake using 9-inch pans will make two 8-inch layers.

LINDA CRANMER      CANYON, TEXAS      PANHANDLE SOUTH PLAINS FAIR

# Orange Poppy Seed Layer Cake

Alice Bird took her favorite white cake recipe, added orange flavoring and lots of crunchy poppy seeds and turned up with a winner. Orange filling and creamy orange frosting give it a more refreshing citrus flavor.

This veteran blue ribbon winner became what she calls a state fair-aholic after she won a blue ribbon for her first cake entry thirty years ago. Her essay, "Confessions of a State Fair-aholic," in which she describes what happens when the premium book arrives in the mail, made such a hit with the Iowa State Fair food supervisor that she had copies made for all the foods contestants.

*2 cups sifted cake flour*
*½ teaspoon baking soda*
*¼ teaspoon baking powder*
*¼ teaspoon salt*
*½ cup margarine, softened*
*1½ cups sugar*
*1 teaspoon pure orange extract*
*1 teaspoon vanilla extract*
*1 cup buttermilk*
*¼ cup (1 ounce) poppy seeds*
*3 egg whites*

*ORANGE FILLING*
*½ cup sugar*
*⅛ teaspoon salt*
*3 tablespoons cornstarch*
*¾ cup water*
*1 tablespoon orange juice*
*1 teaspoon grated orange peel*
*1 teaspoon pure orange extract*
*2 tablespoons margarine*

*CREAMY ORANGE FROSTING*
*⅔ cup butter, softened*
*1 teaspoon pure orange extract*
*3 cups sifted powdered sugar*
*About 2 tablespoons milk*

Preheat oven to 350F (175C). Grease and flour 2 (8-inch-round) baking pans. In a medium bowl, sift together sifted flour, soda, baking powder and salt.

In a mixer bowl, beat together margarine, sugar and orange and vanilla extracts. Add flour mixture alternately with buttermilk, adding poppy seeds with the last addition of flour. Add un-beaten egg whites and beat at medium speed 2 minutes.

Pour batter into prepared baking pans. Bake 30 to 35 minutes or until a wooden pick inserted in the center of a cake comes out clean.

Cool in pans on wire racks 10 minutes. Turn out on racks. Turn layers top side up and cool completely before filling and frosting.

Prepare filling and frosting. Spread filling between the layers and frost the top and sides with the frosting.

**Makes an 8-inch, 2-layer cake, 10 servings.**

**ORANGE FILLING**

In a medium saucepan, mix together sugar, salt and cornstarch. Blend in water, orange juice and orange peel. Cook over medium heat, stirring constantly, until thickened, about 5 minutes. Remove from heat. Stir in orange extract and margarine. Cool at room temperature or refrigerate. The filling will thicken as it cools.

**Makes enough filling for a 2-layer cake.**

**CREAMY ORANGE FROSTING**

In a medium bowl, combine butter, orange extract, powdered sugar and enough milk to make a spreading consistency. Beat about 5 minutes at medium speed until smooth and creamy.

**Makes frosting for the sides and top of a 2-layer cake.**

**NOTE**

Because poppy seeds are such an important ingredient in this cake, be sure they are fresh.

### *Using Cake Flour*

Cake flour is made from soft winter wheat, which is lower in protein and higher in starch than all-purpose flour. It helps give delicate cakes a fine texture and higher volume.

Although the manufacturers say it isn't necessary to sift cake flour before measuring, it has a greater tendency to pack down than higher-protein flours do. But since there is a difference in volume between sifted and unsifted cake flour, follow the recipe, but sift the flour after measuring. Be sure, in either case, to spoon the flour into the measuring cup without packing.

If a recipe calls for cake flour and you don't have it on hand, substitute 2 tablespoons of cornstarch for 2 tablespoons of flour in every cup. (To substitute cake flour for all-purpose flour use 1 cup plus 2 tablespoons cake flour for 1 cup of all-purpose flour.)

Self-rising cake flour is available in some areas. It contains salt and leavening and should not be used in any of these recipes.

If you are making a sturdy cake, like a gingerbread or applesauce cake, choose all-purpose flour.

Store cake flour in an airtight container in a cool, dry place. In hot, humid weather, or if you are only an occasional cake baker, keep the container in the freezer. Cake flour can be stored for about a year.

ALICE BIRD    DES MOINES, IOWA    IOWA STATE FAIR

# Sweet Cherry Layer Cake

Dark-red sweet cherries are an important crop in Oregon. Irene Losey likes them in desserts, so she developed this recipe which uses either fresh or frozen cherries in the cake and the filling. This gently spiced cherry-flavored cake has won blue ribbons many times at the Oregon State Fair. Her lovely Whipped Creamy Frosting is an unusual cooked frosting that looks like whipped cream and is easy to make and spread.

Notice that frozen cherries must be thawed and thoroughly drained in advance.

*1½ cups fresh or frozen sweet cherries*
   *(see Variations, opposite)*
*2¼ cups all-purpose flour*
*1 teaspoon baking soda*
*½ teaspoon pumpkin pie spice*
*½ teaspoon ground cardamom or*
   *¼ teaspoon ground ginger*
*¾ cup butter, softened*
*1½ cups sugar*
*3 eggs*
*½ cup buttermilk*
*½ teaspoon almond extract*

*CHERRY FILLING*
*¼ cup cornstarch*
*1 cup sugar*
*¼ teaspoon salt*
*1½ cups pitted fresh or frozen cherries,*
   *quartered and pureed*
*2 tablespoons butter*
*½ teaspoon almond extract*

*WHIPPED CREAMY FROSTING*
*¼ cup all-purpose flour*
*1 cup milk*
*1 cup butter, softened*
*1 cup sugar*
*1 teaspoon almond extract*

Preheat oven to 350F (175C). Quarter and drain cherries. Line 2 (8-inch-round) cake pans with waxed paper. Lightly grease sides of pans. In a medium bowl, sift together flour, soda, pumpkin pie spice and cardamom.

In a mixer bowl, beat together butter and sugar until light and fluffy. Add eggs, one at a time, beating well after each addition. Mix in buttermilk and almond extract. Add flour mixture and beat at medium speed until blended. Fold in cherries.

Pour batter into prepared pans. Bake about 30 minutes or until the top springs back when lightly touched and a wooden pick inserted in the center of a cake comes out clean. Cool in the pans 10 minutes on a wire rack. Remove from pans and cool completely before filling and frosting.

Prepare filling and frosting. (See Variations, opposite, if using frozen cherries for filling.). Spread about ⅔ of the filling on the bottom cake layer. Place second layer on top. Frost the sides and top of the cake, leaving a 3-inch circle in the center of the cake unfrosted. Carefully spread the remaining filling in the center of the cake.

Makes an 8-inch, 2-layer cake, 10 servings.

## CHERRY FILLING

In a medium saucepan, mix together cornstarch, sugar and salt. Blend in pureed cherries. Cook over medium heat, stirring constantly, about 1 minute or until the mixture is thick. Stir in butter and almond extract and cool.

**Makes filling for a 2-layer cake.**

## WHIPPED CREAMY FROSTING

Blend flour and milk together in a small saucepan. Cook over medium heat, stirring constantly, until the mixture boils. Cook about 1 minute, stirring constantly or until the mixture is like a thick white sauce. Cool.

In a medium bowl, beat butter, sugar and almond flavoring until fluffy. Add cooled milk mixture. With an electric mixer at high speed beat 3 to 5 minutes or until the frosting is light and fluffy and resembles whipped cream.

**Makes frosting for a 2-layer cake.**

## VARIATIONS

If using frozen cherries, use 1 (16-oz.) package (3 cups frozen) for 1½ cups fresh. Quarter the cherries before thawing. After thawing, it will take about 1 hour to drain them thoroughly. Fresh cherries should be rinsed and any liquid drained off.

When Irene Losey makes this cake for her family, she sometimes substitutes either red or black cherry preserves or cherry pie filling for her cooked filling. You'll need at least a 10-ounce jar of preserves. She prefers a generous layer.

### *Importance of Accurate Measurement*

Today's cooks can thank Fannie Farmer, the late-nineteenth-century mother of level measurement and specific baking times and temperatures, for making it easier for even less-experienced bakers to bake successfully.

The professional method of weighing ingredients results in the most accurate measurement, but most Americans prefer to measure by volume. Unfortunately, though, not all measuring equipment is accurate.

Help yourself by selecting good equipment: a stainless steel set rather than plastic for measuring solid and dry ingredients and a good glass cup measure with a spout for liquids.

Lightly spoon flour into the cup rather than dipping. Hold the liquid measure at eye level, rather than look down at it. Then, if you can, avoid distractions while you bake. That's one of the surest ways to make a mistake in measuring.

Fair winners know that accurate measuring can make the difference between a blue ribbon and no ribbon.

IRENE LOSEY    SALEM, OREGON    OREGON STATE FAIR

# Spicy Prune Bundt Cake

Hazel James went from being "pretty unsuccessful" to winning many "Best of Show" rosettes by studying the baked goods that won and then learning by trial and error. Now she also is a judge in the junior department at the Panhandle South Plains Fair and finds it exciting to see young people win.

She also bakes Spicy Prune Bundt Cake as a layer cake and has won a blue ribbon with that. Because the cooked prunes are mashed or pureed rather than being cut up, they blend into the cake batter, adding a subtle fruit flavor to the nicely spiced cake.

*1 cup pitted prunes*
*1 cup water*
*2 cups all-purpose flour*
*1 teaspoon baking soda*
*1 teaspoon salt*
*1 teaspoon ground cinnamon*
*1 teaspoon ground cloves*
*1 teaspoon ground nutmeg*
*2 cups sugar*
*1 cup vegetable oil*
*3 eggs, well beaten*

*1 teaspoon vanilla extract*
*1 cup buttermilk*
*1 cup chopped pecans*

*EASY LEMON OR CARAMEL GLAZE*
*2 tablespoons butter, softened*
*1 cup powdered sugar, sifted*
*½ teaspoon pure lemon extract or*
*    caramel flavoring*
*2 to 3 tablespoons half-and-half*

Simmer prunes in the water in a small saucepan, covered, 7 to 10 minutes or until very tender. Without draining, refrigerate prunes overnight or for several hours. Pour prunes into a strainer and drain off all the liquid. Scrape prunes into a small bowl and mash coarsely with a potato masher. Drain off any juice.

Preheat oven to 350F (175C). Grease and flour a 10-inch Bundt pan.

Sift flour, soda, salt, cinnamon, cloves and nutmeg into a medium bowl. In a large bowl, beat together sugar, oil, eggs and vanilla. Blend in buttermilk and mashed prunes. Stir in flour and mix until well blended.

Pour batter into prepared Bundt pan. Bake 55 to 60 minutes or until a cake tester (see Note, opposite) inserted in the center of the cake comes out clean. Cool the cake in the pan on a wire rack 20 minutes. Remove from the pan and cool completely before glazing.

Prepare glaze. Drizzle glaze over the top of the cake with a spoon, letting it run down the sides of the cake.

**Makes a 10-inch Bundt cake, 12 to 16 servings.**

### EASY LEMON OR CARAMEL GLAZE

In a small bowl, beat butter, powdered sugar, flavoring and enough half-and-half to make a smooth glaze of drizzling consistency.

**NOTE**

To make sure this moist cake is baked, test it with a long bamboo skewer or metal cake tester. A wooden pick isn't long enough.

### Cakes Made with Oil

Cakes made with oil are mixed by the blending method, where all the ingredients are blended together, rather than the sugar and shortening creamed. For the best results, all ingredients should be at room temperature.

Cakes made by this quicker method will be moist and have a denser texture than cakes made by creaming. The method is especially suitable for sturdier cakes like Spicy Prune Bundt Cake.

HAZEL JAMES      LUBBOCK, TEXAS      PANHANDLE SOUTH PLAINS FAIR

# Texas Sheet Cake

The Canfield (Ohio) Fair has a separate category for Texas Sheet Cake, indicating that this regional recipe has infiltrated some other states, although it is virtually unknown in much of the country.

Katrina Wolfe-Whistler says her family believes it tastes even better the second day. They think a glass of milk is the perfect accompaniment for this sweet, moist cake. It's quick to mix and is frosted with a traditional warm icing while the cake is still warm.

| | |
|---|---|
| *2 cups all-purpose flour* | *ICING* |
| *2 cups sugar* | *½ cup butter* |
| *½ teaspoon salt* | *2 tablespoons unsweetened cocoa powder* |
| *1 cup butter* | *⅓ cup milk* |
| *4 tablespoons unsweetened cocoa powder* | *3½ to 4 cups powdered sugar, sifted* |
| *1 cup water* | *½ teaspoon vanilla* |
| *½ cup buttermilk or ½ cup milk plus* | *1 cup sliced almonds or chopped pecans* |
| *1 teaspoon vinegar* | *(optional)* |
| *2 eggs, slightly beaten* | |
| *1 teaspoon baking soda* | |
| *1 teaspoon vanilla extract* | |
| *1 tablespoon vinegar* | |

Preheat oven to 375F (190C). Grease a 15 × 10-inch baking pan.

Sift flour, sugar and salt into a large bowl. In a medium saucepan, bring butter, cocoa and water to a boil, stirring frequently. Pour over flour mixture, beating well. Add buttermilk, eggs, soda, vanilla and vinegar. Mix well.

Pour batter into prepared pan. Bake about 25 minutes or until a wooden pick inserted in the center comes out clean.

When the cake is nearly baked, prepare icing. Spread warm icing on the cake while the cake is warm and in the pan. Sprinkle with nuts, if desired. Cool the cake on a wire rack.

Makes a 15 × 10-inch cake, 15 (3-inch) squares.

**ICING**

In a large saucepan, combine butter, cocoa and milk. Bring to a boil over medium heat, stirring constantly. Heat until butter melts. Remove from heat. Beat in enough powdered sugar to make a spreading consistency. Beat in vanilla and beat until icing is very smooth and creamy. Spread while warm.

### Texas Sheet Cake

A cross between cake, a bar cookie and candy, Texas Sheet Cake seems to be one of those recipes that is seldom found in cookbooks but is passed on from person to person. Newspaper food editors have reported that this mildly flavored chocolate dessert is quite well known in Pennsylvania, Ohio and upper New York State, as well as in Texas.

Some people think it got its name because it's a big cake (baked in a jelly-roll pan) and very rich. It's a favorite party cake for large gatherings, because it makes 15 dessert-size servings or can be cut like a bar.

KATRINA WOLFE-WHISTLER      COLUMBIANA, OHIO      CANFIELD FAIR

# Sweet Spreads & Savory Relishes

*The rule is, jam tomorrow, and jam yesterday, but never jam today.*
Lewis Carroll, *Alice's Adventures in Wonderland*

Condiments, both sweet and savory, have become very popular in specialty food shops and upscale supermarkets. When we are eating quicker and simpler weekday meals, they add variety. Sharing special conserves or pickles with guests when we entertain has long been a hospitable gesture. A signature homemade sweet spread or relish makes a much-appreciated small gift.

Canned fruits and vegetables still have an important place in culinary arts exhibits at state fairs. A display of sparkling clear, colorful jellies always draws admiring glances from the crowds that pass through the exhibits. But the new emphasis and the categories that attract the most new exhibitors now are the specialty conserves, chutneys, marmalades, relishes and herb jellies.

As one blue ribbon winner wrote, "I saw these expensive little jars of pickled asparagus in a specialty food store, and I said I know I can do that at home." Another woman who gives extra jars of her prize-winning marmalade and jams as gifts said her friends always returned the empty preserving jars, as a gentle hint that they hoped to get them back filled with more of her sweet spreads.

This chapter concentrates on specialty condiments. Instead of plain strawberry jam we have a Two-Way Pineapple-Strawberry Jam that you can make with either fresh or frozen and canned fruit; Strawberry-Rhubarb Jam, duplicating the flavors so popular in pie; an unusual Strawberry-Banana Jam; and Strawberry Marmalade.

The simple recipe from an inn famous for its apricot marmalade is revealed. Another winner shares the secret ingredient she adds to her apricot jam to make the blue ribbon difference.

Relishes range from a real Indian chutney to sliced Green Tomato Pickles and a Cucumber-Dill Herb Jelly that will inspire herb growers and vegetable gardeners alike.

Even if you are a novice at canning, by following these tips and recipes you'll find that preserving is no more complicated than making a batch of cookies. Once you have learned the procedures, each recipe is a variation on the same theme.

If you are an experienced preserver, you'll find some distinctive new recipes that might also bring you a blue ribbon.

## Before You Begin

- Assemble canning jars that are free from nicks and cracks and two-piece lids with new center lids.

- You'll need a wide, heavy-bottomed kettle of stainless steel or unchipped enamel. A Dutch oven or a stockpot works well.
- You'll need a water-bath canner.
- A kitchen scale is handy. Ingredients may be listed by weight.
- An accurate timer or clock with a second hand is essential.
- Other small equipment you will want: large metal spoon, jar lifter, funnel, jelly thermometer, hot pads and kitchen towels on which to set hot jars.
- Have all ingredients measured and ready before you start cooking preserves.

## Preserving Basics

**Sterilizing Jars**    Put clean jars right side up in the water-bath canner. Fill it with hot (not boiling) water to 1 inch above the tops. Boil the jars for 10 minutes. Leave them in the water until you are ready to fill them. (Save the water for processing.) Prepare lids and rings according to the manufacturer's directions on the box.

**Full Rolling Boil**    This is a hard boil that doesn't stop when the fruit mixture is stirred.

## Using the Boiling Water–Bath Canner

Fill the canner up to the level of the jars with very hot (not boiling) water. Load the rack with the filled jars. Add boiling water to come at least 1 inch above the top of the lids.

Turn the heat to high until the water boils vigorously. Set the timer for the recommended time and cover the canner. Lower the heat for a gentler boil. When the time is up, remove the jars with a jar lifter and cool on a towel.

## Making Sweet Preserves

- If the recipe calls for pectin, use only the kind and amount specified. They are not interchangeable. Follow the directions exactly. They are different for powdered and liquid pectin. Check the "use by" date on the package to make sure pectin is fresh.
- The final 1-minute boil after you add liquid pectin is to ensure that it is thoroughly mixed in with the other ingredients. It should not be eliminated.
- Without added pectin, preserves are done when they reach 8 degrees above the boiling point of water in your area [e.g. 220F (105C) at sea level to 1,000 feet; 216F (102C) at 2,000 feet; 212F (100C) at 4,000 feet, etc.]. For your own area, check with your county extension service.
- The USDA recommends the use of sterilized jars and the processing of sweet spreads in a boiling water bath for 5 minutes. However, some canning experts recommend a 10-minute processing and some state fairs require it. Our recipes use the time given by the blue ribbon winner.
- If you are making preserves for your own use and don't want to process them, refrigerate them and use them within a few months.

- Achieving the appropriate firmness in sweet preserves is important. You should be able to make a clean cut through jelly with a knife, and a spoonful should spread easily. Jams, conserves and marmalades should be just barely firm.
- Locally grown fruits can vary in the amount of pectin they contain. If the sweet spread is too stiff the first time you make it, you may want to add more fruit, make sure the fruit is fully ripe or even cut back a bit on pectin. Canned and frozen fruit may have less pectin than fresh fruit.
- If the jam or jelly doesn't set up, next time you may need to add lemon juice, even if the recipe doesn't call for it. Acid helps firm up preserves.
- Don't underfill jars. If you don't have enough for a full jar (filled ¼ inch from the top), refrigerate it without processing.

# Blackberry Jam

Edith Martin, now in her eighth decade, has cooked since she was a child. For many years, she was a restaurant pastry cook. Then she and her daughter opened their own restaurant in Indianapolis. After she retired, she kept busy by co-authoring a cookbook with her daughter and found time to enter county and state fair competitions.

If you are fortunate enough to live where blackberries grow abundantly, you know the sweet but tangy berries make exceptionally tasty jam. Edith Martin advises using fully ripe berries for blue ribbon flavor. If fruit is underripe, the jam also may get too stiff.

*8 cups fully-ripe blackberries, rinsed,*
*stemmed and drained*

*1 box powdered fruit pectin*
*7 cups sugar*

Crush blackberries, 1 layer at a time. Sieve 1 cup to remove some of the seeds.

Measure 5 cups crushed berries into a 6- or 8-quart kettle. Mix in pectin. Bring to a full rolling boil over high heat, stirring constantly. Immediately add sugar all at once. Bring to a full rolling boil and boil 1 minute, stirring constantly. Remove from heat. Stir and skim off foam with a metal spoon.

Ladle into hot sterilized jars to within ¼ inch of the top. Wipe off rims of jars; attach lids and firmly screw on bands. Process in a boiling water bath 5 minutes. Remove from the canner.

**Makes about 8 cups.**

**VARIATION**

When Edith Martin doesn't have quite enough prepared fruit, she adds up to ½ cup apple juice.

EDITH MARTIN    MARTINSVILLE, INDIANA    INDIANA STATE FAIR

# Two-Way Pineapple-Strawberry Jam

When Cristy Pitts was married, the only thing she knew how to cook was spaghetti sauce. Despite her friends' concerns, her husband didn't starve, and she learned to cook from the two hundred cookbooks she gradually collected.

Her cooking experiments soon encompassed interesting jams and relishes. This versatile recipe for her sweepstakes-winning pineapple-strawberry jam can be made either with fresh fruit, canned and frozen fruit or a combination. The jam firms up after 24 hours but does not get stiff, a quality which gives it a lot of homemade appeal.

*4 cups prepared fruit (from 1 fully-ripe*          *7 cups sugar*
*    medium pineapple and 1 quart*                 *1 pouch liquid fruit pectin*
*    strawberries)*

Prepare pineapple by paring and coring and cutting out the eyes. Finely chop or grind. Hull and crush strawberries.

Measure 4 cups prepared fruit into a 6- or 8-quart kettle. Mix in sugar. Bring to a full rolling boil over high heat. Boil hard 1 minute, stirring constantly. Stir in liquid pectin. Bring to a boil and boil 1 minute, stirring constantly. Remove from heat. Stir and skim off foam with a metal spoon for 5 minutes.

Ladle into hot sterilized jars to within ¼ inch of the top. Wipe off rims of jars; attach lids and firmly screw on bands. Process in a boiling water bath 5 minutes. Remove from the canner. If you have floating fruit, invert jars 5 minutes, then turn upright. Let jam set in a cool place, out of drafts, 24 hours before removing bands.

**Makes about 8 cups.**

### Variation

Use 1 (1-lb. 13-oz.) can crushed pineapple, drained, and 1 (20-oz.) bag frozen strawberries, thawed, drained and crushed, to make 4 cups of prepared fruit.

CRISTY PITTS     ANDERSON, INDIANA     INDIANA STATE FAIR

# Strawberry-Rhubarb Jam

Myrl DuPuis won with her entries of pie crust and gingerbread the first time she exhibited at a county fair in Kansas more than sixty-five years ago. After moving to Washington, she has entered both state fairs, the Puyallup Fair and the Evergreen Fair. Now she concentrates on the Evergreen, only ten miles from home. She wins sweepstakes awards in both baking and canning and also has been picked to demonstrate making dinner rolls at the Evergreen Fair.

She grows her own pink strawberry rhubarb and recommends using that any time it's available. She prefers the tender young stalks that are available early in the summer. The small amount of butter in the recipe helps prevent foaming.

*4 cups strawberries, stemmed and crushed*
*2 cups sliced rhubarb, preferably strawberry*
  *rhubarb*
*¼ cup lemon juice*

*1 box powdered fruit pectin*
*¼ teaspoon butter*
*5½ cups sugar*

Mix together fruit, lemon juice and pectin in a 6- to 8-quart kettle. Add butter and bring to a full rolling boil over high heat, stirring constantly. Immediately stir in all the sugar. Bring to a full rolling boil and boil 1 minute, stirring constantly. Remove from heat; skim off foam with a metal spoon.

Ladle into hot sterilized jars to within ¼ inch of the top. Wipe off rims of jars, attach lids and firmly screw on bands. Process in a boiling water bath 5 minutes. Remove from the canner. Invert jars 5 minutes, then turn upright to distribute fruit.

**Makes about 6 cups.**

MYRL DUPUIS    SNOHOMISH, WASHINGTON    EVERGREEN FAIR

# Strawberry-Banana "Happiness Jam"

Kenneth Buis has been cooking at home for more than forty years, but he didn't take up fair competition until he retired. He has collected an impressive number of blue ribbons, including the sweepstakes ribbon for his "Happiness Jam." But this takes up only a small amount of his spare time. He writes Westerns, has two inventions in the works and has just taken up oil painting.

Many of his favorite recipes are from his mother, but this delicious jam is a slightly modified version of a recipe he was given by a friend in Las Vegas. You will need about 2 quarts of strawberries and 3 bananas to make up the prepared fruit.

*3½ cups thoroughly crushed strawberries*      *1 box powdered fruit pectin*
*1½ cups mashed bananas*                        *½ teaspoon margarine*
*3 tablespoons lemon juice*                     *6¾ cups sugar*

In a 6- to 8-quart kettle, combine strawberries, bananas and lemon juice. Stir pectin into fruit. Add margarine and bring to a full rolling boil over high heat, stirring constantly. Immediately stir in all the sugar. Bring to a full rolling boil and boil 1 minute, stirring constantly. Remove from heat, skim off foam with a metal spoon.

Ladle into hot sterilized jars to within ¼ inch of the top. Remove air bubbles. Wipe off rims of jars, attach lids and firmly screw on bands. Process in a boiling water bath 15 minutes. Remove from the canner.

**Makes about 8 cups.**

### Using Paraffin
In line with the latest food safety guidelines, none of the blue ribbon winners used paraffin to seal their preserves. Fairs no longer will accept entries that use it.

Paraffin-sealed products are more likely to develop mold. Research now indicates that mold may not be as harmless as we once thought. It no longer is considered safe to scrape it off and eat the food.

Use regular canning jars and new lids. Metal ring bands can be reused as long as they are in good condition.

KENNETH L. BUIS      HENRYVILLE, INDIANA      INDIANA STATE FAIR

# Nectarine Jam

Karen Dammer has been a consistent blue ribbon winner with her beautiful Nectarine Jam. The judges also gave her a perfect rating on flavor and commented on the excellent fresh taste.

She chooses nectarines with the most red color, careful to pick out ones that are at the same stage of ripeness. Then she cuts off the flesh as close to the pit as she can to get the most red color. It will take about 3 pounds of nectarines for this recipe.

*4 cups finely chopped nectarines*     *1 box powdered fruit pectin*
*2 tablespoons fresh lemon juice*      *5½ cups sugar*
*½ teaspoon butter*

Mix nectarines and lemon juice in a 6- to 8-quart saucepan. Stir in butter and pectin. Bring to a full rolling boil over high heat, stirring constantly. Immediately stir in all the sugar. Allow mixture to return to a full rolling boil; boil 1 minute, stirring constantly. Remove from heat. Skim off foam with a metal spoon.

Ladle into hot sterilized jars to within ¼ inch of the top. Wipe off rims of jars, attach lids and firmly screw on bands. Process in a boiling water bath 5 minutes. Remove from the canner.

**Makes about 7 cups.**

KAREN DAMMER        ST. PAUL, MINNESOTA        MINNESOTA STATE FAIR

# Kiwi Jam

Lisa Carter started entering jams at the Los Angeles County Fair soon after her first child was born. Now, with three children, she has branched out to include baking "everything with calories" and to take part in many of the special commercial food company contests.

Kiwi fruit is available year-round, so you can make up this small-batch recipe any time. The fruit has enough natural pectin, so you don't need to add any. Choose ripe fruit for flavor, but since ripe kiwi have less pectin, also include some less ripe fruit.

If you are making the fresh-flavored, not-too-sweet jam for your own use and don't want to process it, just store it in the refrigerator.

*2 pounds ripe kiwi fruit (about 10)*          *2 cups sugar*
*Grated peel of 1 large lemon*

Peel and quarter fruit. Slice thin. Place in a heavy 4-quart saucepan. Mix in lemon peel. Bring to a full rolling boil over high heat, stirring constantly. Reduce heat and simmer 10 minutes, stirring often. Add the sugar ½ cup at a time. Cook, stirring and reducing heat to prevent sticking, until it reaches the gel point, about 10 minutes. Remove from heat, skim off foam.

Ladle into hot sterilized jars to within ¼ inch of the top. Wipe off rims of jars, attach lids and firmly screw on bands. Process in a boiling water bath 10 minutes. Remove from the canner.

**Makes about 2½ cups.**

LISA CARTER     LONG BEACH, CALIFORNIA     LOS ANGELES COUNTY FAIR

# Louise Piper's Apricot Jam

If you are not an expert, it can be tricky making up your own jam recipe. But Louise Piper is so experienced at food preparation, she developed this apricot jam recipe and won a blue ribbon at the Iowa State Fair. The judges commented particularly on the good apricot flavor, which is enhanced by the added apricot gelatin and the grated orange peel.

*5 cups finely chopped ripe apricots*
*(3 to 3½ lbs.) (see Note, below)*
*¼ cup fresh lemon juice*
*2 tablespoons grated orange peel*

*1 box powdered fruit pectin*
*6½ cups sugar*
*1 (3-oz.) package apricot-flavored gelatin*

Mix apricots, lemon juice, orange peel and pectin in a 6- to 8-quart saucepan. Bring to a full rolling boil over high heat, stirring constantly. Immediately stir in sugar and gelatin. Bring to a full rolling boil and boil 1 minute, stirring constantly. Remove from the heat. Skim off foam with a metal spoon.

Ladle into hot sterilized jars to within ¼ inch of the top. Wipe off rims of jars, attach lids and firmly screw on bands. Process in a boiling water bath 10 minutes. Remove from the canner.

**Makes 9 cups.**

**NOTE**

Prepare fruit by grinding pitted, unpeeled apricots using the coarse blade of a food grinder or by chopping by hand or in the food processor.

### *What's in a Name?*

*Jams* are made from crushed or chopped fruit. They are cooked until thick enough to spread but not as stiff as jelly.

*Marmalades* are soft jellies containing suspended pieces of citrus peel and/or fruit.

*Preserves* are made with larger pieces of fruit or small whole fruits in a clear, slightly jellied syrup.

*Conserves* usually contain two or more fruits and may include raisins and nuts.

*Butters* are fruit pulp and sugar, thickened to a good spreading consistency with long, slow cooking.

LOUISE PIPER      ROLFE, IOWA      IOWA STATE FAIR

# Durbin Inn Apricot Marmalade

Madonna Alderson's bright-flavored spread is the re-creation of a marmalade served at the Durbin Inn in Rushville, Indiana. She says the flavor is best when it's made with very ripe apricots. When they are out of season, she uses frozen or drained, canned apricots and sometimes uses fresh pineapple instead of canned. The marmalade also makes a nice topping for ice cream.

Madonna's mother has exhibited preserves and pies that have won the grand championship, and she is following in her footsteps. She finds it is relaxing to spend time away from work preserving the fruit and vegetables the Aldersons raise on their farm.

*2 cups finely chopped fully ripe apricots*
  *(about 1½ pounds)*
*2 tablespoons fresh lemon juice*

*1 cup well drained, juice-packed pineapple*
*3 cups sugar*

Mix apricots and lemon juice. Combine with pineapple and sugar in a heavy 4-quart saucepan. Bring to a full rolling boil over high heat, stirring constantly. Reduce the heat to medium and simmer, stirring constantly, until the mixture begins to thicken, about 10 minutes. (The marmalade will thicken more as it cools.)

Ladle into hot sterilized jars to within ¼ inch of the top. Wipe off rims of jars, attach lids and firmly screw on bands. Process in a boiling water bath 10 minutes. Remove from the canner.

If you have floating fruit, invert jars 5 minutes, then turn upright. Let jam set 24 hours in a cool place before removing bands. This marmalade sets up slowly.

**Makes about 3 cups.**

MADONNA ALDERSON      SHARPSVILLE, INDIANA      INDIANA STATE FAIR

# Strawberry Marmalade

Anna Davis became a Master Food Preserver (MFP) with the University of California in 1984. She is a volunteer teacher for several groups and puts on preservation demonstrations for the public.

Her family doesn't like orange marmalade. When she tried this recipe from a newspaper food column, she finally found a marmalade they all enjoy. It has a lovely color and is not too sweet.

It has won the best of class for marmalade a number of times, in addition to being a frequent blue ribbon winner.

| | |
|---|---|
| *1 medium orange* | *1 quart fully ripe strawberries* |
| *1 medium lemon* | *7 cups sugar* |
| *½ cup water* | *1 pouch liquid pectin* |
| *⅛ teaspoon baking soda* | |

Cut orange and lemon into quarters and remove the seeds. Cut into very thin slices. In an 8- to 10-quart kettle, mix citrus fruit, water and soda. Bring to a boil, reduce heat and simmer, covered, 30 minutes, stirring occasionally.

Thoroughly crush strawberries, 1 layer at a time. Measure strawberries, cooked citrus slices and juices to make 4 cups. In the large kettle, thoroughly mix fruit with sugar. Bring to a full rolling boil over high heat and boil hard 1 minute, stirring constantly. Stir in pectin all at once, boil 1 minute and remove from the heat. Skim off foam with a metal spoon.

Ladle into hot sterilized jars to within ¼ inch of the top. Wipe off rims of jars, attach lids and firmly screw on bands. Process in a boiling water bath 10 minutes. Remove from the canner.

**Makes 8 cups.**

ANNA DAVIS        FAIR OAKS, CALIFORNIA        CALIFORNIA STATE FAIR

# Peach Melba Conserve

Anna Davis first learned about preserving food as a young child by working with her mother. She has carried on that tradition with her own daughter, who also has become a prize-winning competitor at the California State Fair.

This beautifully colored conserve is made with frozen fruit. This not only saves preparation time, but you can make it year-round, not just when the fresh fruit is available.

Serve this versatile conserve as a topping for ice cream or angel food cake or as an accompaniment to ham, as well as a spread for toast or hot biscuits.

*2 (16-oz.) bags frozen peaches, thawed,*
*    drained and chopped*
*1 cup raspberries, fresh or thawed frozen*
*3 tablespoons lemon juice*
*1 teaspoon grated lemon peel*

*1 box powdered fruit pectin*
*6 cups sugar*
*⅜ cup slivered almonds, broken and*
*    toasted*

In a 6- to 8-quart kettle, combine the peaches, raspberries, lemon juice, lemon peel and pectin and mix well. Bring mixture to a full rolling boil over high heat, stirring constantly. Add sugar all at once. Cook, stirring, until the conserve comes to a rolling boil. Boil hard 1 minute. Remove from the heat. Using a metal spoon, stir and skim the foam from the mixture for 5 minutes. Stir in toasted almonds.

Ladle into hot sterilized jars to within ¼ inch of the top. Wipe off rims of jars, attach lids and firmly screw on bands. Process in a boiling water bath 10 minutes. Remove from the canner.

**Makes 7 to 8 cups.**

ANNA DAVIS      FAIR OAKS, CALIFORNIA      CALIFORNIA STATE FAIR

# Grape Butter

Mary Ann Hildreth goes to a local orchard to pick her grapes and then rushes home to turn them into grape butter. This extra care gives her entry the exceptional flavor that won her the top award in eight classes of jams, butters and marmalades at the 1996 Ohio State Fair.

In addition to her fair entries, Mary Ann makes relishes and preserves for her church bazaar.

*About 4 pounds fully ripe concord grapes*          *1 box powdered fruit pectin*
*1 cup water*          *7½ cups sugar*

Prepare grape pulp by slipping skin from grapes by squeezing until the pulp slips out. Set skins aside. Place pulp in a saucepan. Add water and bring to a boil over medium heat. Reduce heat and simmer 5 minutes, stirring occasionally. Press pulp through a sieve to remove seeds. Finely chop or grind skins and add to the pulp.

Measure 6 cups of prepared fruit into a 6- to 8-quart kettle. Stir in pectin. Bring to a full rolling boil over high heat. Boil 1 minute, stirring constantly. Add sugar all at once. Bring to a boil and boil 1 minute, stirring constantly. Remove from heat. Skim off the foam with a metal spoon.

Ladle into hot sterilized jars to within ¼ inch of the top. Wipe off rims of jars, attach lids and firmly screw on bands. Process in a boiling water bath 10 minutes. Remove from the canner.

Makes about 10 cups.

### If You Plan to Exhibit

Write for the fair premium book well in advance. Fairs have specific rules for preserved foods to be exhibited, and these can vary slightly from year to year. For example, some of the fairs that previously have not required that jams and jellies be processed might add that rule. Fairs also add new categories from time to time.

The premium book also will tell how products will be judged. For example, color, texture and appearance count heavily. You will want to take special care with any product you plan to exhibit.

Our blue ribbon winners tell us that some fair judges are very fussy about certain details, e.g., that jars of preserves be filled exactly ¼ inch from the top. On the other hand, some judges are more interested in the quality and appearance of the product. Your best chance of getting a high score is to follow all the prescribed procedures, plus make the best preserves that you can.

Hide the jars you plan to exhibit in a cool, dark place, so they aren't used by mistake.

MARY ANN HILDRETH     FAIRBORN, OHIO     OHIO STATE FAIR

SAVORY RELISHES

## Making Piquant Relishes

See "Before You Begin" (page 187) and "Preserving Basics" (page 188).

- For pickling, you will want a nonmetallic tool like a plastic knife to get rid of air bubbles in the filled jars.
- The fresher the produce, the better your product will be. Small cucumbers and zucchini, under 5 inches, are best for pickles. Avoid bitter-tasting cucumbers or zucchini. They will make off-flavored pickles.
- Canning salt will make the clearest brine. You can use other kinds of salt, but the additives in them may make the brine slightly cloudy. (Some canning salts also contain an anticaking additive. Check the label.) Iodized salt may darken some pickles.
- Salt isn't necessary for food safety in these recipes, but cutting down on salt can affect texture and flavor.
- Apple cider vinegar has a more mellow flavor than distilled white vinegar, but it may discolor some vegetables. Use only good-quality commercial vinegar of at least 4 to 6 percent acidity.
- Cider-flavored vinegar is distilled white vinegar with coloring added. It does not have the flavor of real apple cider vinegar.
- If your tap water is very hard or contains a high level of iron, use distilled water. Extremely hard water can discolor these relishes.
- Use stainless steel or unchipped enamelware for heating pickling liquids. Other metals can react with acids or salts and galvanized containers might even form toxic compounds.
- Fill jars to within ½ inch of the top. Don't overpack the jars. You need to leave space for the liquid, because it contains the acid that keeps your relishes safe to eat.
- Clean fruit and vegetables well before processing but don't use detergent.

## Defining Pickles

*Fermented* or *brined pickles* go through a long curing process in which various fermentative bacteria produce a characteristic lactic acid flavor. Fermented dills and sauerkraut are examples. This method takes a long time and requires greater skills than do those for other kinds of pickles. None of these recipes use this method.

*Fresh pack pickles* are made from cucumbers and other vegetables and fruits. The method uses a boiling hot vinegar solution which increases the acidity of the vegetables or fruit and various seasonings. These pickles are quicker and easier to make. Bread & Butter Pickles and Pickled Peppers are examples.

*Relishes* are piquant blends of vegetables, fruits, spices and vinegar, chopped and cooked to a desired consistency.

*Chutney* is of East Indian origin. It is a fruit or vegetable relish ranging from smooth to chunky and from sweet to spicy-hot.

*Salsa* is a highly seasoned sauce, generally chunky in texture and usually containing tomatoes and chiles.

# Mango Chutney

The best-known commercial brand of chutney is a mango chutney, but you will find there is no comparison between that and Anna Davis's slightly tangy homemade winner.

Her list of seasonings and spices is long, but it gives the same subtle blend of flavors East Indians accomplish when they make their own curry powder by blending individual spices.

Some Indian chutneys are made with unripe mangoes, which gives them a sweet-sour flavor. Anna prefers using a mixture of green and firm-ripe fruit. Her recipe is an adaptation of the Mango Chutney from Helen Witty's *Fancy Pantry*.

*1 cup chopped onion*
*1¼ cups golden raisins*
*1 cup dried currants*
*4 large garlic cloves*
*Grated peel of 1 lemon*
*¼ cup lemon juice*
*1 teaspoon ground ginger*
*2 teaspoons ground cinnamon*
*¼ teaspoon ground cloves*
*2 tablespoons mustard seeds*

*1 teaspoon crushed dried hot peppers*
*½ teaspoon turmeric*
*½ teaspoon salt*
*2 cups packed light brown sugar*
*½ cup granulated sugar*
*2 large and 2 medium mangoes*
  *(4 pounds), peeled and cubed*
*1½ cups white vinegar*
*1 cup water*

Combine all ingredients in a 6- to 8-quart kettle. Bring the mixture to a boil over medium heat. Reduce heat so mixture simmers and cook, uncovered, stirring often, until the mango and onion pieces are translucent and the chutney has thickened to the consistency of preserves, 1 to 2 hours.

Ladle into hot sterilized jars leaving ¼ inch headspace. Wipe off rims of jars, attach lids and firmly screw on bands. Process in a boiling water bath 10 minutes. Remove from canner.

Makes 7 cups.

### About Mangoes

Rarely seen in produce departments in many parts of the country a few years ago, this tropical fruit now is available in most large supermarkets. It is most abundant and lower in price in the summer.

The flavor is somewhat similar to that of peaches, but ripe mangoes have an even richer, almost perfumey flavor. The skin color can range from green to yellow and red, so it can be difficult to tell ripeness just from the color.

The mango chutney recipe calls for green and firm-ripe fruit. A fully ripe mango will smell fruity and feel just slightly soft when pressed. Pick these for eating but not for this recipe. Your produce manager also can advise you.

Mangoes have a large, flat seed. The flesh clings to the seed. One of the easiest ways to release it is to run a thin knife horizontally around the circumference from the outer peel and through the fruit to the seed. Then take the knife and cut gently down between the seed and the fruit. Do the same with the other half of the mango. Now score the fruit like a checkerboard to the peel, but not through the peel. Push the peel forward so the cubes of fruit can easily be cut from the peel.

ANNA DAVIS     FAIR OAKS, CALIFORNIA     CALIFORNIA STATE FAIR

# Curried Apricot Chutney

Karen Dammer was born into a family of good cooks accustomed to eating foods from many different countries. She grew up enjoying dishes like curried turkey with wild rice for Thanksgiving instead of the traditional roast turkey. Commercial fruit chutney always was served with it, until Karen found this recipe and learned how much better homemade chutney can be. She often makes it and refrigerates it, but also processes some for her blue ribbon fair entry.

She has used fresh peaches but prefers dried apricots, so she can make it year-round. To give the spicy fruit relish its chunky texture, she quarters the apricots instead of chopping them. She stresses that it is very important to use a good brand of fresh curry powder.

*4 cups dried apricots, cut into quarters*
  *(1½ pounds)*
*1⅔ cups coarsely chopped yellow onions*
*½ cup sugar*
*4 cups water*
*3 cups golden raisins*

*2 teaspoons ground ginger*
*2½ teaspoons curry powder*
*2 (2-inch) cinnamon sticks*
*¾ teaspoon kosher salt*
*3 cups distilled white vinegar*

Mix together apricots, onions, sugar and water in a 6- to 8-quart kettle. Over medium heat, simmer 5 minutes, stirring occasionally.

Add raisins, ginger, curry powder, cinnamon sticks, salt and vinegar. Return to a simmer and cook 10 minutes, stirring occasionally, until onions are translucent and apricots and raisins are plump. Remove cinnamon sticks.

Ladle into hot sterilized jars leaving ¼ inch headspace. Wipe off rims of jars, attach hot lids and firmly screw on bands. Process in a boiling water bath 10 minutes. Remove from canner.
**Makes 4 pints.**

**VARIATION**
For fresh chutney, refrigerate unprocessed chutney. Use within 2 to 3 weeks.

KAREN DAMMER     ST. PAUL, MINNESOTA     MINNESOTA STATE FAIR

# Cucumber Dill Herb Jelly

Frances Morgenstern taught microbiology at the State University of New York's College of Health Related Professions for twenty-two years. She also raised six children and lived on a farm where they raised most of the food they ate.

She entered state fair competition sporadically even during those busy days. Now retired from teaching and a widow with grown children, she has time to indulge her love of cooking and state fair competition.

One of her interests, shared with an increasing number of herb growers, is making herb jelly. To make the herb infusion, she purees cucumber and the leaves, flowers and green seeds of dill, then strains out the liquid.

You can use large pieces of cucumber for this and include some tender seeds to make the puree, but be sure to taste the cucumber first. The jelly has the delicate flavor of the cucumbers and dill. Any bitterness will come through in the jelly. Because some of the fine pulp remains in the juice and gives the jelly its distinctive flavor, it will not be sparkling clear.

Be sure to rinse the dill thoroughly by dunking it in a bowl of water to get rid of dust and minute insects.

*4 large cucumbers (about 2 pounds)*
*3 stalks dill (use the leaves, flowers and tender green seeds only)*
*5 cups sugar*
*⅓ cup lemon juice*
*1 drop green food coloring (optional)*
*1 pouch liquid fruit pectin*
*1 head of dill in flower or with green seeds*

Peel cucumbers, discarding the biggest seeds. Cut in large chunks and puree with the dill in a blender. Strain the liquid through cheesecloth and measure 2 cups of juice into a 4-quart saucepan. (The juice will be cloudy and contain very small particles of pureed cucumber.) Stir in sugar, lemon juice and food color, if desired. Bring to a full rolling boil over high heat and boil 1 minute. Stir in fruit pectin and boil 1 minute, stirring constantly. Remove from the heat. Skim off foam with a metal spoon.

Ladle into hot, sterilized jars to within ¼ inch of the top. If desired, place a well-washed small stem of dill flowers or green seeds in each jar. Wipe jar rims, attach hot lids and firmly screw on bands. Process in a simmering water bath 5 minutes or invert jars 5 minutes, then turn upright.

Makes about 5 cups.

### Notes

The New York State Fair did not require jelly to be processed, but many fairs use the USDA guidelines and require processing. If you do not process the jelly, it's best to refrigerate it after 24 hours.

Do not use dried (brown) dill seed in this recipe.

### Making Herb Jellies

With the increasing interest in raising culinary herbs in the home garden, herbs no longer are confined to the horticulture exhibits at fairs.

Herb vinegars were the first to make the move to culinary arts, joining mint jelly, the one herb-flavored jelly that has always been exhibited along with the traditional fruit flavors.

Now the category has been expanded to include herb jellies other than mint, leaving the door open for experimentation and creativity. As microbiologist Frances Morgenstern knew, she could start out by using a standard ratio of juice to sugar to pectin. Her intriguing difference was to make the juice from cucumbers. Other possibilities are grape juice flavored with thyme or apple cider flavored with sage or any of the lemon-flavored herbs like lemon verbena, lemon balm or lemon thyme.

Start with a basic recipe using commercial pectin and experiment with your favorite herb flavors. Harvest the herbs at the same stage you would for drying, since you want optimum herb flavor. Pick them when the oil content is highest, just when flower buds are beginning to open. (Mints are the exception. Their flavor is strongest when the plant is in full flower.) Cut them on a sunny day.

Besides serving herb jellies with meat and poultry, use them to season vegetables. (Think of mint jelly and peas, thyme jelly with carrots.) Many herb jellies make a tasty appetizer combined with cream cheese on crackers or melba toast.

FRANCES MORGENSTERN     CATO, NEW YORK     NEW YORK STATE FAIR

# Vidalia Onion Relish

Scott McGowan says in today's fast-paced life it's good to slow down and do something the old-fashioned way. For him that is making jellies, pickles and relishes. Not only is preserving relaxing for him, but he says it's impossible to match the quality of these homemade products with commercial versions.

One of the secrets that made this relish the grand prize winner in all the canned vegetable categories is using all sweet, mild Vidalia onions. He chops them coarsely in the food processor, then finishes chopping small batches by hand to the size he wants.

Scott serves his relish with roast beef and pork, and after a really bad day he says it is great to eat by the spoonful, right from the jar.

| | |
|---|---|
| *10 cups finely chopped sweet onions, preferably Vidalia (about 5 to 10, medium to large onions)* | *½ cup canning salt* |
| | *3 cups cider vinegar* |
| | *3 cups sugar* |
| *2 large red bell peppers, chopped* | *2 teaspoons mustard seeds* |
| *1 hot pepper, seeds removed and chopped (optional)* | *2 teaspoons celery seeds* |
| | *1 teaspoon turmeric* |

Place chopped onions, peppers and salt in a large stainless steel, glass or unchipped enamel bowl; cover with ice water and let stand 1 hour. Drain, rinse well and drain again.

In a 4- to 6-quart stainless steel or unchipped enamel kettle, mix vinegar, sugar, mustard seed, celery seed and turmeric. Bring to a boil over high heat, stirring to dissolve sugar. Add onions and peppers; boil gently 10 minutes.

Pack into hot, sterilized pint jars, leaving ½ inch headspace. Wipe the rims, seal with hot lids and firmly screw on bands. Process in a boiling water bath 15 minutes. Remove from canner.

**Makes about 10 cups.**

### About Sweet Onions

Gourmet spring-to-summer onions like Vidalia, Walla Walla and Texas 1015 are large, mild and sweet-flavored. You can chop them without weeping, and some claim you can eat them like an apple.

Unfortunately, the characteristics that give these varieties their good eating qualities mean they aren't good keepers. You have to use them during the few months they are available. Sometimes produce departments will have banners announcing their arrival. They always are displayed separately and may be identified by a name sticker.

SCOTT MCGOWAN      ROCHESTER, NEW YORK      NEW YORK STATE FAIR

# Delicious Zucchini Relish

When your zucchini plants have outpaced your ability to find ways to use them, look no further. Mary Ann Hildreth's zippy relish is a perfect accompaniment for any grilled meat or poultry. You'll find a spoonful or two will add interest to potato and pasta salads and many sandwich spreads.

While you might be tempted to grind up your bigger zucchini, Mary Ann uses zucchini at their peak eating quality for her blue ribbon results. Soaking the ground vegetable helps keep them crisp and gives the relish mouth-watering crunchiness.

Grind the zucchini, onions and peppers in a food chopper, using a coarse blade, or chop in a food processor.

| | |
|---|---|
| *2 quarts ground zucchini* | *2¼ cups distilled white vinegar* |
| *4 medium onions, ground* | *½ teaspoon ground cloves* |
| *2 large green bell peppers, seeds removed and ground* | *1 teaspoon turmeric* |
| | *1 teaspoon dry mustard* |
| *¼ cup canning salt* | *1 teaspoon celery seeds* |
| *2¼ cups sugar* | *1 teaspoon mustard seeds* |

Place vegetables in a stoneware crock or a large stainless steel or glass bowl. Mix salt with just enough water to dissolve. Add to vegetable mixture and add enough cold water to just cover the vegetables. Let stand in a cool place overnight or at least 3 hours. Drain, rinse with cold water and drain again, pressing the vegetables to extract as much water as possible.

In a 4- to 6-quart stainless steel or unchipped enamel kettle, mix sugar, vinegar, cloves, turmeric, dry mustard, celery seeds and mustard seeds. Add vegetable mixture and mix well. Bring to a boil over high heat. Boil gently 5 minutes, stirring occasionally.

Pack into hot sterilized pint jars, leaving ½ inch headspace. Wipe the rims, seal with hot lids and firmly screw on bands. Process in a boiling water bath 10 minutes. Remove from canner.

**Makes 8 to 10 cups.**

MARY ANN HILDRETH    FAIRBORN, OHIO    OHIO STATE FAIR

# Perfectly Pickled Asparagus

Susan Moser saw jars of pickled asparagus in a gourmet food shop and knew she could duplicate the pricey relish at a fraction of the cost. Since the Mosers have a large hobby garden, she could use her own freshly picked asparagus. If you have to buy it, she suggests going directly to a grower or a farmers' market for the best product. She uses fresh dill weed, not dried, for best flavor.

She cans the spears in wide-mouth half-pint jars, cutting the tips and tender spears into lengths that just fit in the jars.

*2 pounds asparagus*
*2½ cups distilled white vinegar*
*2½ cups water*
*¼ cup canning salt*

*4 teaspoons fresh dill weed*
*4 garlic cloves, peeled and halved*
*1 teaspoon ground hot (cayenne) pepper*

Choose tender, tight-tipped fresh asparagus. Remove tough ends and scales. Cut into lengths to fit ½-pint canning jars, leaving ½ inch headspace.

In a medium saucepan, combine vinegar, water and salt. Bring to a boil and keep hot while packing asparagus into hot, sterilized jars. To each jar, add ½ teaspoon dill weed; ½ garlic clove, cut in half; and ⅛ teaspoon hot pepper.

Pour boiling liquid over asparagus, leaving ½ inch headspace. Remove air bubbles with a plastic knife. Wipe rims, attach hot lids and firmly screw on bands. Process in a boiling water bath 10 minutes. Remove from canner.

Makes 8 (½-pint) jars.

**NOTE**

Wide-mouth jars are the easiest to pack. Avoid overpacking the jars. Leave space for the preserving liquid.

SUSAN MOSER        KING, NORTH CAROLINA        NORTH CAROLINA STATE FAIR

# Green Tomato Pickles

Dee Hansen works in the County District Attorney's office. She brings the foods she plans to make for the state fair to work and lets her colleagues be her practice judges. They apparently do a very good job. In addition to many blue ribbons, she has won the top Sweepstakes Award for the most total ribbon points won in a combination of baked goods and preserving.

With Oregon's normally cool, wet summers, there's never a lack of green tomatoes in late summer. Dee layers the tomatoes, onions, green and red peppers in the jars, so the pickles are as attractive as they are tasty. Use tomatoes that are green all the way through. If they are large, halve the slices.

*3 cups distilled white vinegar*
*2½ cups sugar*
*1 tablespoon canning salt*
*1 tablespoon celery seeds*
*1 tablespoon mustard seeds*

*10 cups ¼-inch-thick slices cored*
 *green tomatoes*
*2 cups thinly sliced onions*
*2 cups chopped green bell peppers*
*2 cups chopped red bell peppers*

In a 4- to 6-quart stainless steel or unchipped enamel kettle, combine vinegar, sugar, salt, celery seeds and mustard seeds. Heat to boiling. Add tomatoes, onions and green and red peppers. Return syrup to boiling and simmer 10 minutes, stirring occasionally.

Keep mixture just at a simmer while packing 1 hot, sterilized jar at a time. Fill to within ½ inch of the top, making sure vinegar solution covers the vegetables.

Run a plastic knife between the vegetables and jar sides to release air bubbles. Wipe rims, attach hot lids and firmly screw on bands. Process 10 minutes in a boiling water bath. Remove from canner.

**Makes 4 to 5 pints.**

**NOTE**

Wide-mouth jars are easiest to pack. If desired, layer the vegetables in the jar. The flavor of these pickles is best if you let them mellow for a month before using.

DEE HANSEN    KEIZER, OREGON    OREGON STATE FAIR

# Zucchini Pickle Slices

Helen Kirsch's pickles are similar to bread and butter pickles, but they are a little sweeter and less spicy than some. Use garden-fresh zucchini with a small seed cavity for the crunchiest texture. This is a small recipe, so you can make them when your zucchini plants get just ahead of you.

Helen's pickles are especially attractive because she uses a ripple-edged knife to slice the zucchini. Blue ribbon winners like to hand-cut their vegetables rather than use a food processor to get the most uniform slices.

*2 pounds zucchini (about 8 small),*
*cut into ¼-inch-thick slices*
*1 medium onion, quartered and*
*sliced very thin*
*¼ cup canning salt*

*2 cups sugar*
*3 cups distilled white vinegar*
*2 teaspoons mustard seeds*
*1 teaspoon celery salt*
*1 teaspoon turmeric*

Place zucchini and onion in a stainless steel, ceramic or glass bowl. Sprinkle with salt and cover with cold water. Let stand 2 hours in a cool place. Drain, rinse and drain thoroughly.

In a large saucepan, combine sugar, vinegar, mustard seeds, celery salt and turmeric; bring to a boil. Remove from the heat and add zucchini and onion. Let stand 2 hours.

Return mixture to a boil over high heat. Reduce heat and simmer 5 minutes, stirring occasionally.

Immediately pack into hot, sterilized ½-pint jars, leaving ½ inch headspace. Be sure vegetables are covered with liquid. Run a plastic knife between the vegetables and the jar sides to release air bubbles. Wipe the rims, seal with hot lids and firmly screw on bands. Process in a boiling water bath 10 minutes. Remove from canner.

Makes about 4 cups.

HELEN KIRSCH     ALBUQUERQUE, NEW MEXICO     NEW MEXICO STATE FAIR

# Plain Old Bread & Butter Pickles

Susan Moser can pick the perfect cucumbers and home-grown onions from her big vegetable garden. She slices them right away and then chills them in saltwater overnight in the refrigerator. This helps keep them crisp without using pickling lime, a standby in the South.

If you have to buy cucumbers, if possible, get the spiny pickling cucumbers instead of slicers. They can be full size (4 to 6 inches) for these sliced pickles but should be as freshly picked as possible.

*6 pounds medium cucumbers*
*1¼ cups thinly sliced onions*
*2 large cloves garlic, peeled*
*⅓ cup canning salt*
*2 trays ice cubes*

*5 cups sugar*
*1½ teaspoons turmeric*
*1½ teaspoons celery seeds*
*2 tablespoons mustard seeds*
*3 cups distilled white vinegar*

Cut washed, unpeeled cucumbers into ¼-inch-thick slices. In a large stainless steel, glass or ceramic bowl, mix together cucumbers, onions, garlic and salt. Cover with ice cubes. Cover bowl and refrigerate overnight. Thoroughly drain off liquid and discard garlic.

In a 4- to 6-quart kettle, combine sugar, turmeric, celery seeds, mustard seeds and vinegar. Heat just to boiling, stirring to dissolve sugar. Add the cucumbers and onions; simmer 10 minutes.

Pack loosely into hot sterilized pint jars, leaving ½ inch headspace. Be sure vegetables are covered with liquid. With a plastic knife remove air bubbles. Wipe the rims, seal with hot lids and firmly screw on bands. Process in a boiling water bath 10 minutes. Remove from canner.

**Makes 7 pints.**

SUSAN MOSER　　KING, NORTH CAROLINA　　NORTH CAROLINA STATE FAIR

# Pickled Jalapeño Chiles

Irlene Yarbrough likes to preserve pickled chiles, but she lets her family eat them. If you also prefer less heat, you can substitute mild ancho chiles or even bell peppers cut into strips.

She has learned by experience that if you keep the water in the canner at a full rolling boil, you can boil out some of the liquid in the jars. Fair exhibitors know judges are quick to take off points when this happens. Once the water comes to a full boil, she turns the heat down to get a gentle boil—and a blue ribbon product.

| | |
|---|---|
| *4 pounds fresh jalapeño chiles* | *1½ cups water* |
| *6 cups apple cider vinegar* | *1 tablespoon canning salt* |

Leave jalapeños (or any other small chiles) whole and do not cut off stems. Prick the end with a large needle or cut a small slit in the chile.

In a 6- to 8-quart stainless steel or unchipped enamel kettle, combine the vinegar, water and salt. Bring to a boil over high heat, reduce heat and simmer 5 minutes. Add the chiles, return to a boil and remove from heat.

Pack chiles into hot, sterilized, wide-mouth pint jars, leaving ½ inch headspace. Cover with hot vinegar solution, leaving ½ inch headspace. Be sure chiles are covered with liquid. Gently run a plastic knife between the chiles and the jar sides to release air bubbles. Wipe rims, seal with hot lids and firmly screw on bands. Process in a boiling water bath 10 minutes. Remove from canner.

**Makes about 8 pints.**

IRLENE YARBROUGH        STRAFFORD, MISSOURI        OZARK EMPIRE FAIR

# Sassy Salsa

Harvey Moser decided to join his wife, Susan, in exhibiting at the North Carolina State Fair. At first he entered some of the vegetables that they raise in their big hobby garden. Then he moved on to baking and canning, where he brought home a blue ribbon for his salsa.

Few of us could duplicate his winning entry, because the sweet peppers included a mixture of eye-catching colors from their garden: yellow, purple, lilac, light and dark green and chocolate. However, the flavor is just as good with plain green bell peppers.

*4 cups peeled, cored, chopped firm-ripe tomatoes*
*1½ cups seeded, chopped bell peppers*
*¾ cup seeded, chopped jalepeño chiles*
*1 cup chopped onion*

*2 garlic cloves, chopped*
*1 teaspoon hot (cayenne) pepper*
*1½ teaspoons salt*
*1½ cups distilled white vinegar*

In a 6- to 8-quart nonaluminum kettle, combine tomatoes, peppers, chiles, onion, garlic, cayenne, salt and vinegar. Bring to a boil over high heat, stirring often. Reduce heat and simmer until thickened, about 20 minutes.

Fill hot, sterilized jars, leaving ½ inch headspace. Wipe rims, attach hot lids and firmly screw on bands. Process in a boiling water bath 30 minutes.

**Makes about 6 cups.**

**NOTE**

Wear rubber gloves when handling the jalapeño chiles.

North Carolina guidelines call for 30 minutes processing for salsa. Other state extension guidelines are for 20 minutes for pint or half-pint jars.

### *Safe Salsa*

Devotees of fiery salsa complain that recipes for processed salsa aren't hot enough. This may be frustrating, but the problem is that getting a zippier salsa always seems to involve adding more chiles, onion and garlic. Adding too much of these low-acid foods to tomato-based salsa lowers the acid level to the point where the only safe way to preserve it is to process the salsa in a pressure canner, as you would do for corn or green beans.

One thing you can do is change the ratio of hot to sweet peppers, as long as the total is no higher. You can also add the extra ingredients to the salsa when you are ready to serve it.

HARVEY MOSER     KING, NORTH CAROLINA     NORTH CAROLINA STATE FAIR

# Simple Salsa

LaVerne Schmidt is a retired registered nurse with four adult children and fifteen grand-children. She studied advanced nutrition as a nurse. As a 4-H Club leader she learned more about cooking techniques as she taught from the state extension pamphlets and booklets.

She has won many of the top preserving awards at the Wisconsin State Fair, including the Best of Fair jam and jelly award. Her salsa recipe came from a publication of the Wisconsin Agriculture Department. If you prefer a milder salsa, use some bell peppers instead of the jalepeño chiles, but don't use more than 3 cups total. She likes to use Roma tomatoes for her salsa. These remain firm when fully ripe, so it's important to choose firm-ripe Romas. (See the following tip, "Acid in Tomatoes," below.)

Use rubber gloves while handling hot chiles.

*2 quarts peeled, seeded, chopped*
*   firm-ripe tomatoes*
*3 cups seeded and chopped fresh*
*   jalepeño chiles*

*¾ cup chopped onion*
*3 cloves garlic, minced*
*1½ cups distilled white vinegar*
*1½ teaspoons salt*

In a 6- to 8-quart nonaluminum kettle, combine tomatoes, chiles, onion, garlic, vinegar and salt. Bring to a boil over high heat, stirring often. Reduce heat and simmer, uncovered, stirring occasionally, about 5 minutes or until mixture begins to thicken.

Fill hot, sterilized pint jars with hot salsa, leaving ½ inch headspace. Wipe the rims, seal with hot lids and firmly screw on bands. Process in a boiling water bath 20 minutes. Remove from canner.

**Makes 5 to 6 pints.**

### Acid in Tomatoes

Americans have developed a taste for sweeter tomatoes, and horticulturists have obliged by developing tomatoes with a higher sugar content that masks the acid flavor.

When tomatoes were tested at the firm-ripe stage by the USDA and the University of Minnesota, they found none had a pH greater than 4.6, which is considered the safe level for processing in a water bath canner. However, they learned that when all tomatoes became fully ripe, the amount of acid decreased enough to make the tomatoes unsafe for canning by the boiling water bath method, unless an acid such as lemon juice was added.

*C. botulinum* spores will germinate and grow, producing their deadly poison, unless low-acid foods are processed at temperatures over 212F (100C). No matter how long you process a product in a water bath canner, the temperature will not go above boiling (212F; 100C). When other low-acid vegetables like celery, onion and peppers are included with the tomatoes, this lowers the acid level even further.

In making relishes like salsa, it's especially important to use recipes from reliable sources that contain enough acid to be safe. You also want to be sure that the recipe has a safe proportion of added low-acid ingredients.

University of Minnesota research emphasizes that it's essential to use disease-free, firm-ripe tomatoes. Never use soft tomatoes or ones with any decay, even though you discard those parts. It is not safe to process tomatoes from dead or frost-killed vines.

LaVerne Schmidt      Richfield, Wisconsin      Wisconsin State Fair

# Contributors of Blue Ribbon—Winning Recipes

Madonna Alderson
Cheryl Ashwill
Thelma Atkinson
Lori A. Beach
Alice Bird
Ruth Bristol
Mary Lou Brousil
Tina Brown
Kenneth L. Buis
Debra Burk
Lisa Carter
Shirley Casity
John D. Chovan
Cheryl Christiansen
Cynthia Clarke
Lucile G. Cline
Karen Cope
Jacqueline Core
Donna Craig
Linda Cranmer
Marge Cuff
Karen L. Dammer
Becky Daugherty
Anna Davis
Maryn DeBoer
Julie Dilleshaw-Canada
Paula S. Downing
Joyce Dubois
Myrl DuPuis
Ellen Ebner
Mary Ann Ferguson-Rich
Nancy Gabriel
David George
Brenda Gray

JoEllen Hall
Dee Hansen
Linda L. Hemond
Norma Herring
Mary Ann Hildreth
Mary Linda Horn
Fran Hurayt
Thelma Huston
Hazel James
Lola M. Jean
Pauline Jenkins
Marjorie Johnson
Nancy Johnson
Michelle Keim
Helen Kirsch
Kathy Klass
Elaine M. Klempay
Helen A. Lambert
Orville Lawson
Virginia Lawson
Emily K. Lewis
Tracy Penn Liberatore
Paula Lonnberg
Irene Losey
Leisa J. Lower
Scott McGowan
Lynda Mackey
Edith J. Martin
Ruth A. Maugeri
Jean Meiers
Frances Morgenstern
Harvey E. Moser
Susan C. Moser
Florence Neavoll

Fran Neavoll
Vicki Neuharth
Bonnie Orlando
Janet Parkhurst
Linda Pauls
Fay Peterson
Louise Piper
Cristy Pitts
Barbara Polk
Joan Randall
Lee Rathbone
Charlene C. Reardon
Alan Reid
Shirley Stafford Roberson
Marjorie K. Rose
Peggy A. Russell
Geraldine Sandoval
LaVerne J. Schmidt
Louise Schneiderman
Mary Schuman
Berta Shapiro
Linda Shaw
Susan Smart
Roy S. Struve
Gladys Sykes
Ruth Taylor
Marian Tobin
Denise Turnbull
Valalee Weber
Margaret White
Katrina Wolf-Whistler
Irlene Yarbrough
Martha York

# Metric Conversion Charts

## Comparison to Metric Measure

| When You Know | Symbol | Multiply By | To Find | Symbol |
|---|---|---|---|---|
| teaspoons | tsp. | 5.0 | milliliter | ml |
| tablespoons | tbsp. | 15.0f | milliliters | ml |
| fluid ounces | fl. oz. | 30.0 | milliliters | ml |
| cups | c | 0.24 | liters | 1 |
| pints | pt. | 0.47 | liters | 1 |
| quarts | qt. | 0.95 | liters | 1 |
| ounces | oz. | 28.0 | grams | g |
| pounds | lb. | 0.45 | kilograms | kg |
| Fahrenheit | F | 5/9 (after subtracting 32) | Celsius | C |

## Fahrenheit to Celsius

| F | C |
|---|---|
| 200–205 | 95 |
| 220–225 | 105 |
| 245–250 | 120 |
| 275 | 135 |
| 300–305 | 150 |
| 325–330 | 165 |
| 345–350 | 175 |
| 370–375 | 190 |
| 400–405 | 205 |
| 425–430 | 220 |
| 445–450 | 230 |
| 470–475 | 245 |
| 500 | 260 |

## Liquid Measure to Liters

| 1/4 | cup | = | 0.06 liters |
|---|---|---|---|
| 1/2 | cup | = | 0.12 liters |
| 3/4 | cup | = | 0.18 liters |
| 1 | cup | = | 0.24 liters |
| 1-1/4 | cups | = | 0.30 liters |
| 1-1/2 | cups | = | 0.36 liters |
| 2 | cups | = | 0.48 liters |
| 2-1/2 | cups | = | 0.60 liters |
| 3 | cups | = | 0.72 liters |
| 3-1/2 | cups | = | 0.84 liters |
| 4 | cups | = | 0.96 liters |
| 4-1/2 | cups | = | 1.08 liters |
| 5 | cups | = | 1.20 liters |
| 5-1/2 | cups | = | 1.32 liters |

## Liquid Measure to Milliliters

| 1/4 teaspoon | = | 1.25 milliliters |
|---|---|---|
| 1/2 teaspoon | = | 2.50 milliliters |
| 3/4 teaspoon | = | 3.75 milliliters |
| 1 teaspoon | = | 5.00 milliliters |
| 1-1/4 teaspoons | = | 6.25 milliliters |
| 1-1/2 teaspoons | = | 7.50 milliliters |
| 1-3/4 teaspoons | = | 8.75 milliliters |
| 2 teaspoons | = | 10.0 milliliters |
| 1 tablespoon | = | 15.0 milliliters |
| 2 tablespoons | = | 30.0 milliliters |

# Index